VOLUME
1

RADIO NOWHERE

STEPHANIE PHILLIPS

TONY SHASTEEN

JD METTLER

TROY PETERI

N U C L E A R

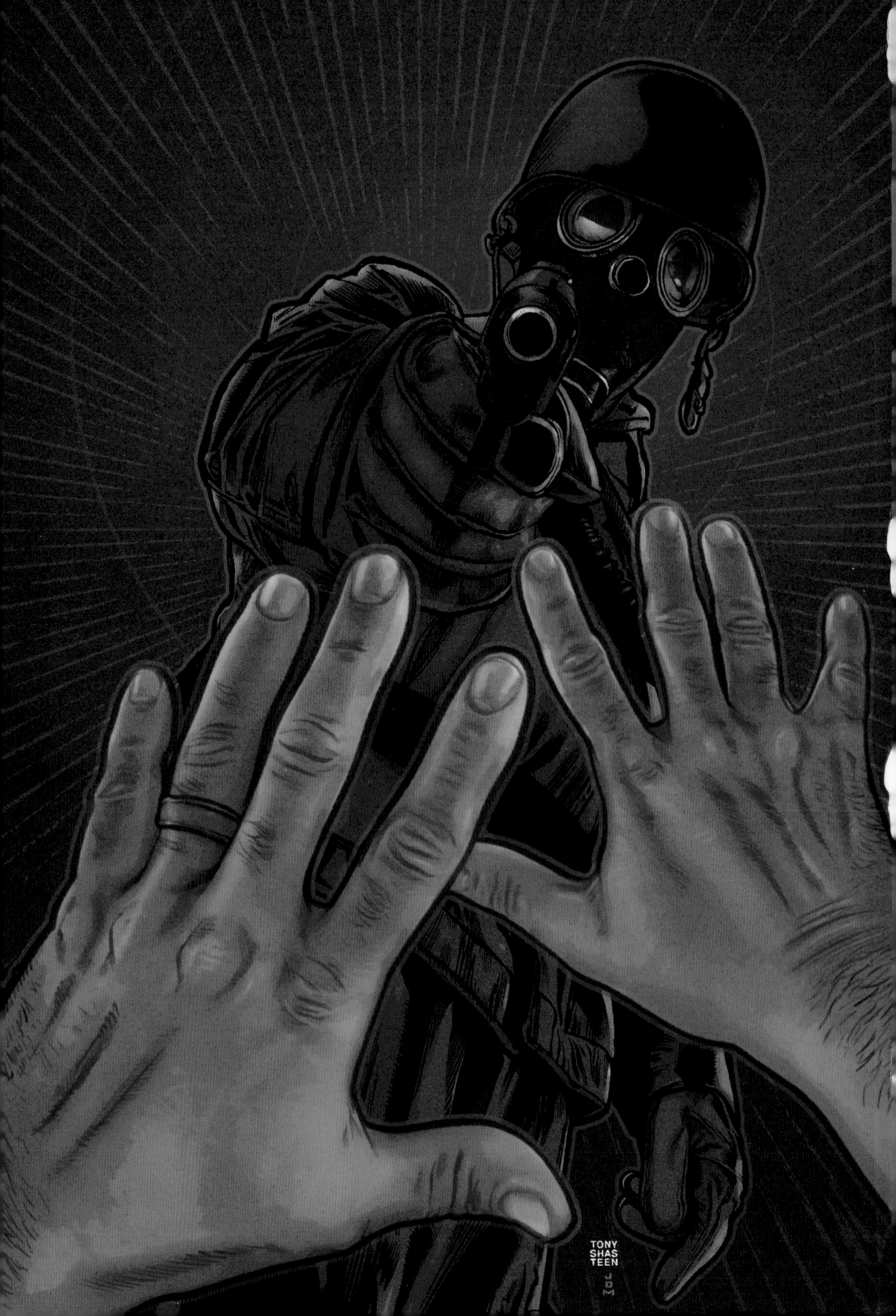
TONY
SHAS
TEEN

FAMILY™

VOL.1

RADIO NOWHERE

STEPHANIE PHILLIPS writer

TONY SHASTEEN artist

JD METTLER colorist

TROY PETERI letterer

TONY SHASTEEN w/ **JD METTLER** front & original covers

RYAN GARY BROWNE, **JUAN DOE**, **TONY HARRIS** & **NEIL NELSON** variant covers

TONY SHASTEEN logo designer

CHARLES PRITCHETT issue #1 backmatter designer

COREY BREEN book designer

MIKE MARTS editor

based on the **PHILIP K. DICK** short story *Breakfast at Twilight*

developed by **ERIC BROMBERG**

AFTERSHOCK™

MIKE MARTS - Editor-in-Chief • JOE PRUETT - Publisher/CCO • LEE KRAMER - President • JON KRAMER - Chief Executive Officer
STEVE ROTTERDAM - SVP, Sales & Marketing • DAN SHIRES - VP, Film & Television UK • CHRISTINA HARRINGTON - Managing Editor
MARC HAMMOND - Sr. Retail Sales Development Manager • RUTHANN THOMPSON - Sr. Retailer Relations Manager
KATHERINE JAMISON - Marketing Manager • KELLY DIODATI - Ambassador Outreach Manager • BLAKE STOCKER - VP, Finance
AARON MARION - Publicist • LISA MOODY - Finance • RYAN CARROLL - Director, Comics/Film/TV Liaison • JAWAD QURESHI - Technology Advisor/Strategist
RACHEL PINNELAS - Social Community Manager • CHARLES PRITCHETT - Design & Production Manager • COREY BREEN - Collections Production
TEODORO LEO - Associate Editor • STEPHANIE CASEBIER & SARAH PRUETT - Publishing Assistants

AfterShock Logo Design by COMICRAFT
Publicity: contact AARON MARION (aaron@publichausagency.com) & RYAN CROY (ryan@publichausagency.com) at PUBLICHAUS
Special thanks to: ATOM! FREEMAN, IRA KURGAN, MARINE KSADZHIKYAN, KEITH MANZELLA, ANTHONY MILITANO, ANTONIA LIANOS, STEPHAN NILSON & ED ZAREMBA

NUCLEAR FAMILY VOL.1: RADIO NOWHERE Published by AfterShock Comics, LLC, 15300 Ventura Boulevard Suite 507, Sherman Oaks, CA 91403. Originally published as Nuclear Family #1-5.
PRINTED IN KOREA. First Printing: October 2021. 10 9 8 7 6 5 4 3 2 1

AFTERSHOCKCOMICS.COM Follow us on social media

INTRODUCTION

I've always been interested in the notion of the American Dream and the false reality of American exceptionalism—how America sees itself and what America is in reality are often very disparate concepts. Shows like M*A*S*H or The Twilight Zone always struck me for their ability to offer that kind of critique wrapped in science-fiction, comedy and drama. The 1950s are such a ripe time period in American history to dig into that kind of discussion because the rhetoric about the "nuclear family" and American idealism was so prevalent, but this same rhetoric was also used as a mask to hide a deep-seated distrust and fear of each other's neighbors and unknown communist threats.

NUCLEAR FAMILY was born from this mindset: once you start peeling back the layers of propaganda and exceptionalism rhetoric, there's something rotten underneath. What better way to explore those layers than watching a quintessential nuclear family thrust into unknown territory, and forced to confront the very worst that their country has to offer.

This series has been a special book to work on. From the amazing creative team of Tony Shasteen, JD Mettler and Troy Peteri, to getting to play in a sandbox that the incredible Philip K. Dick established, this project has been a dream. I can't say enough good things about how Tony and JD brought this world to life visually—letting the reader quite literally dig deeper as we descend layers into this world of American idealism gone wrong.

I'm also excited to tease that this is not be the end for the McClean family... **stay tuned.**

STEPHANIE PHILLIPS
July 2021

1

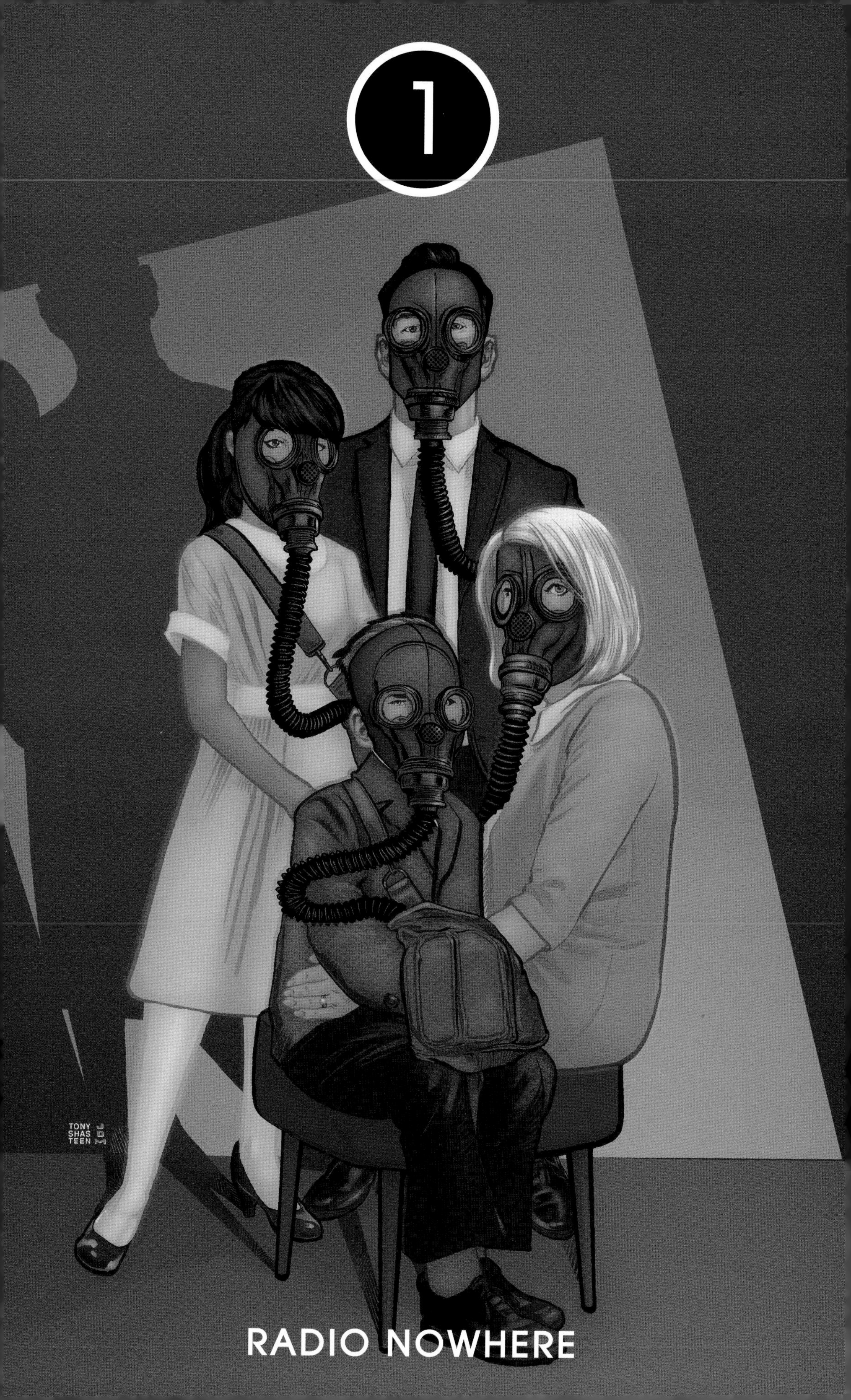
TONY
SHAS
TEEN

RADIO NOWHERE

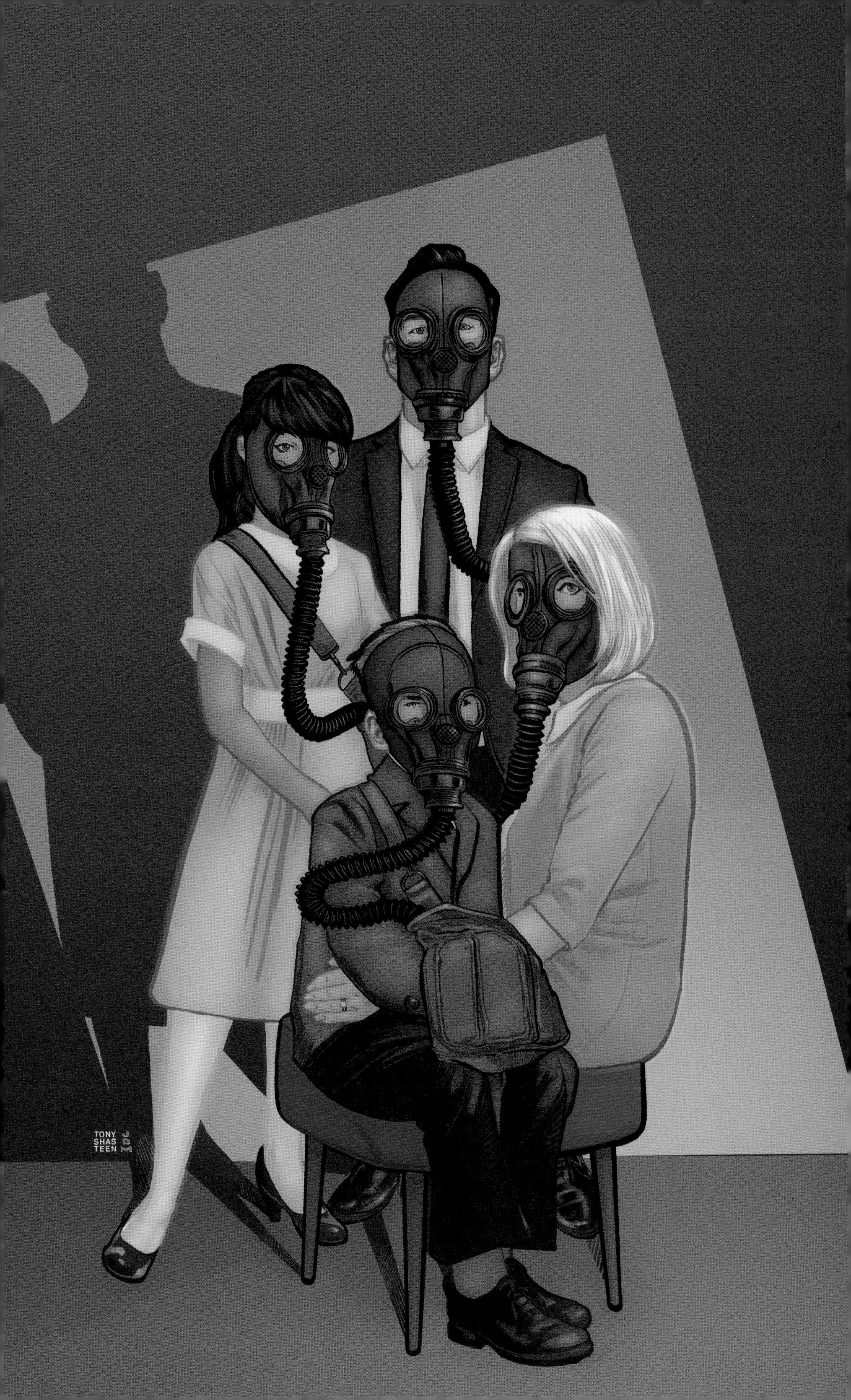
TONY
SHAS
TEEN

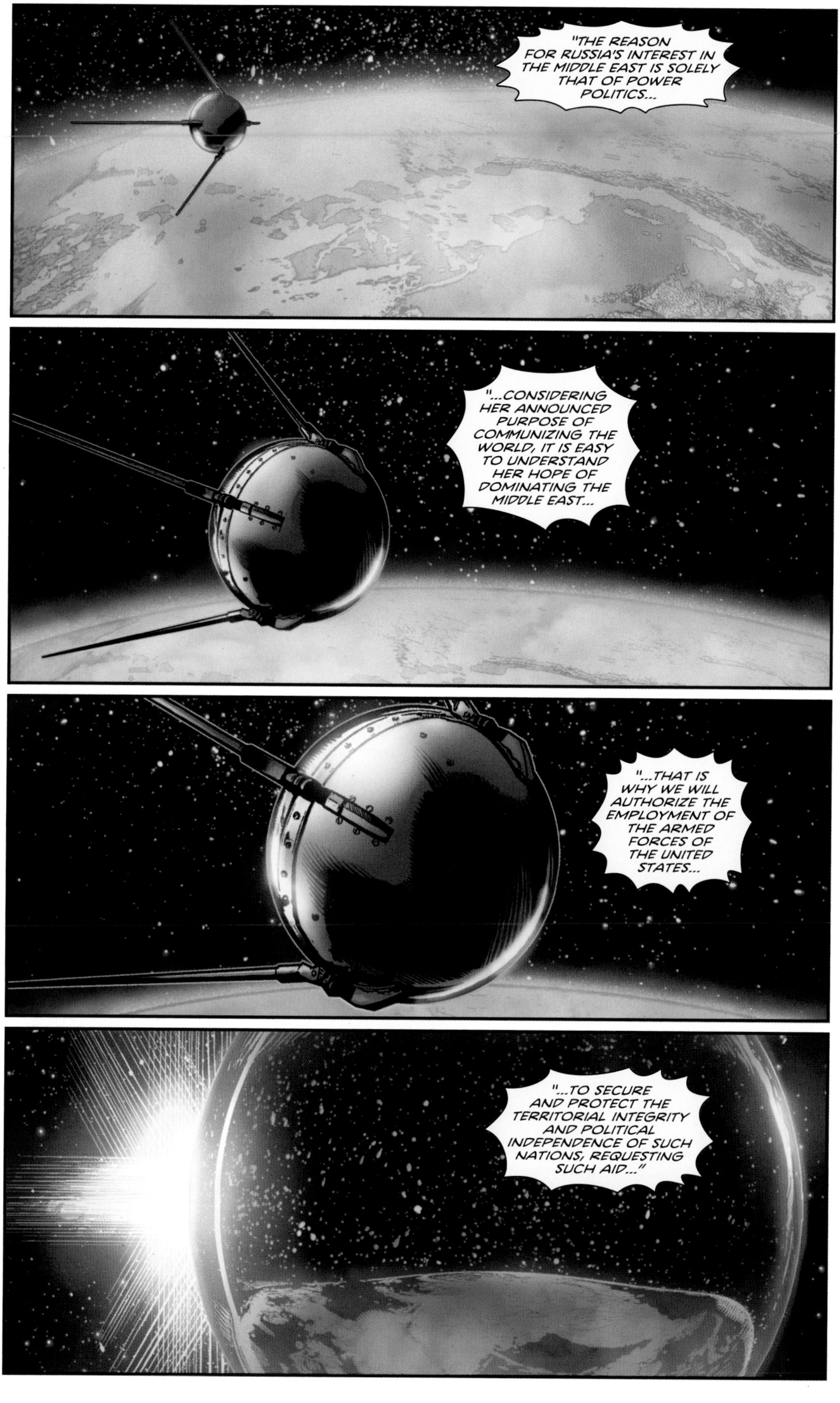
"THE REASON FOR RUSSIA'S INTEREST IN THE MIDDLE EAST IS SOLELY THAT OF POWER POLITICS...
"...CONSIDERING HER ANNOUNCED PURPOSE OF COMMUNIZING THE WORLD, IT IS EASY TO UNDERSTAND HER HOPE OF DOMINATING THE MIDDLE EAST...
"...THAT IS WHY WE WILL AUTHORIZE THE EMPLOYMENT OF THE ARMED FORCES OF THE UNITED STATES...
"...TO SECURE AND PROTECT THE TERRITORIAL INTEGRITY AND POLITICAL INDEPENDENCE OF SUCH NATIONS, REQUESTING SUCH AID..."

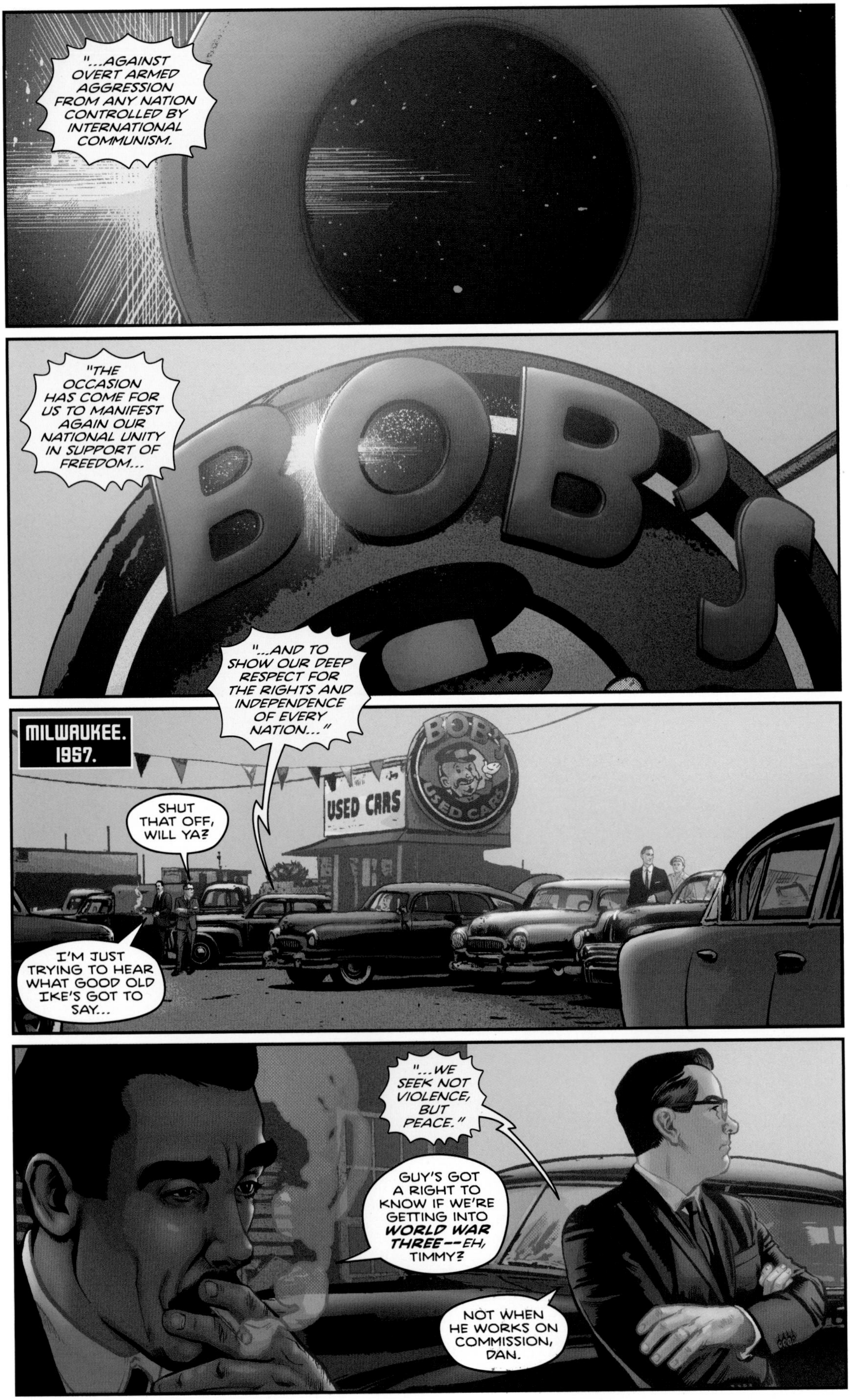
"...AGAINST OVERT ARMED AGGRESSION FROM ANY NATION CONTROLLED BY INTERNATIONAL COMMUNISM.
BOB'S
"THE OCCASION HAS COME FOR US TO MANIFEST AGAIN OUR NATIONAL UNITY IN SUPPORT OF FREEDOM...
"...AND TO SHOW OUR DEEP RESPECT FOR THE RIGHTS AND INDEPENDENCE OF EVERY NATION..."
MILWAUKEE. 1957.
BOB'S USED CARS
USED CARS
SHUT THAT OFF, WILL YA?
I'M JUST TRYING TO HEAR WHAT GOOD OLD IKE'S GOT TO SAY...
"...WE SEEK NOT VIOLENCE, BUT PEACE."
GUY'S GOT A RIGHT TO KNOW IF WE'RE GETTING INTO WORLD WAR THREE--EH, TIMMY?
NOT WHEN HE WORKS ON COMMISSION, DAN.

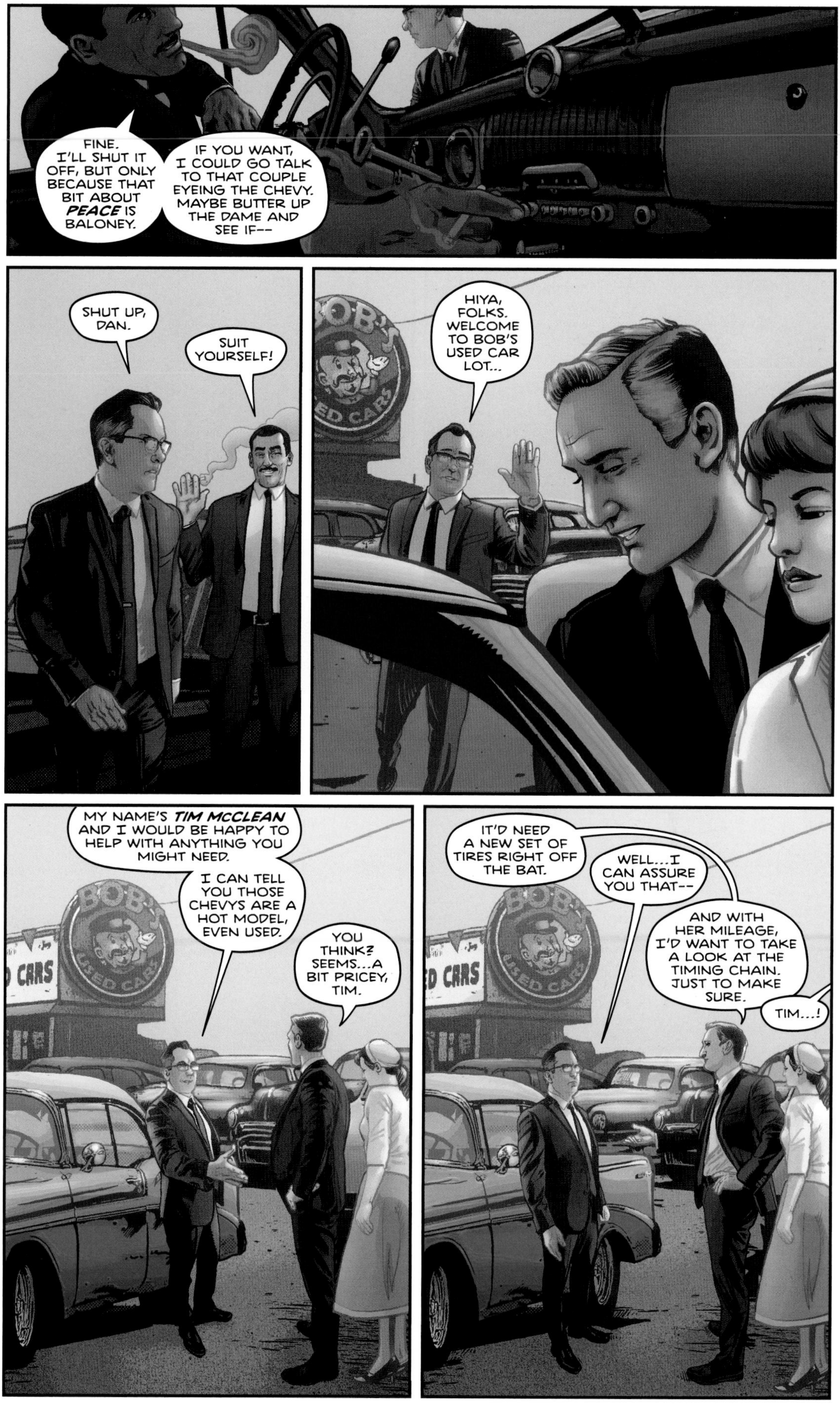
FINE. I'LL SHUT IT OFF, BUT ONLY BECAUSE THAT BIT ABOUT *PEACE* IS BALONEY.
IF YOU WANT, I COULD GO TALK TO THAT COUPLE EYEING THE CHEVY. MAYBE BUTTER UP THE DAME AND SEE IF--
SHUT UP, DAN.
SUIT YOURSELF!
HIYA, FOLKS. WELCOME TO BOB'S USED CAR LOT...
BOB'S
USED CARS
MY NAME'S *TIM McCLEAN* AND I WOULD BE HAPPY TO HELP WITH ANYTHING YOU MIGHT NEED.
I CAN TELL YOU THOSE CHEVYS ARE A HOT MODEL, EVEN USED.
YOU THINK? SEEMS...A BIT PRICEY, TIM.
IT'D NEED A NEW SET OF TIRES RIGHT OFF THE BAT.
WELL...I CAN ASSURE YOU THAT--
AND WITH HER MILEAGE, I'D WANT TO TAKE A LOOK AT THE TIMING CHAIN. JUST TO MAKE SURE.
TIM...!

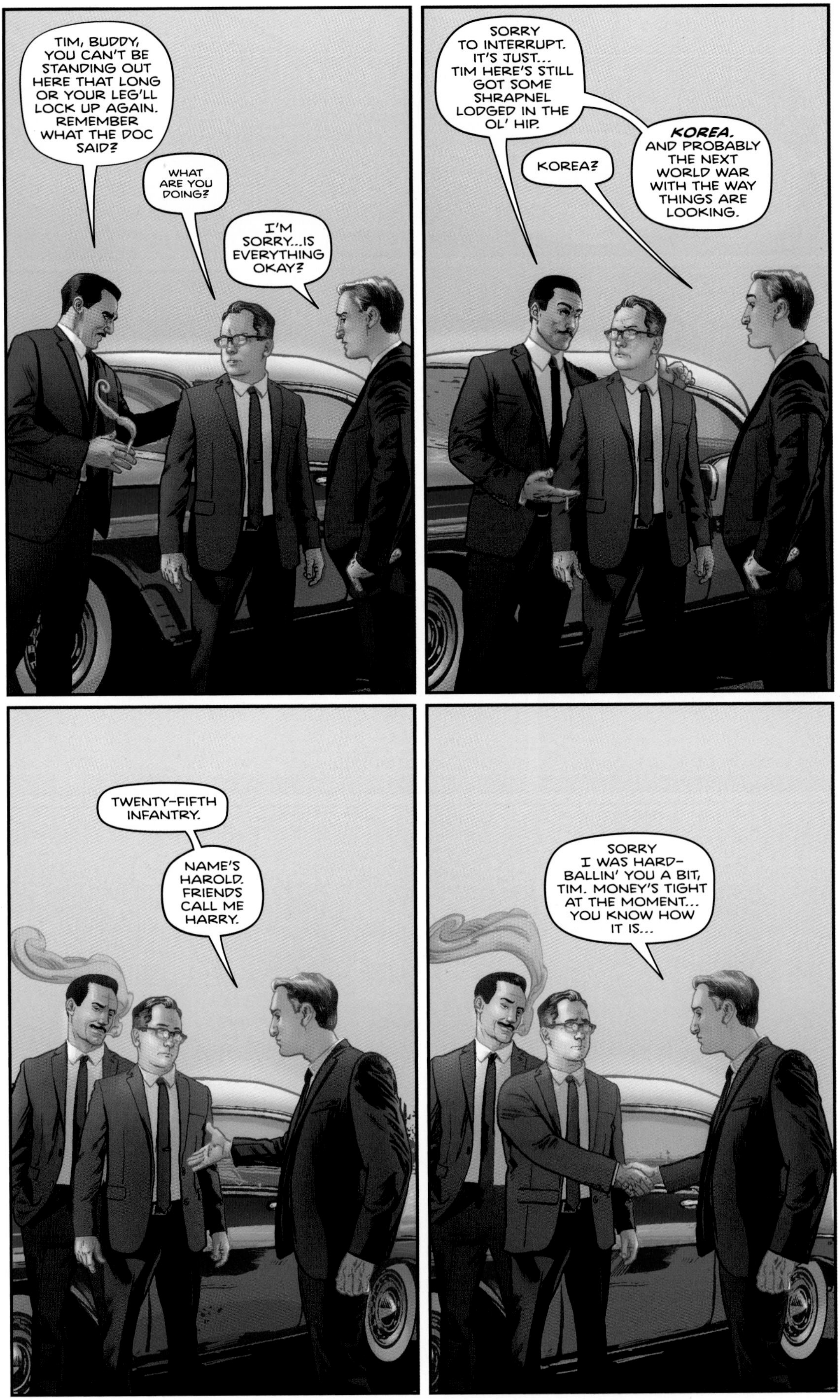
TIM, BUDDY, YOU CAN'T BE STANDING OUT HERE THAT LONG OR YOUR LEG'LL LOCK UP AGAIN. REMEMBER WHAT THE DOC SAID?
WHAT ARE YOU DOING?
I'M SORRY...IS EVERYTHING OKAY?
SORRY TO INTERRUPT. IT'S JUST... TIM HERE'S STILL GOT SOME SHRAPNEL LODGED IN THE OL' HIP.
KOREA?
KOREA. AND PROBABLY THE NEXT WORLD WAR WITH THE WAY THINGS ARE LOOKING.
TWENTY-FIFTH INFANTRY.
NAME'S HAROLD. FRIENDS CALL ME HARRY.
SORRY I WAS HARD-BALLIN' YOU A BIT, TIM. MONEY'S TIGHT AT THE MOMENT... YOU KNOW HOW IT IS...

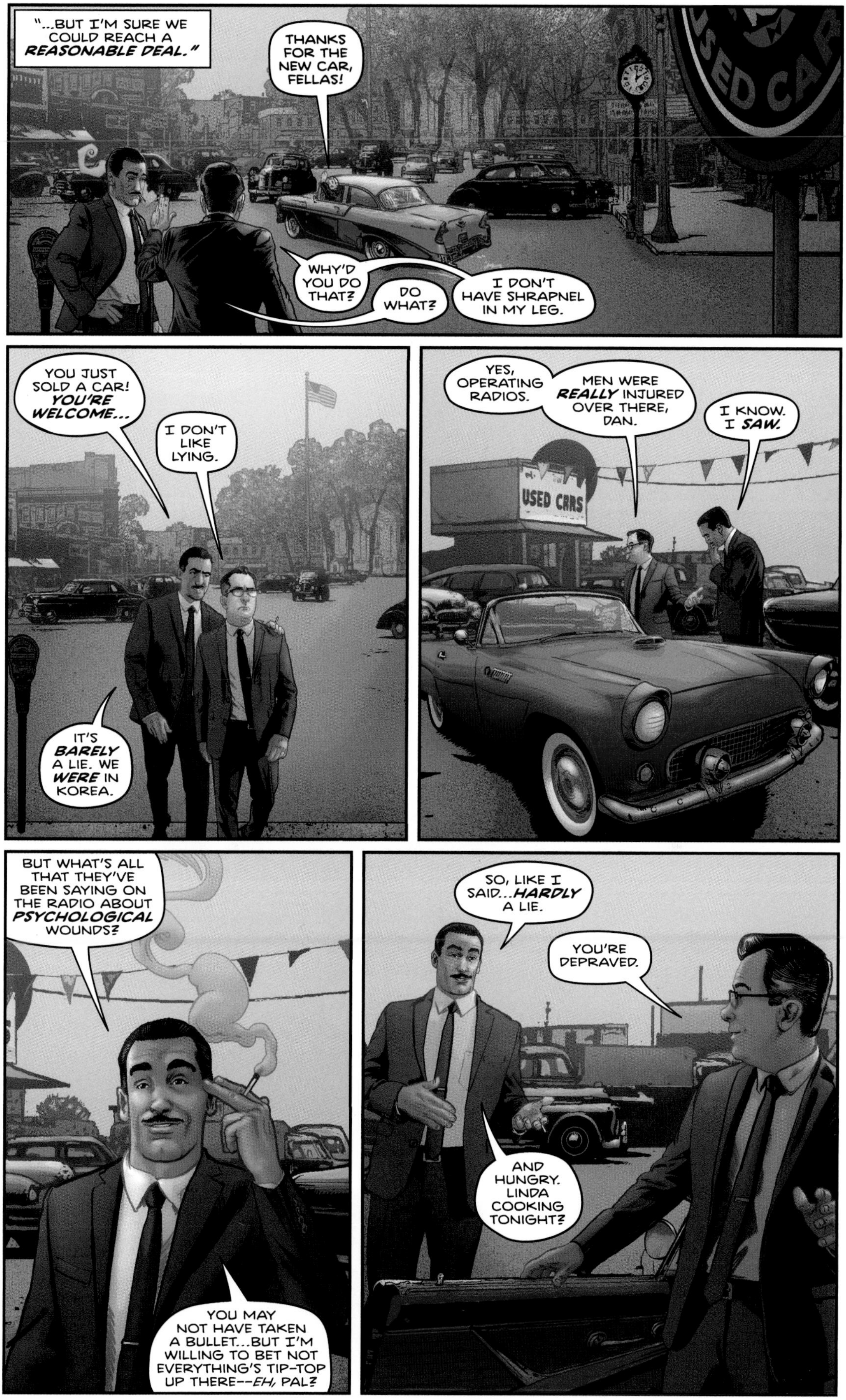
"...BUT I'M SURE WE COULD REACH A *REASONABLE DEAL.*"
THANKS FOR THE NEW CAR, FELLAS!
USED CAR
WHY'D YOU DO THAT?
DO WHAT?
I DON'T HAVE SHRAPNEL IN MY LEG.
YOU JUST SOLD A CAR! *YOU'RE WELCOME...*
I DON'T LIKE LYING.
IT'S *BARELY* A LIE. WE *WERE* IN KOREA.
YES, OPERATING RADIOS.
MEN WERE *REALLY* INJURED OVER THERE, DAN.
I KNOW. I *SAW.*
USED CARS
BUT WHAT'S ALL THAT THEY'VE BEEN SAYING ON THE RADIO ABOUT *PSYCHOLOGICAL* WOUNDS?
YOU MAY NOT HAVE TAKEN A BULLET...BUT I'M WILLING TO BET NOT EVERYTHING'S TIP-TOP UP THERE--*EH,* PAL?
SO, LIKE I SAID...*HARDLY* A LIE.
YOU'RE DEPRAVED.
AND HUNGRY. LINDA COOKING TONIGHT?

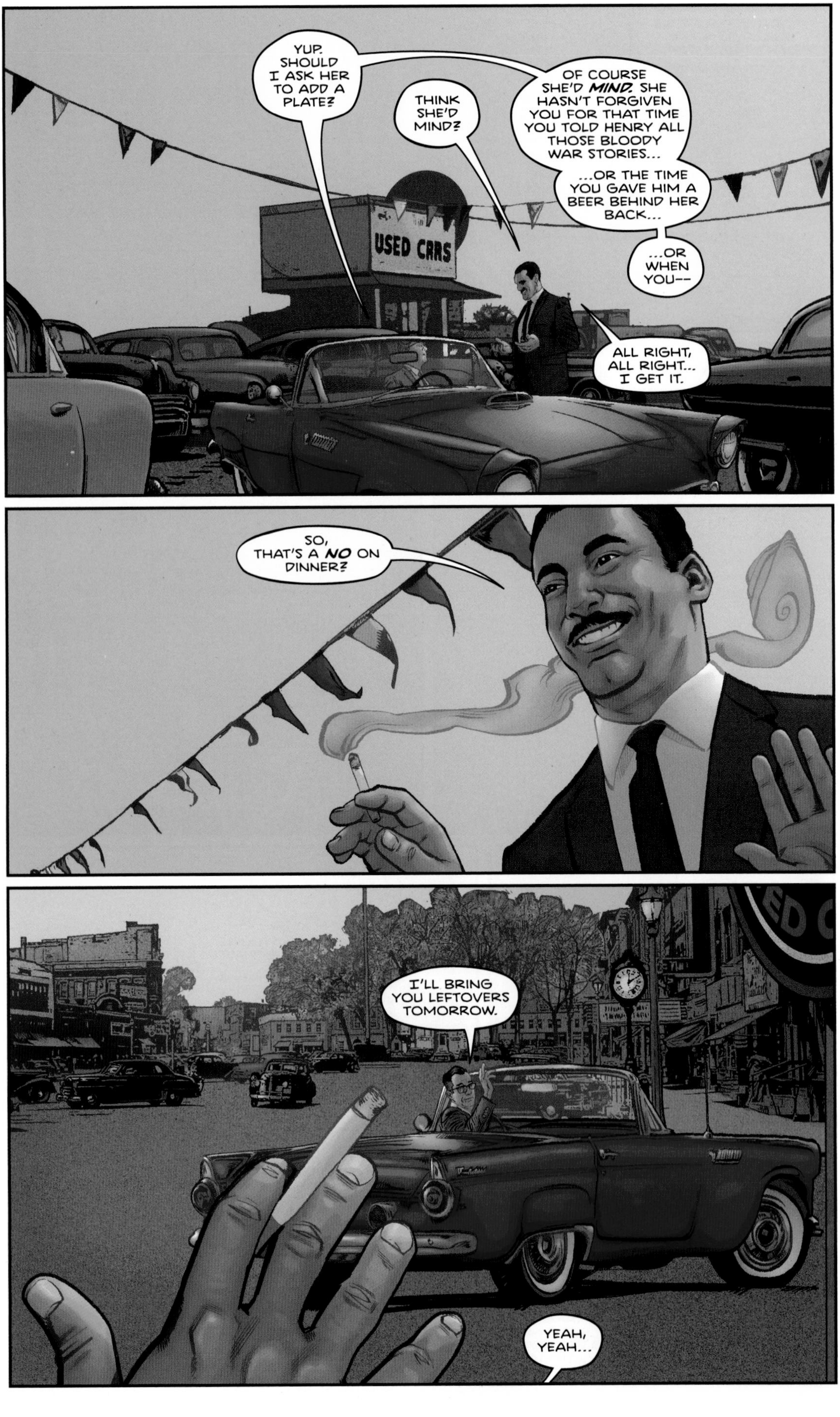
YUP. SHOULD I ASK HER TO ADD A PLATE?
THINK SHE'D MIND?
OF COURSE SHE'D MIND. SHE HASN'T FORGIVEN YOU FOR THAT TIME YOU TOLD HENRY ALL THOSE BLOODY WAR STORIES...
...OR THE TIME YOU GAVE HIM A BEER BEHIND HER BACK...
...OR WHEN YOU--
USED CARS
ALL RIGHT, ALL RIGHT... I GET IT.
SO, THAT'S A NO ON DINNER?
I'LL BRING YOU LEFTOVERS TOMORROW.
YEAH, YEAH...

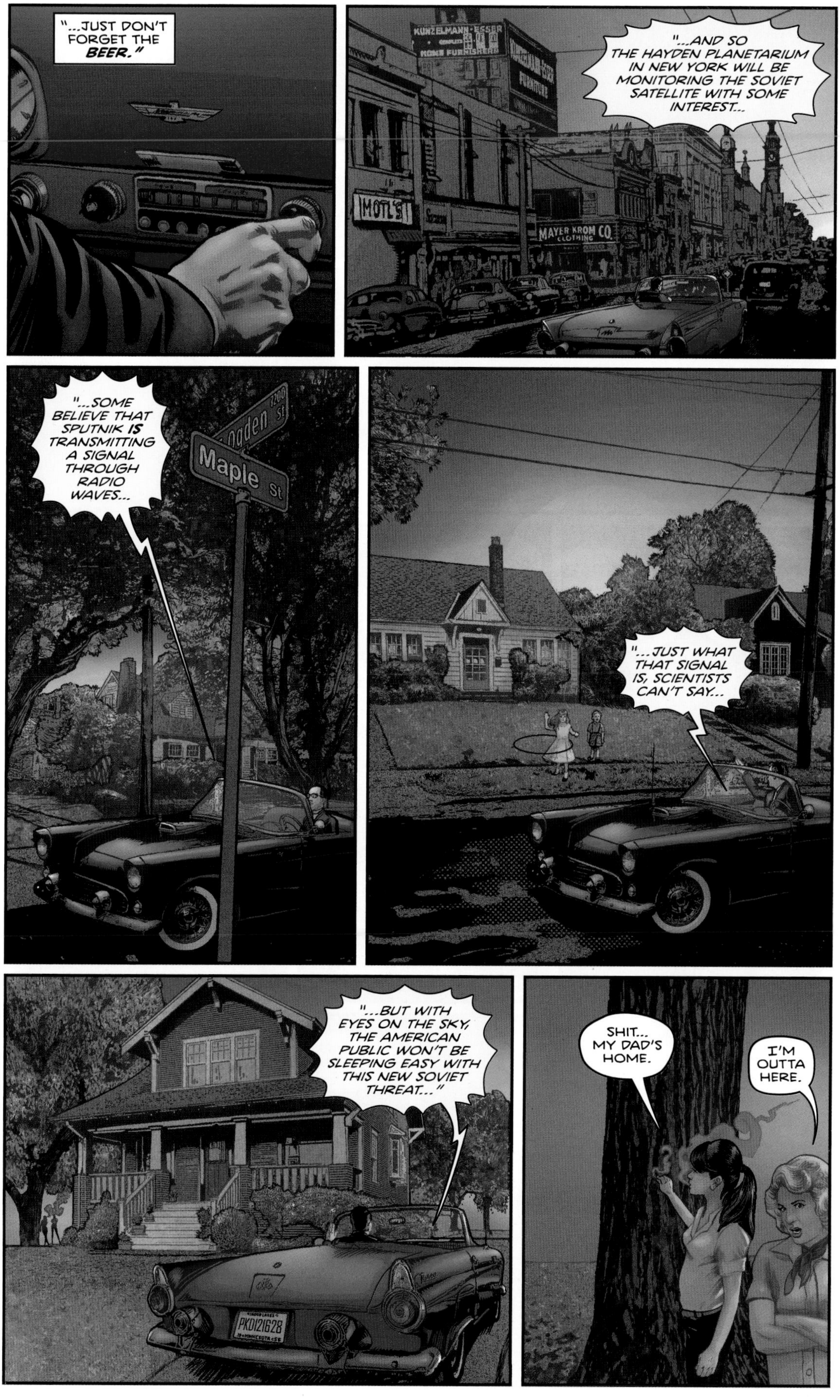
"...JUST DON'T FORGET THE **BEER.**"
KUNZELMANN-ESSER
HOME FURNISHERS
"...AND SO THE HAYDEN PLANETARIUM IN NEW YORK WILL BE MONITORING THE SOVIET SATELLITE WITH SOME INTEREST...
MOTL'S
MAYER KROM CO.
CLOTHING
"...SOME BELIEVE THAT SPUTNIK **IS** TRANSMITTING A SIGNAL THROUGH RADIO WAVES...
Maple St
"...JUST WHAT THAT SIGNAL IS, SCIENTISTS CAN'T SAY...
"...BUT WITH EYES ON THE SKY, THE AMERICAN PUBLIC WON'T BE SLEEPING EASY WITH THIS NEW SOVIET THREAT..."
PKD121628
SHIT... MY DAD'S HOME.
I'M OUTTA HERE.

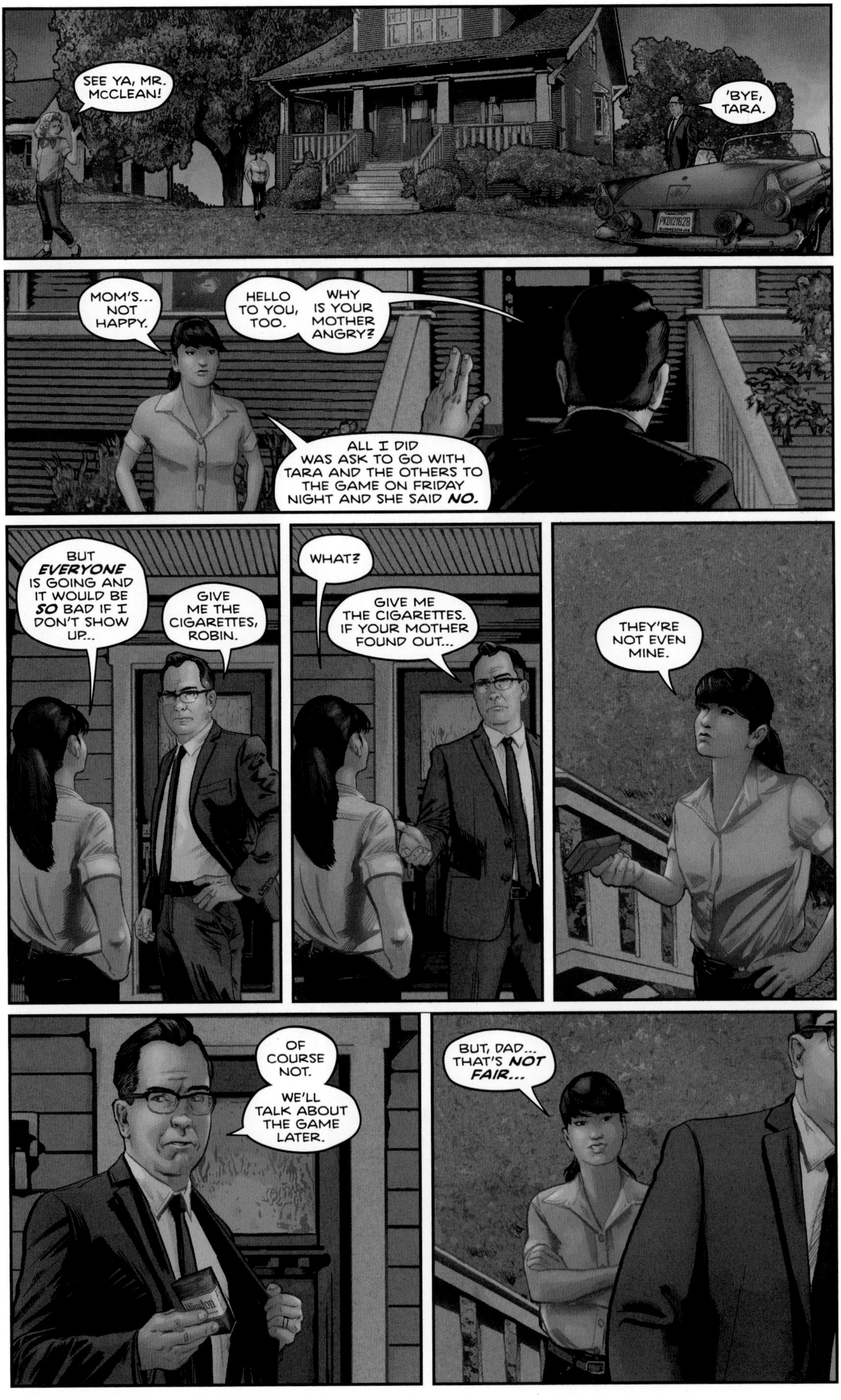
SEE YA, MR. MCCLEAN!
'BYE, TARA.
MOM'S... NOT HAPPY.
HELLO TO YOU, TOO.
WHY IS YOUR MOTHER ANGRY?
ALL I DID WAS ASK TO GO WITH TARA AND THE OTHERS TO THE GAME ON FRIDAY NIGHT AND SHE SAID NO.
BUT EVERYONE IS GOING AND IT WOULD BE SO BAD IF I DON'T SHOW UP...
GIVE ME THE CIGARETTES, ROBIN.
WHAT?
GIVE ME THE CIGARETTES. IF YOUR MOTHER FOUND OUT...
THEY'RE NOT EVEN MINE.
OF COURSE NOT.
WE'LL TALK ABOUT THE GAME LATER.
BUT, DAD... THAT'S NOT FAIR...

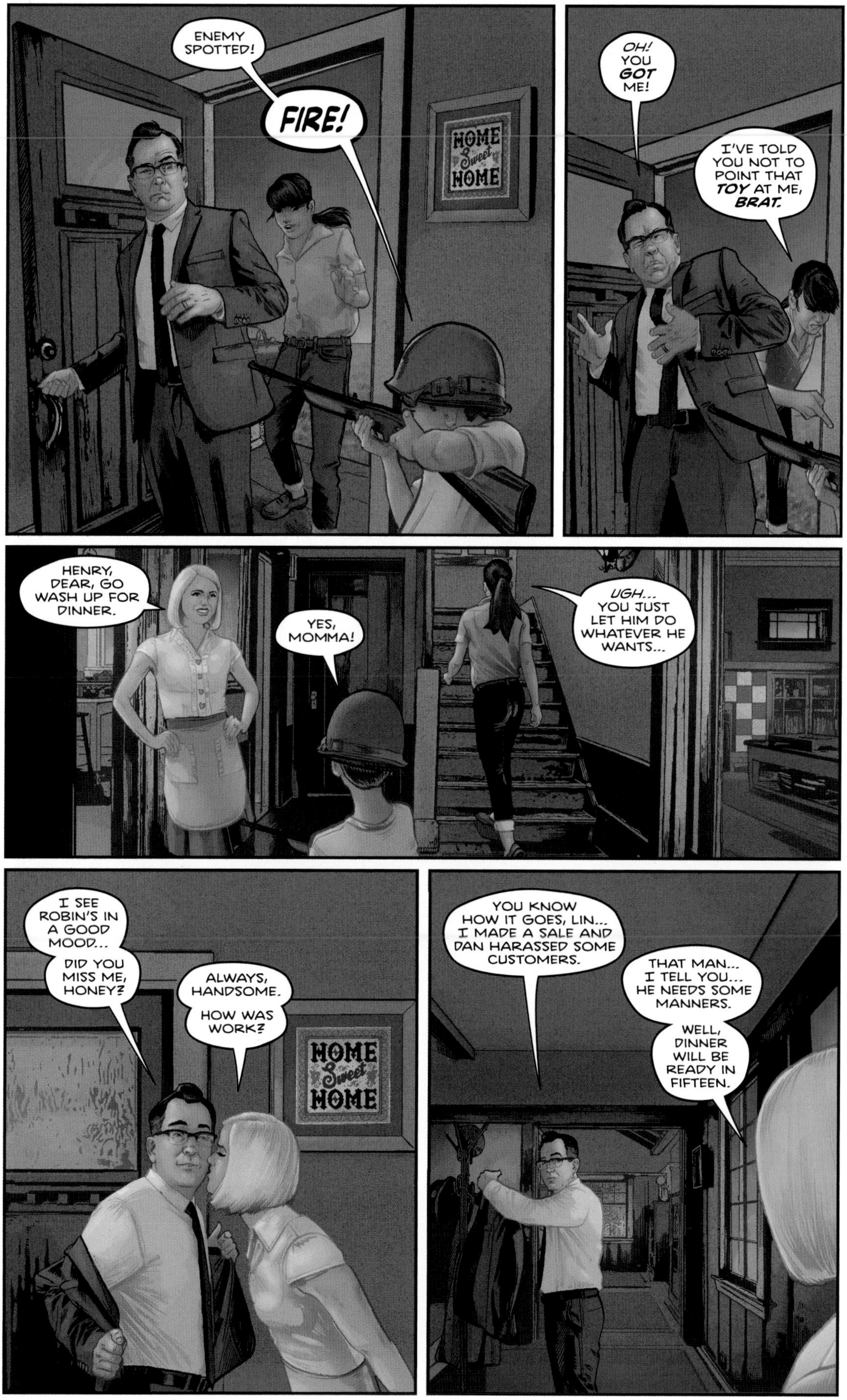
ENEMY SPOTTED!
FIRE!
HOME Sweet HOME
OH! YOU GOT ME!
I'VE TOLD YOU NOT TO POINT THAT TOY AT ME, BRAT.
HENRY, DEAR, GO WASH UP FOR DINNER.
YES, MOMMA!
UGH... YOU JUST LET HIM DO WHATEVER HE WANTS...
I SEE ROBIN'S IN A GOOD MOOD...
DID YOU MISS ME, HONEY?
ALWAYS, HANDSOME.
HOW WAS WORK?
HOME Sweet HOME
YOU KNOW HOW IT GOES, LIN... I MADE A SALE AND DAN HARASSED SOME CUSTOMERS.
THAT MAN... I TELL YOU... HE NEEDS SOME MANNERS.
WELL, DINNER WILL BE READY IN FIFTEEN.

SOUNDS GREAT, DARLING. I'M JUST GOING TO POP INTO THE BASEMENT.

I INSTALLED THAT NEW ANTENNA LAST NIGHT AND CAN'T WAIT TO SEE WHAT THAT BABY CAN DO.

BOYS AND THEIR TOYS...

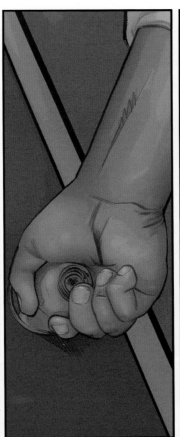

KLICK

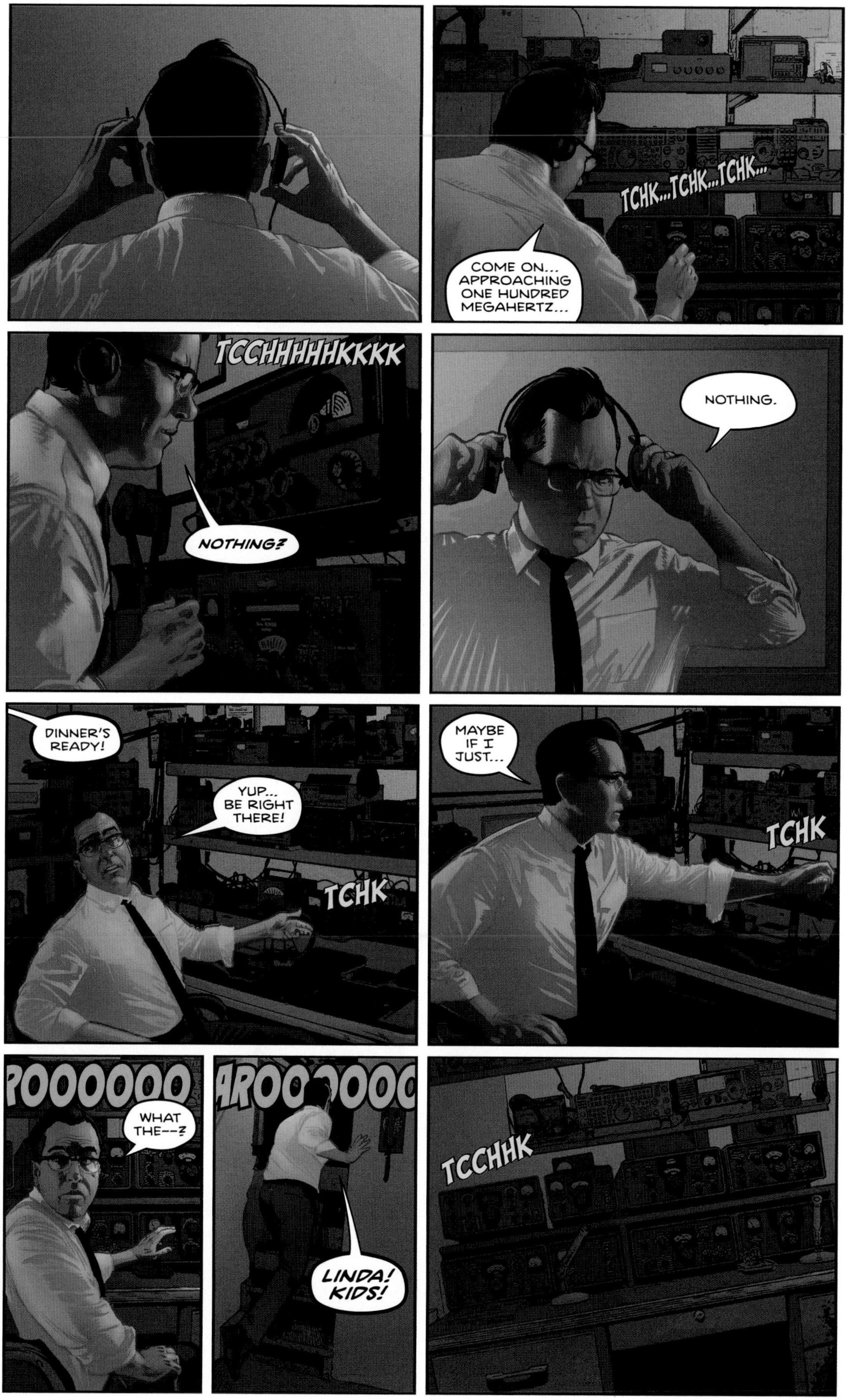
TCHK...TCHK...TCHK...
COME ON... APPROACHING ONE HUNDRED MEGAHERTZ...
TCCHHHHHKKKK
NOTHING?
NOTHING.
DINNER'S READY!
YUP... BE RIGHT THERE!
TCHK
MAYBE IF I JUST...
TCHK
ROOOOOO
WHAT THE--?
AROOOOOO
LINDA! KIDS!
TCCHHK

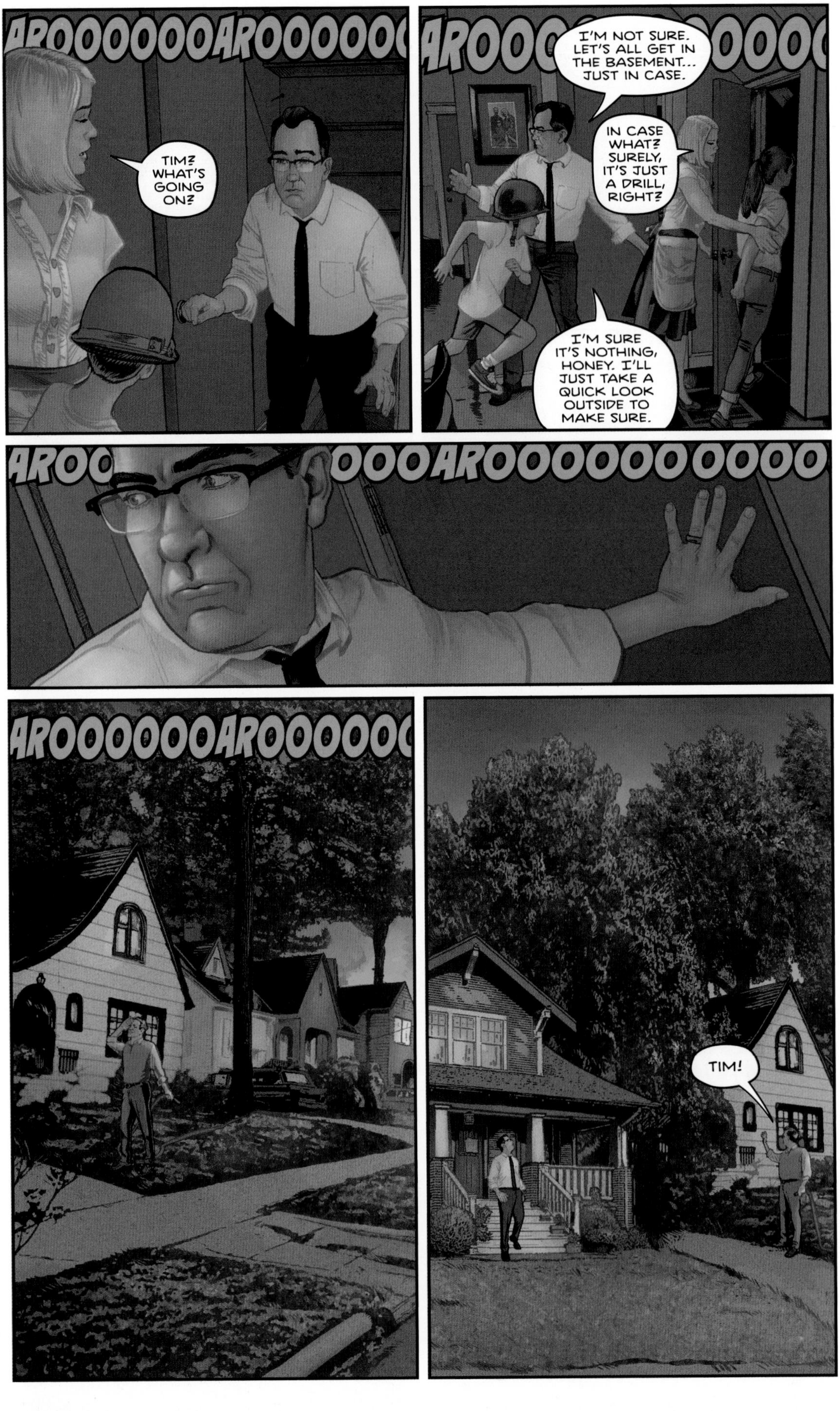
AROOOOOOAROOOOOO
TIM? WHAT'S GOING ON?
AROOO OOOOO
I'M NOT SURE. LET'S ALL GET IN THE BASEMENT... JUST IN CASE.
IN CASE WHAT? SURELY, IT'S JUST A DRILL, RIGHT?
I'M SURE IT'S NOTHING, HONEY. I'LL JUST TAKE A QUICK LOOK OUTSIDE TO MAKE SURE.
AROO OOOAROOOOOOOOOOOO
AROOOOOOAROOOOOO
TIM!

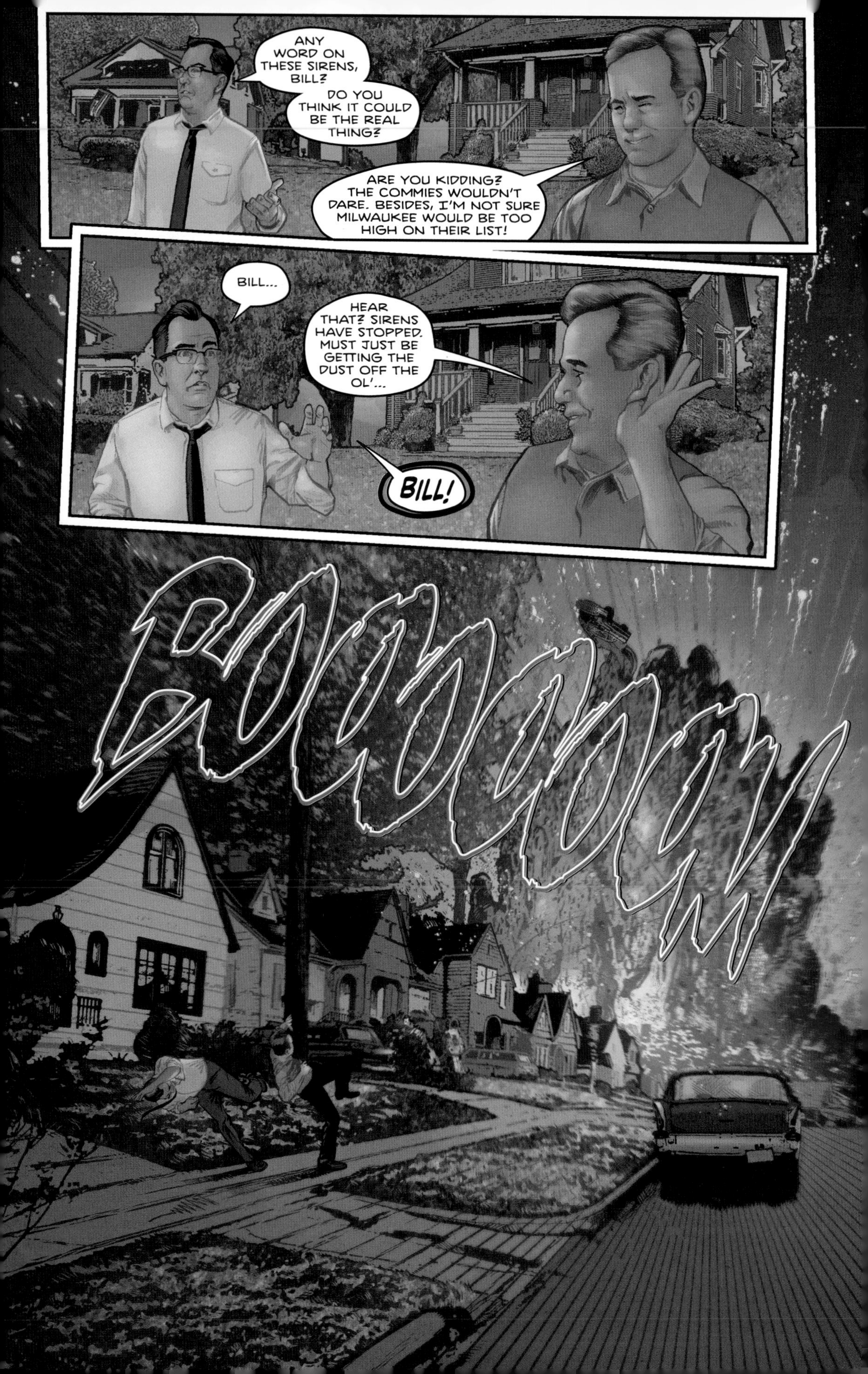
ANY WORD ON THESE SIRENS, BILL?
DO YOU THINK IT COULD BE THE REAL THING?
ARE YOU KIDDING? THE COMMIES WOULDN'T DARE. BESIDES, I'M NOT SURE MILWAUKEE WOULD BE TOO HIGH ON THEIR LIST!
BILL...
HEAR THAT? SIRENS HAVE STOPPED. MUST JUST BE GETTING THE DUST OFF THE OL'...
BILL!
BOOOOOOM

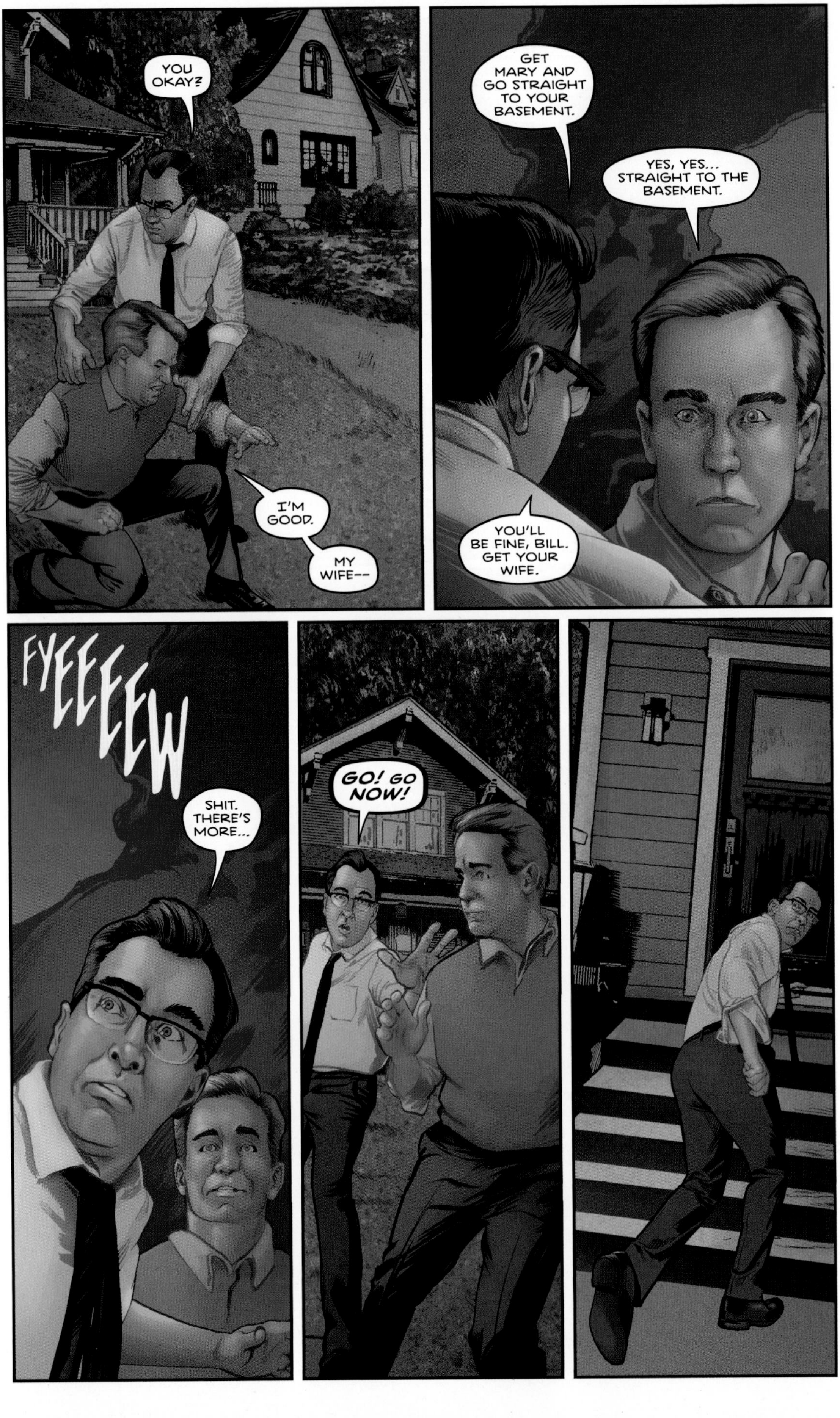
YOU OKAY?
I'M GOOD.
MY WIFE--
GET MARY AND GO STRAIGHT TO YOUR BASEMENT.
YES, YES... STRAIGHT TO THE BASEMENT.
YOU'LL BE FINE, BILL. GET YOUR WIFE.
FYEEEEW
SHIT. THERE'S MORE...
GO! GO NOW!

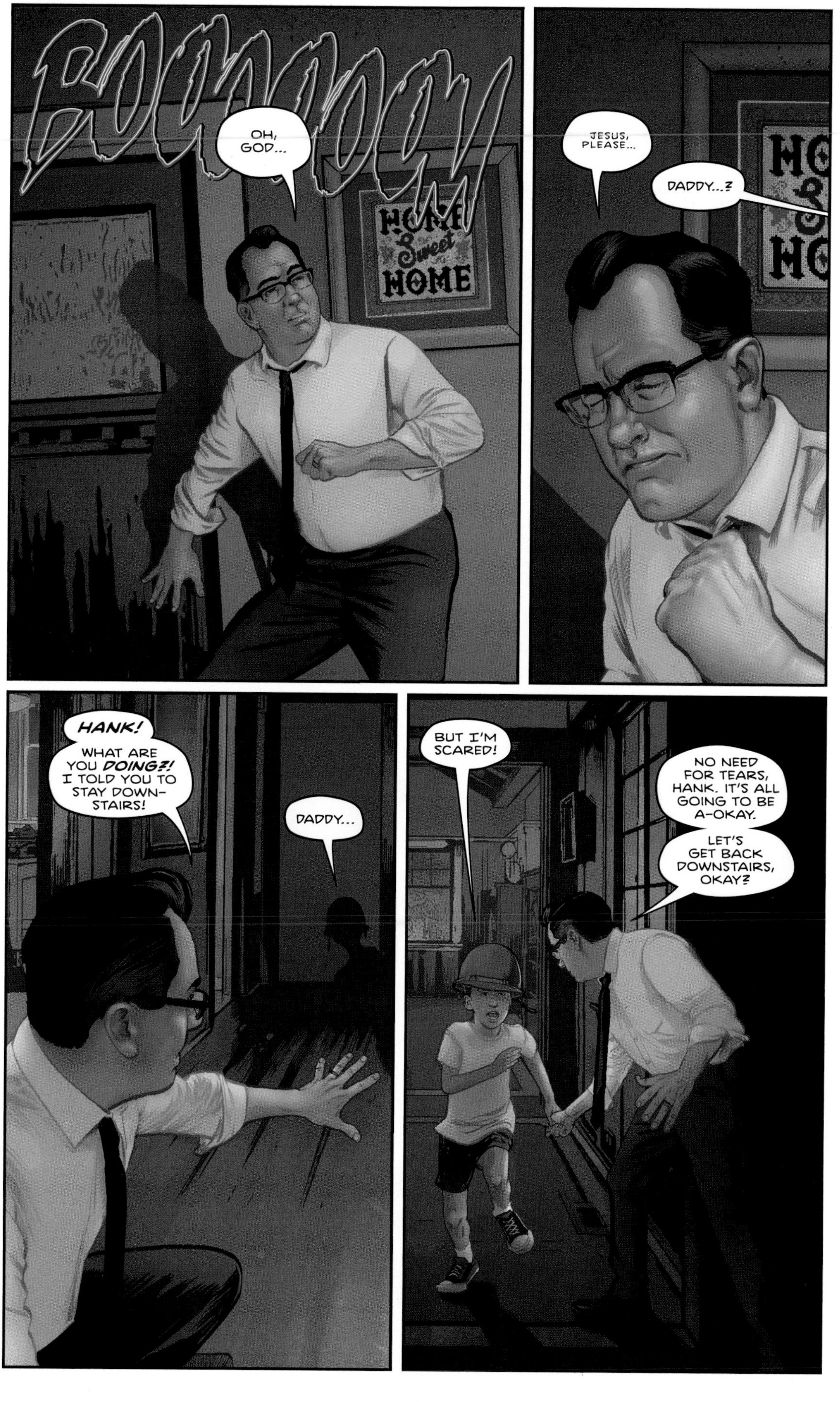
BOOOOOM
OH, GOD...
JESUS, PLEASE...
DADDY...?
HANK!
WHAT ARE YOU DOING?! I TOLD YOU TO STAY DOWN-STAIRS!
DADDY...
BUT I'M SCARED!
NO NEED FOR TEARS, HANK. IT'S ALL GOING TO BE A-OKAY.
LET'S GET BACK DOWNSTAIRS, OKAY?

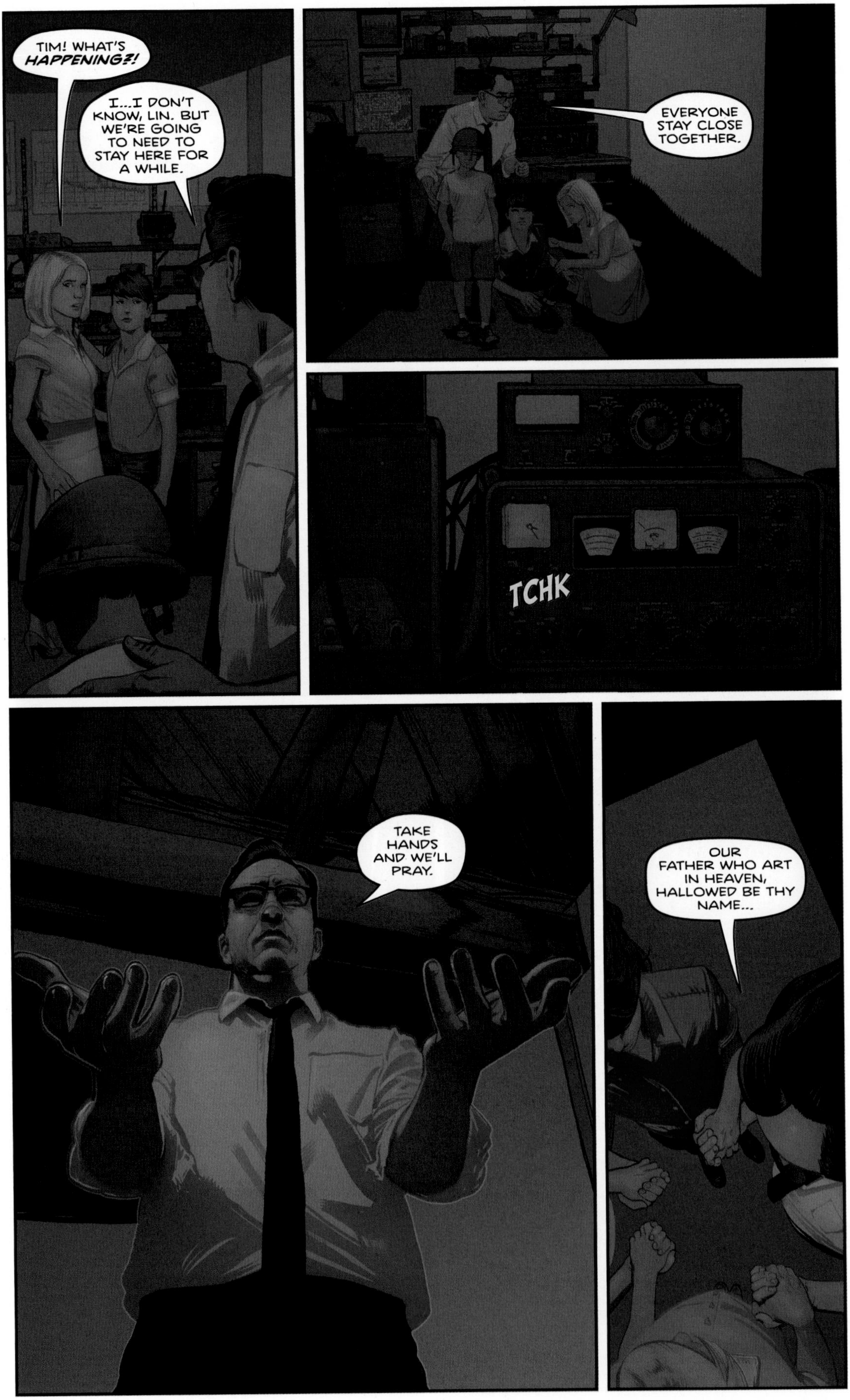
TIM! WHAT'S *HAPPENING?!*
I...I DON'T KNOW, LIN. BUT WE'RE GOING TO NEED TO STAY HERE FOR A WHILE.
EVERYONE STAY CLOSE TOGETHER.
TCHK
TAKE HANDS AND WE'LL PRAY.
OUR FATHER WHO ART IN HEAVEN, HALLOWED BE THY NAME...

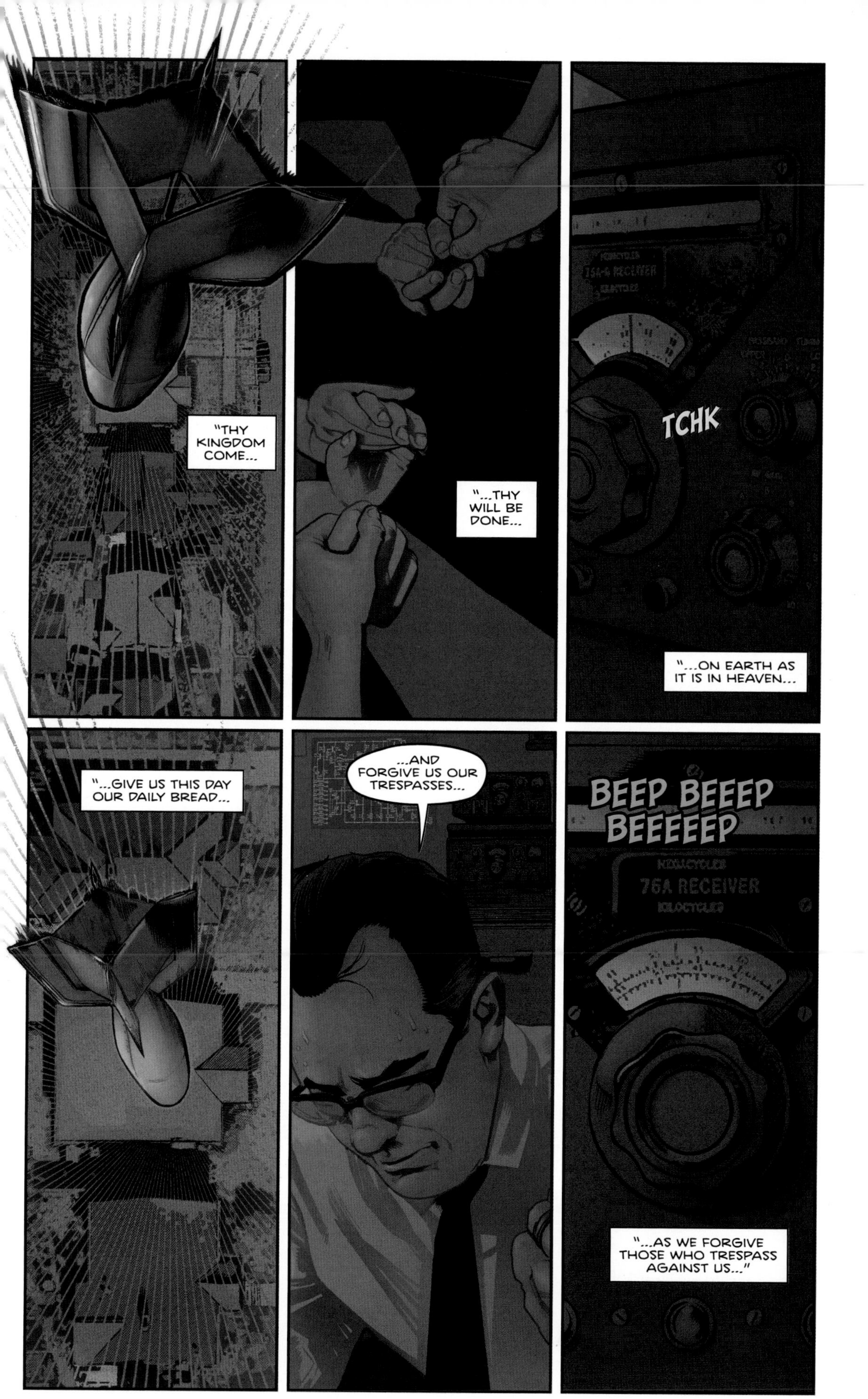
"THY KINGDOM COME...
"...THY WILL BE DONE...
TCHK
"...ON EARTH AS IT IS IN HEAVEN...
"...GIVE US THIS DAY OUR DAILY BREAD...
...AND FORGIVE US OUR TRESPASSES...
BEEP BEEEP BEEEEEP
76A RECEIVER
"...AS WE FORGIVE THOSE WHO TRESPASS AGAINST US..."

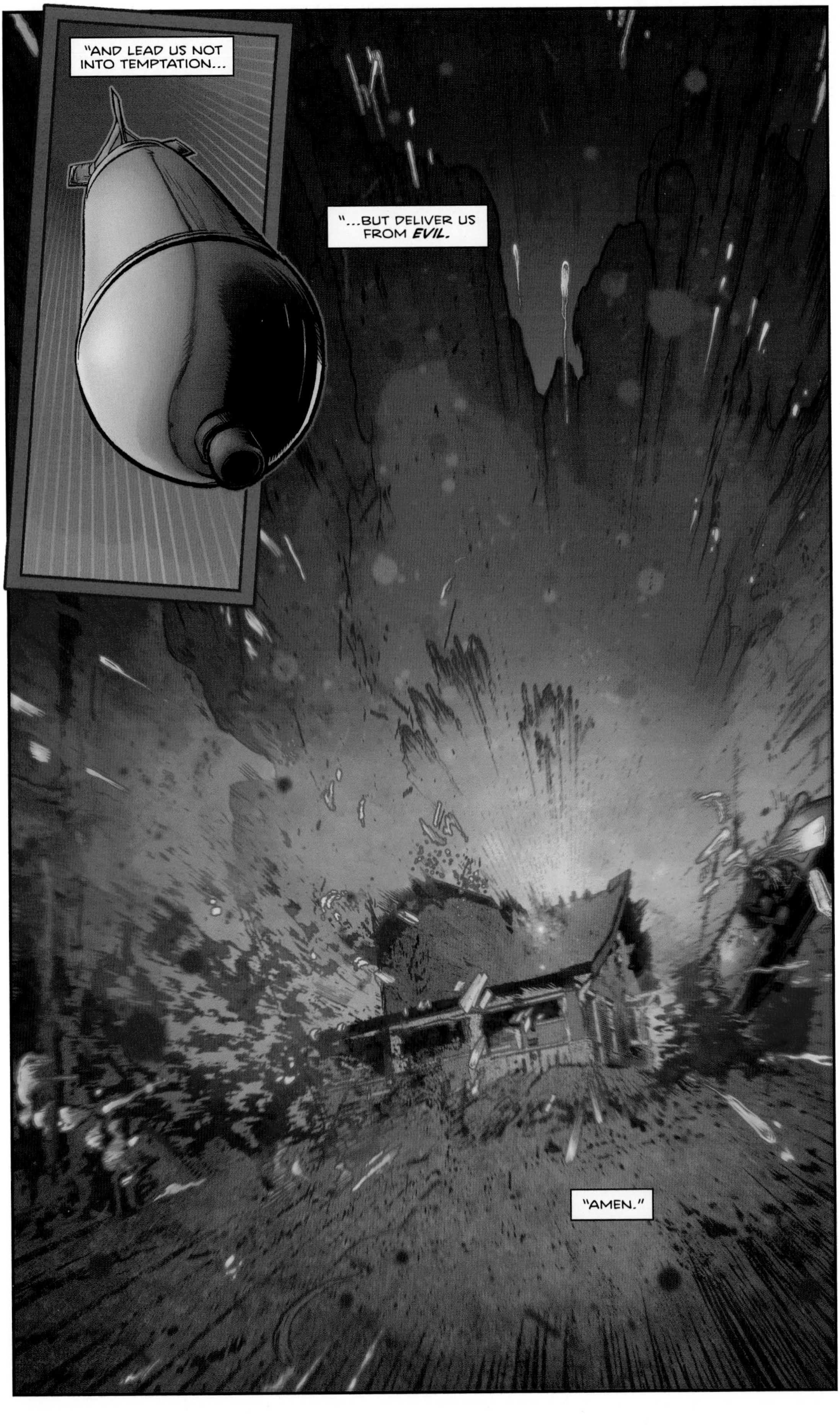
"AND LEAD US NOT INTO TEMPTATION...
"...BUT DELIVER US FROM *EVIL.*
"AMEN."

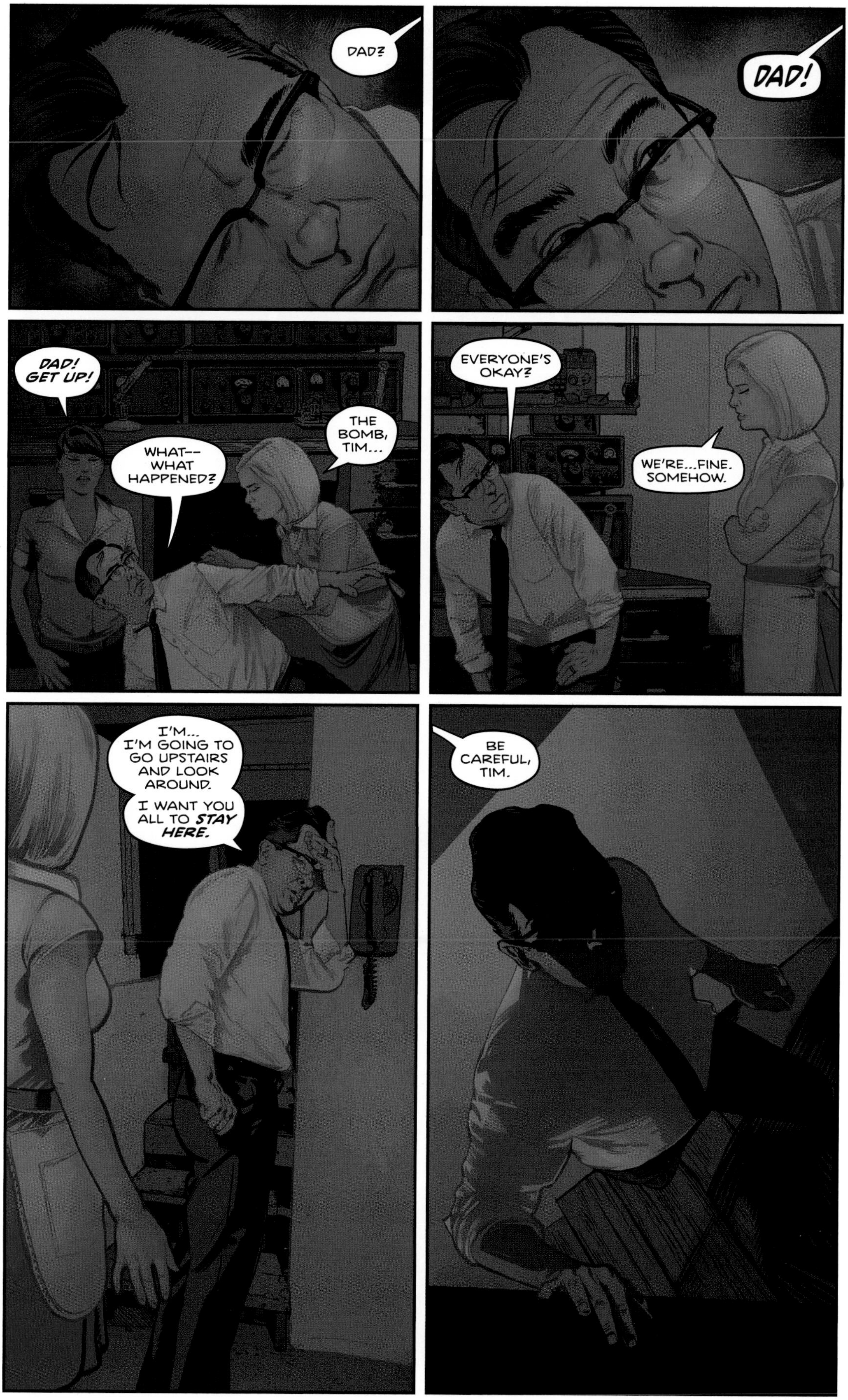
DAD?
DAD!
DAD! GET UP!
WHAT-- WHAT HAPPENED?
THE BOMB, TIM...
EVERYONE'S OKAY?
WE'RE...FINE. SOMEHOW.
I'M... I'M GOING TO GO UPSTAIRS AND LOOK AROUND.
I WANT YOU ALL TO STAY HERE.
BE CAREFUL, TIM.

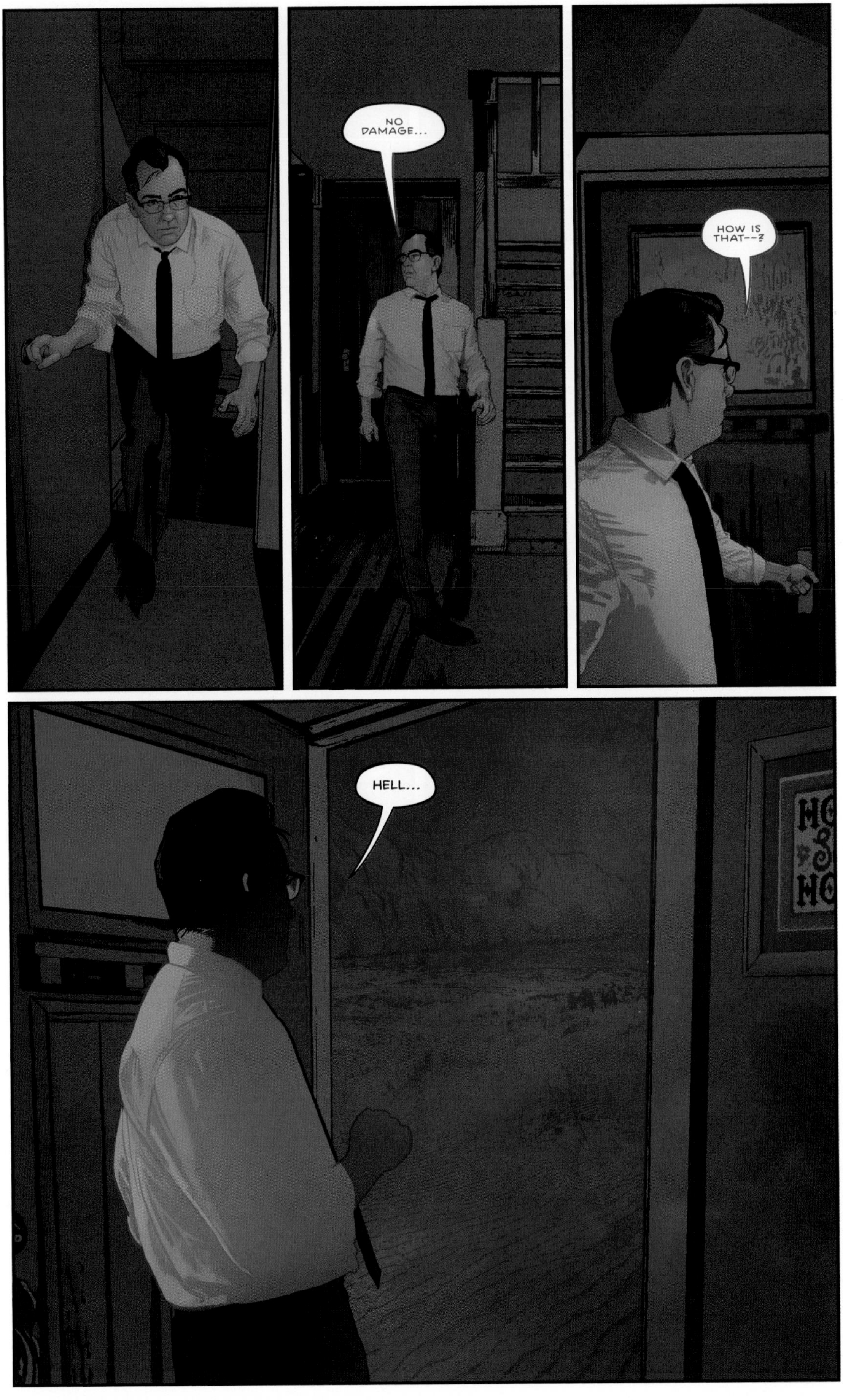
NO DAMAGE...
HOW IS THAT--?
HELL...

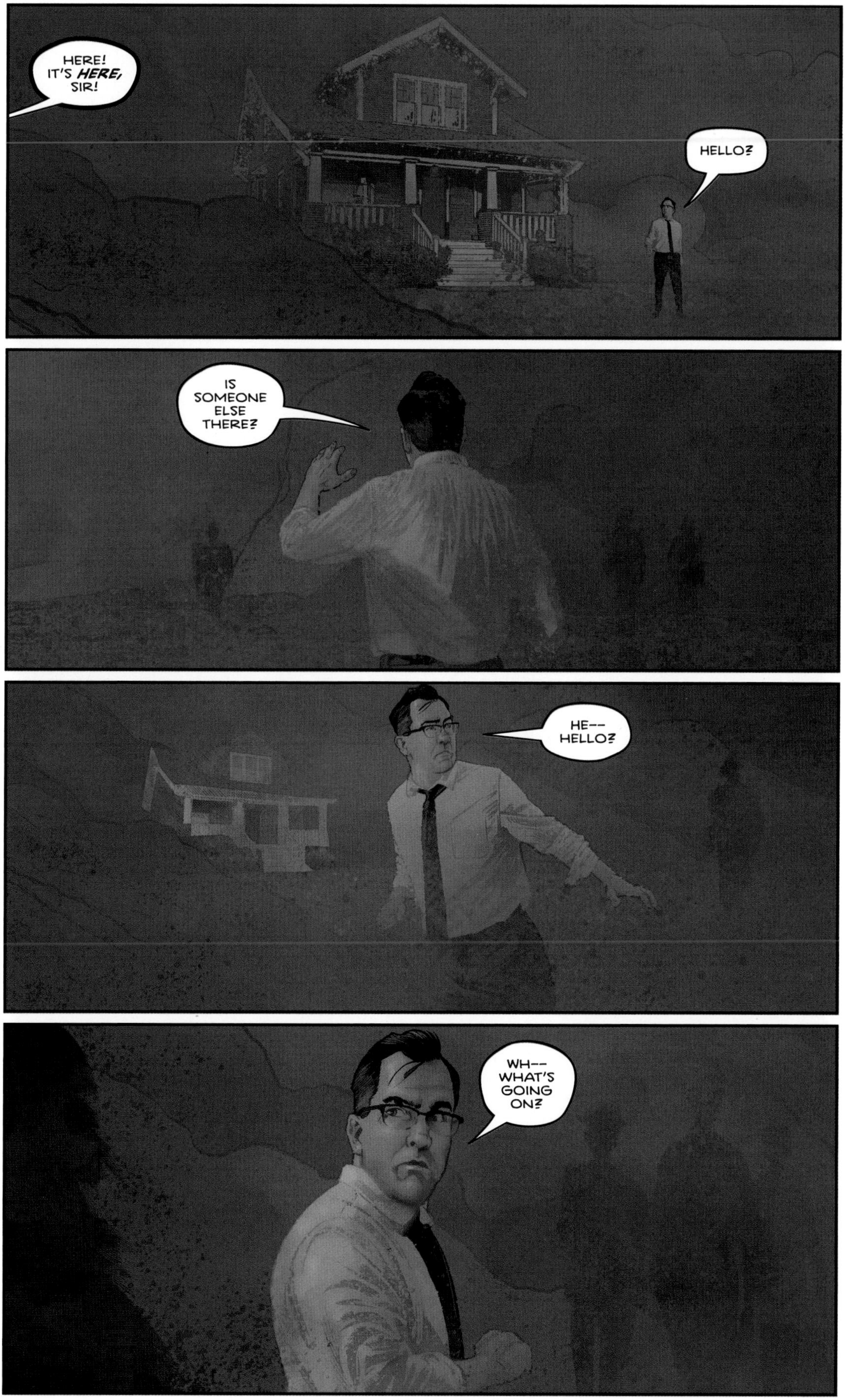
HERE! IT'S *HERE,* SIR!
HELLO?
IS SOMEONE ELSE THERE?
HE-- HELLO?
WH-- WHAT'S GOING ON?

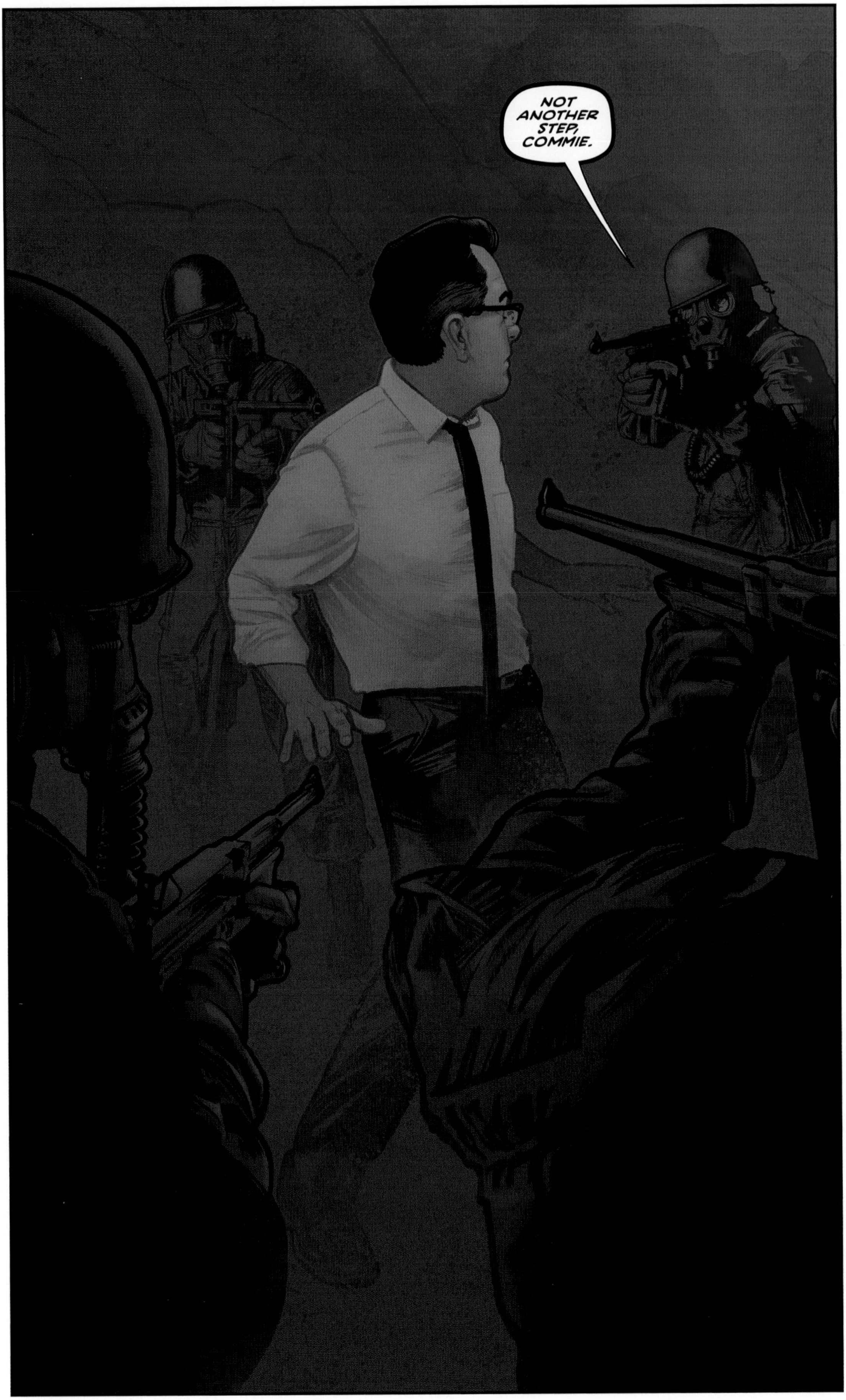
NOT ANOTHER STEP, COMMIE.

2

BAD TRANSMISSION

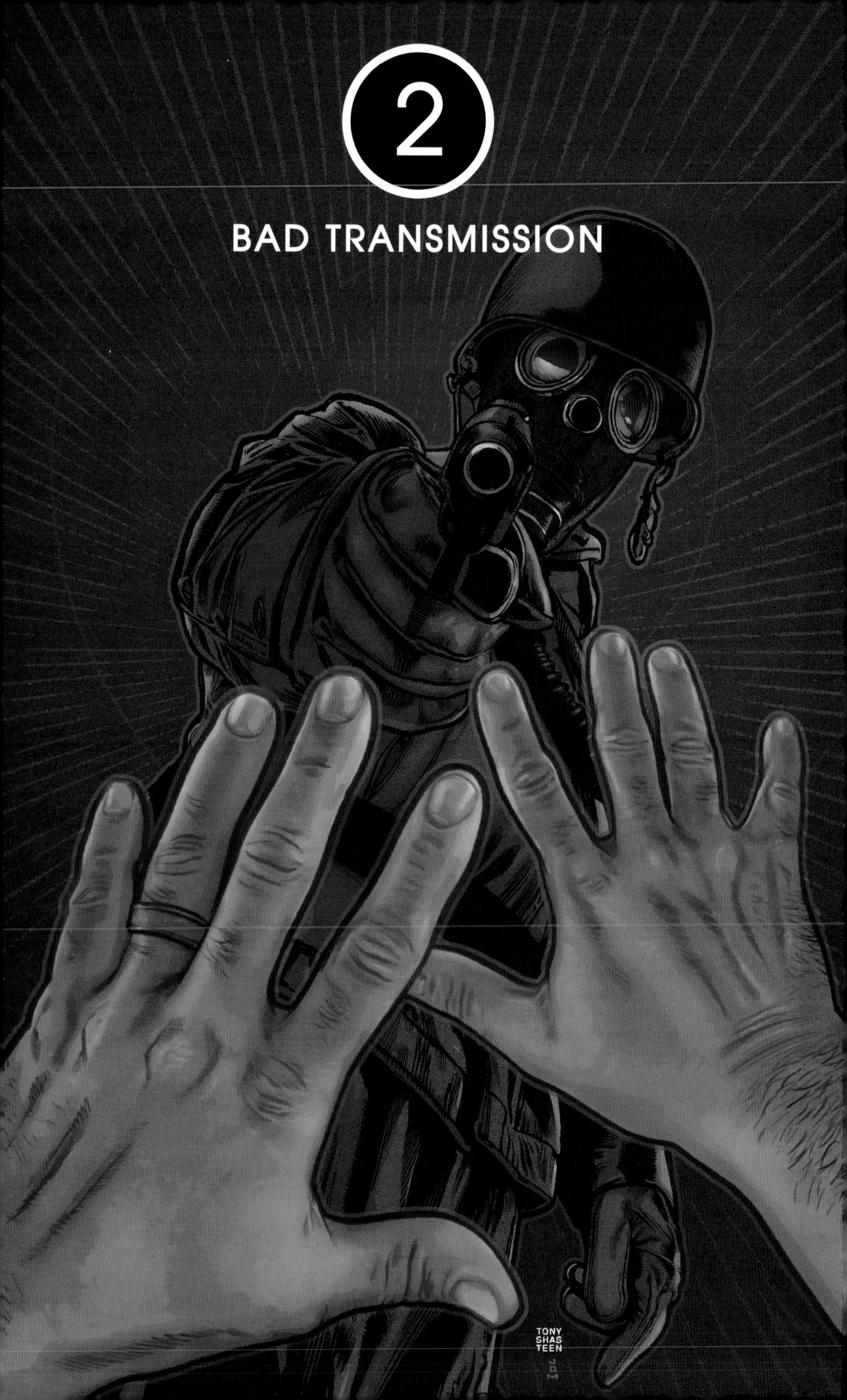
TONY
SHAS
TEEN

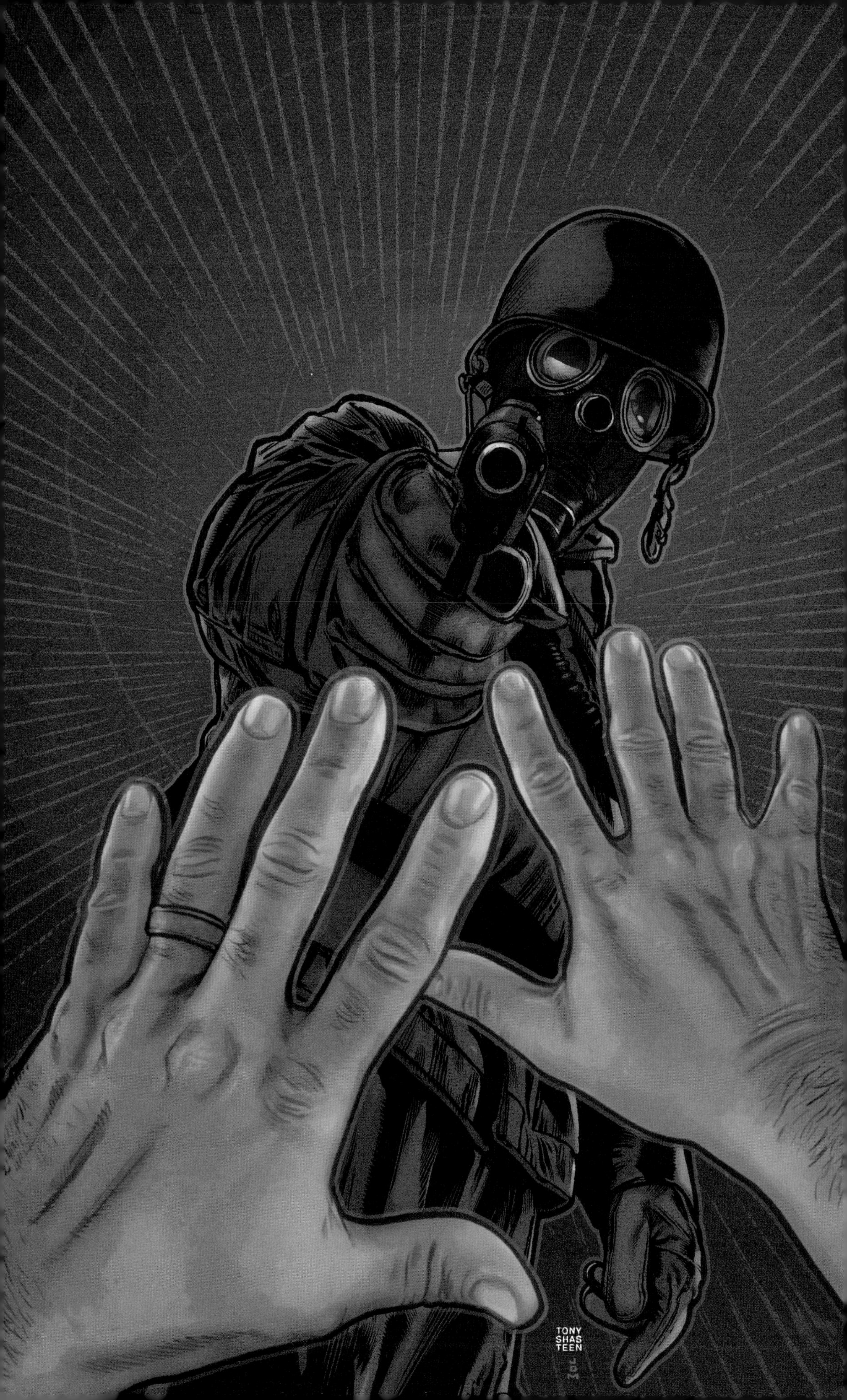
TONY
SHAS
TEEN

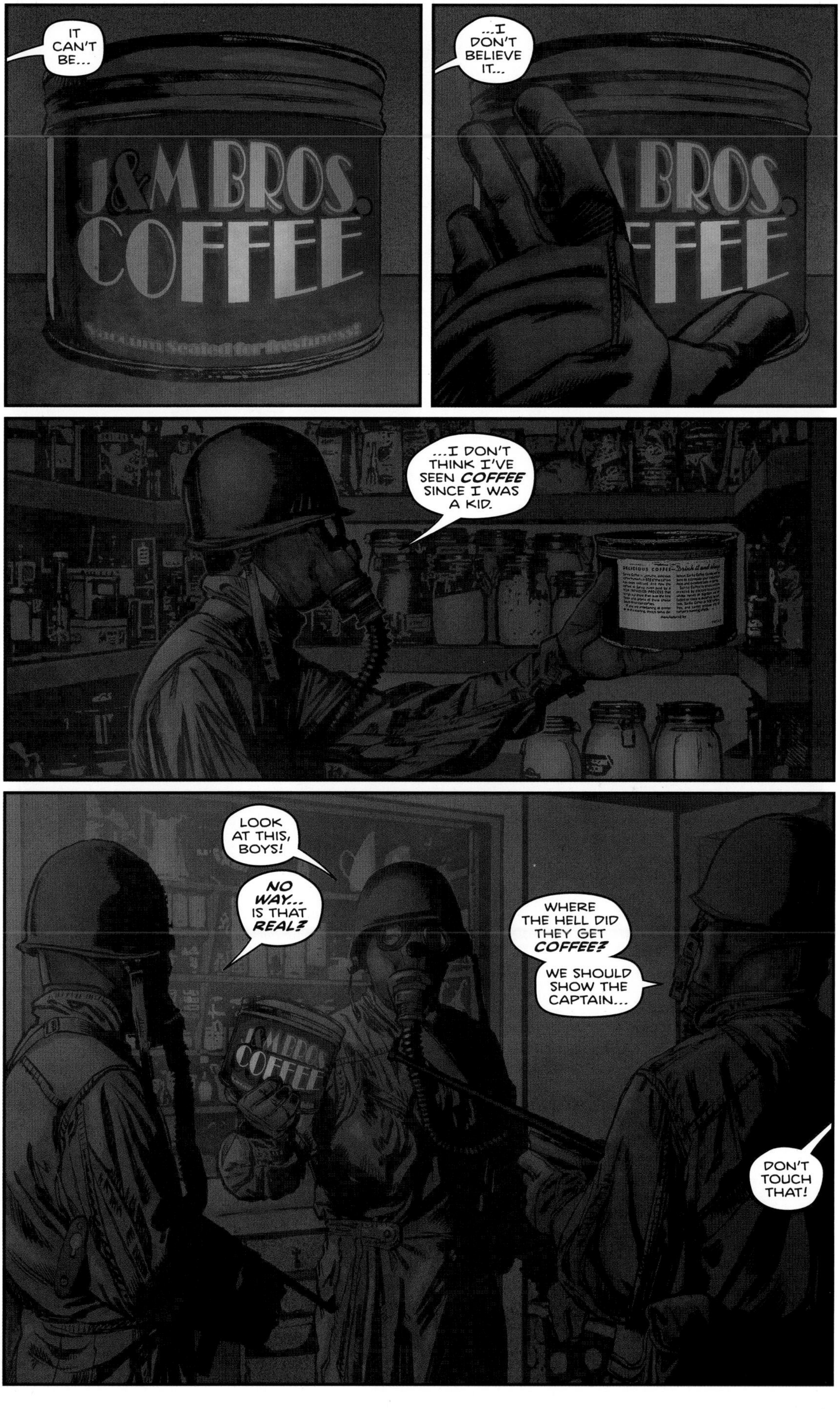
IT CAN'T BE...
J&M BROS. COFFEE
...I DON'T BELIEVE IT...
BROS.
FFEE
...I DON'T THINK I'VE SEEN *COFFEE* SINCE I WAS A KID.
LOOK AT THIS, BOYS!
NO WAY... IS THAT *REAL?*
WHERE THE HELL DID THEY GET *COFFEE?*
WE SHOULD SHOW THE CAPTAIN...
J&M BROS. COFFEE
DON'T TOUCH THAT!

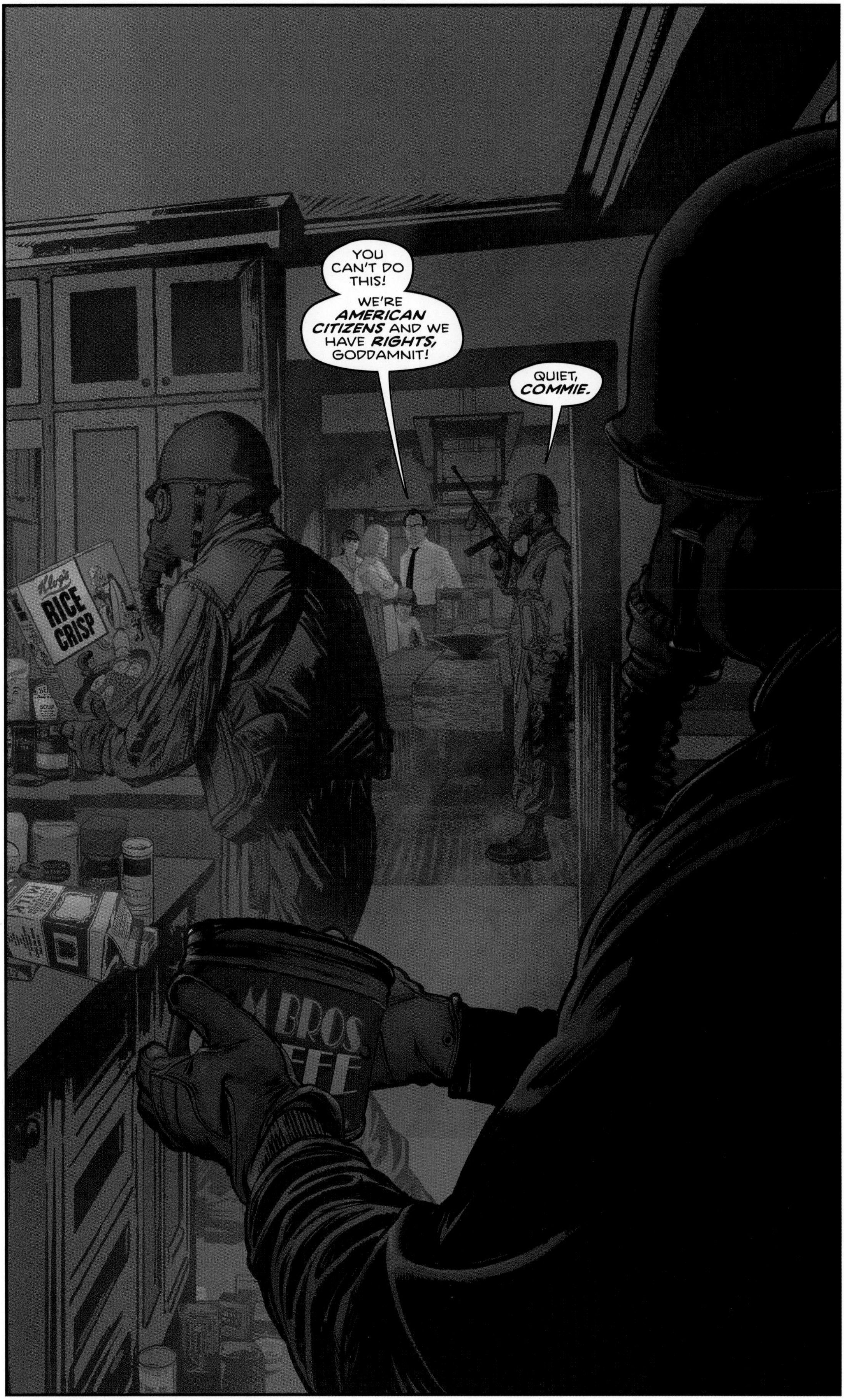
YOU CAN'T DO THIS!
WE'RE **AMERICAN CITIZENS** AND WE HAVE **RIGHTS,** GODDAMNIT!
QUIET, **COMMIE.**
RICE CRISP

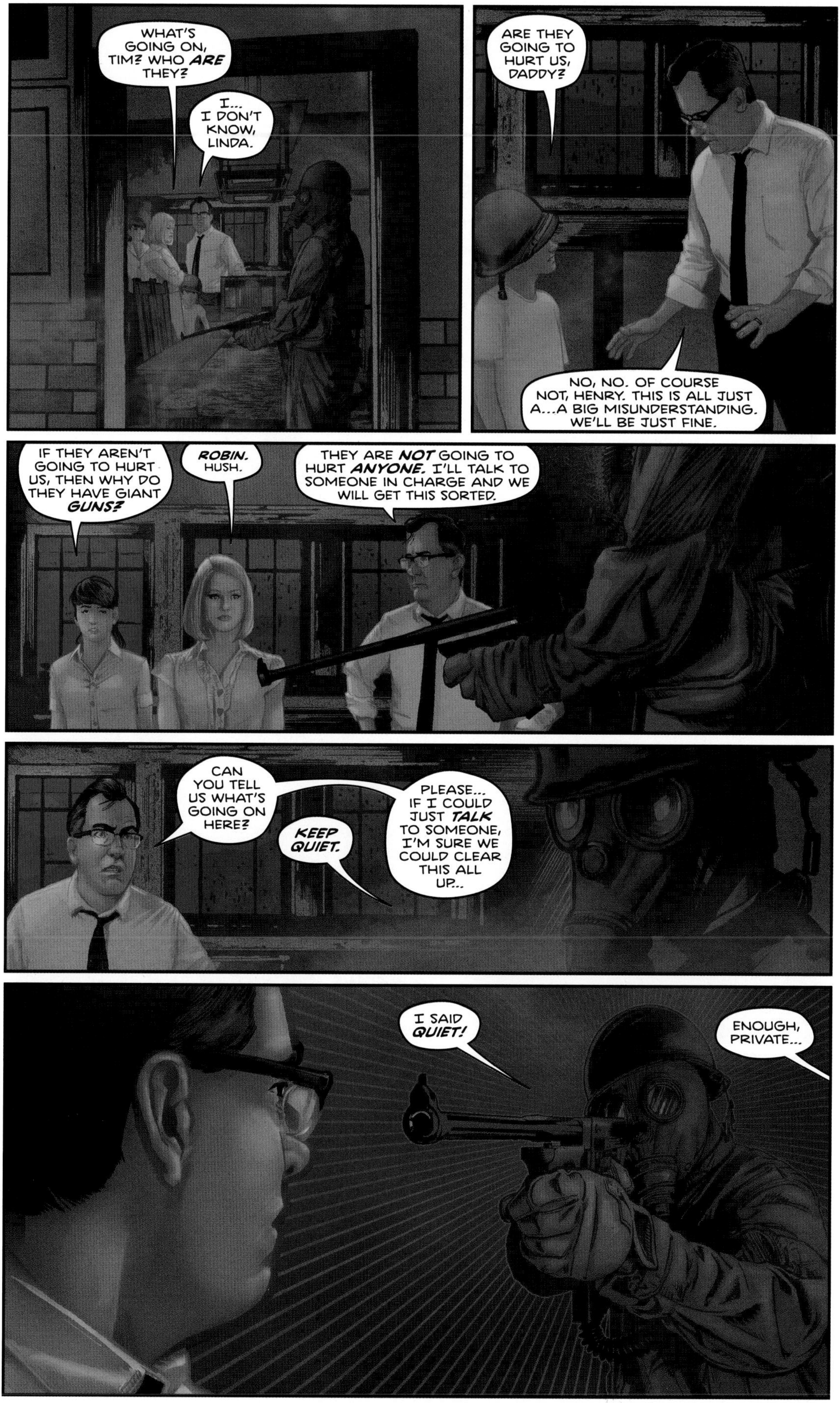

WHAT'S GOING ON, TIM? WHO ARE THEY?
I... I DON'T KNOW, LINDA.
ARE THEY GOING TO HURT US, DADDY?
NO, NO. OF COURSE NOT, HENRY. THIS IS ALL JUST A...A BIG MISUNDERSTANDING. WE'LL BE JUST FINE.
IF THEY AREN'T GOING TO HURT US, THEN WHY DO THEY HAVE GIANT GUNS?
ROBIN. HUSH.
THEY ARE NOT GOING TO HURT ANYONE. I'LL TALK TO SOMEONE IN CHARGE AND WE WILL GET THIS SORTED.
CAN YOU TELL US WHAT'S GOING ON HERE?
PLEASE... IF I COULD JUST TALK TO SOMEONE, I'M SURE WE COULD CLEAR THIS ALL UP...
KEEP QUIET.
I SAID QUIET!
ENOUGH, PRIVATE...

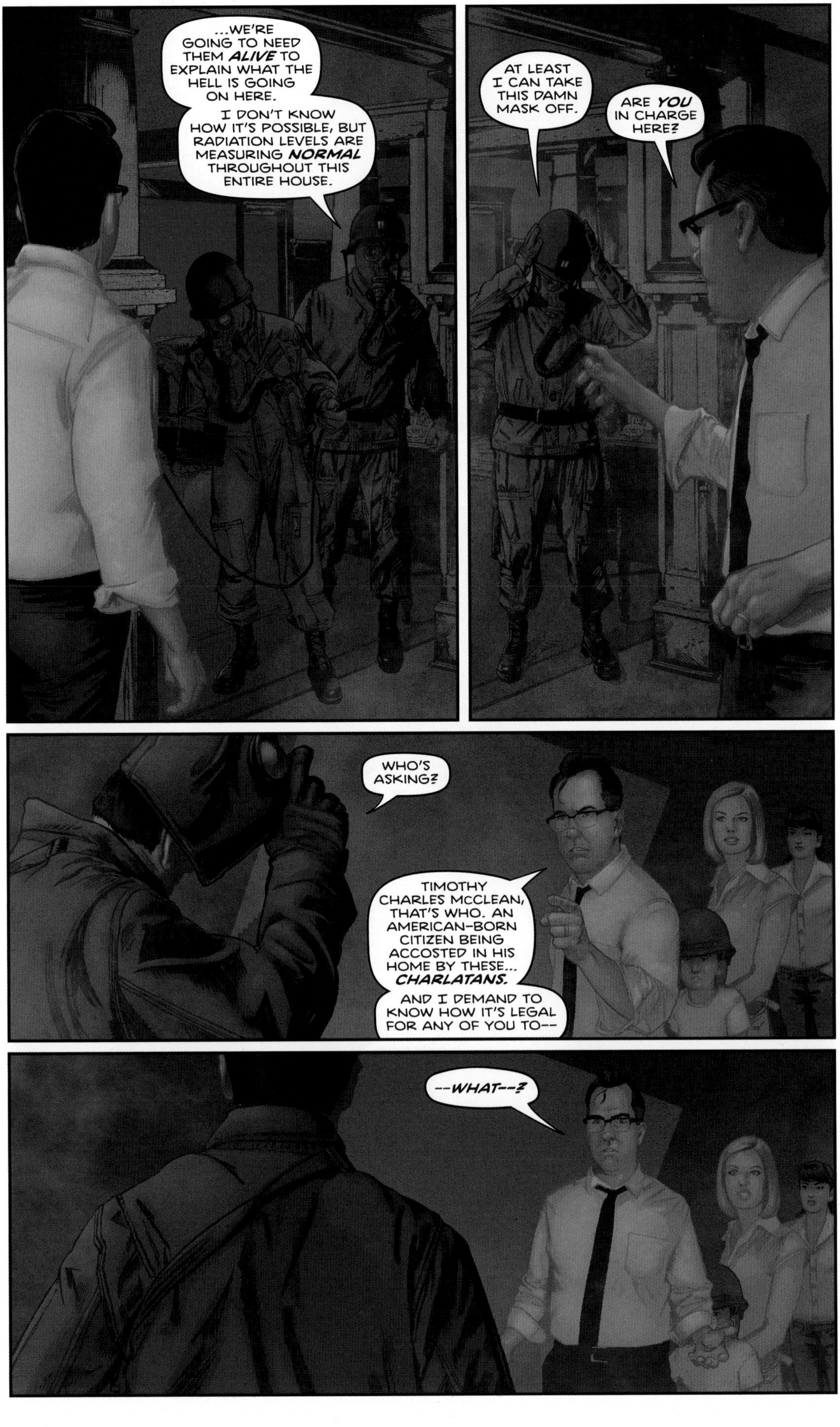
...WE'RE GOING TO NEED THEM ALIVE TO EXPLAIN WHAT THE HELL IS GOING ON HERE.
I DON'T KNOW HOW IT'S POSSIBLE, BUT RADIATION LEVELS ARE MEASURING NORMAL THROUGHOUT THIS ENTIRE HOUSE.
AT LEAST I CAN TAKE THIS DAMN MASK OFF.
ARE YOU IN CHARGE HERE?
WHO'S ASKING?
TIMOTHY CHARLES McCLEAN, THAT'S WHO. AN AMERICAN-BORN CITIZEN BEING ACCOSTED IN HIS HOME BY THESE... CHARLATANS.
AND I DEMAND TO KNOW HOW IT'S LEGAL FOR ANY OF YOU TO--
--WHAT--?

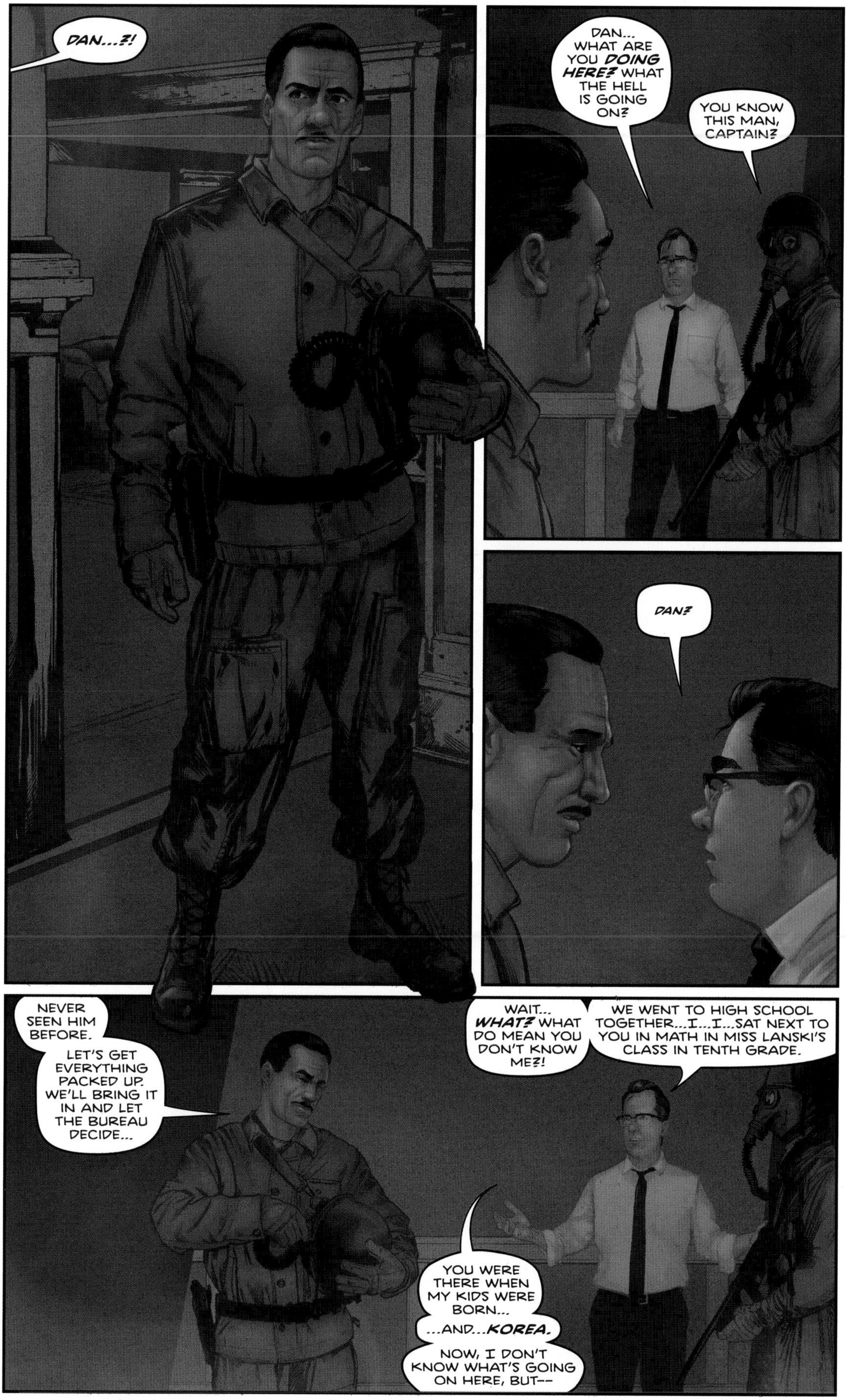
DAN...?!
DAN... WHAT ARE YOU DOING HERE? WHAT THE HELL IS GOING ON?
YOU KNOW THIS MAN, CAPTAIN?
DAN?
NEVER SEEN HIM BEFORE.
LET'S GET EVERYTHING PACKED UP. WE'LL BRING IT IN AND LET THE BUREAU DECIDE...
WAIT... WHAT? WHAT DO MEAN YOU DON'T KNOW ME?!
WE WENT TO HIGH SCHOOL TOGETHER...I...I...SAT NEXT TO YOU IN MATH IN MISS LANSKI'S CLASS IN TENTH GRADE.
YOU WERE THERE WHEN MY KIDS WERE BORN...
...AND...KOREA.
NOW, I DON'T KNOW WHAT'S GOING ON HERE, BUT--

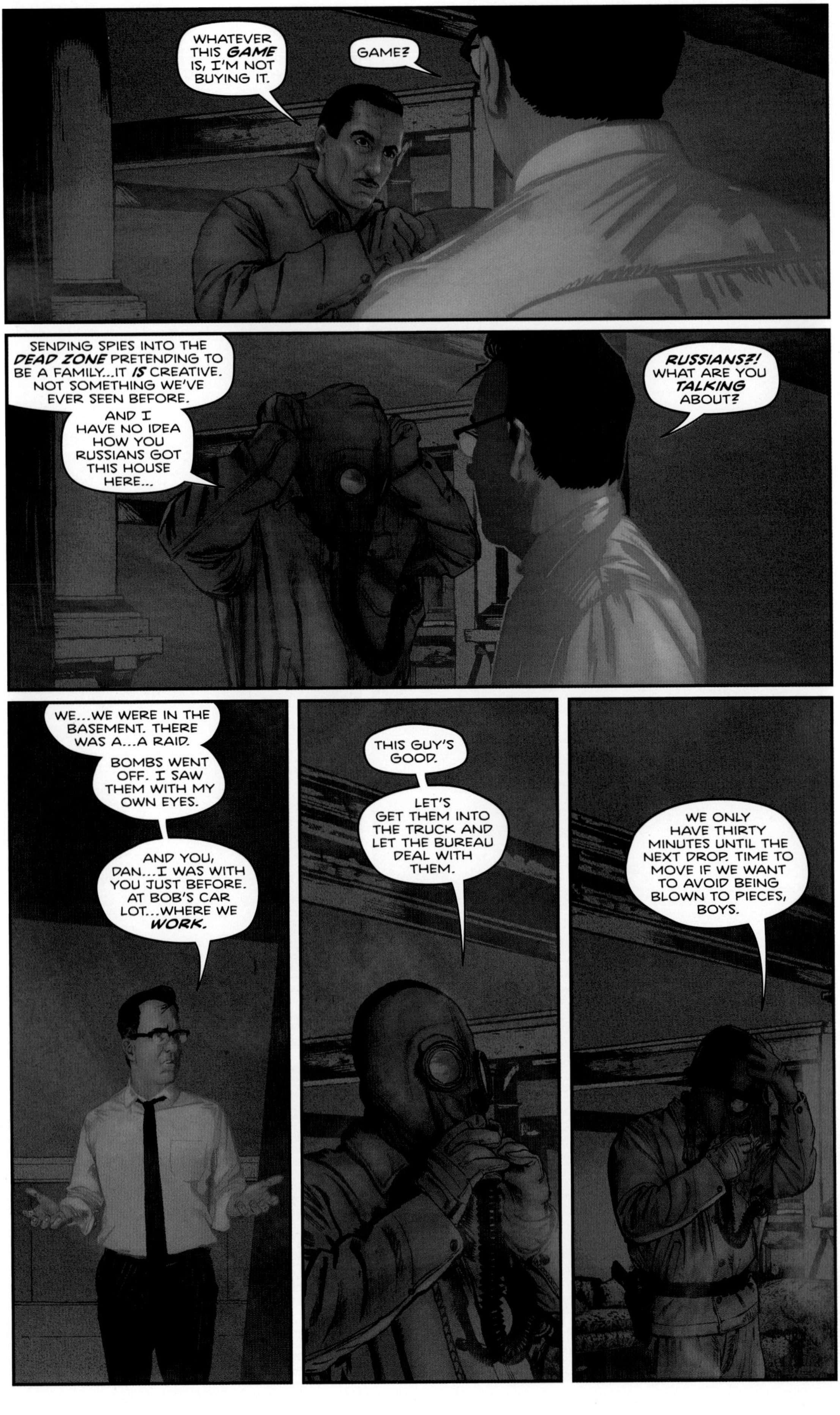
WHATEVER THIS GAME IS, I'M NOT BUYING IT.
GAME?
SENDING SPIES INTO THE DEAD ZONE PRETENDING TO BE A FAMILY...IT IS CREATIVE. NOT SOMETHING WE'VE EVER SEEN BEFORE.
AND I HAVE NO IDEA HOW YOU RUSSIANS GOT THIS HOUSE HERE...
RUSSIANS?! WHAT ARE YOU TALKING ABOUT?
WE...WE WERE IN THE BASEMENT. THERE WAS A...A RAID.
BOMBS WENT OFF. I SAW THEM WITH MY OWN EYES.
AND YOU, DAN...I WAS WITH YOU JUST BEFORE. AT BOB'S CAR LOT...WHERE WE WORK.
THIS GUY'S GOOD.
LET'S GET THEM INTO THE TRUCK AND LET THE BUREAU DEAL WITH THEM.
WE ONLY HAVE THIRTY MINUTES UNTIL THE NEXT DROP. TIME TO MOVE IF WE WANT TO AVOID BEING BLOWN TO PIECES, BOYS.

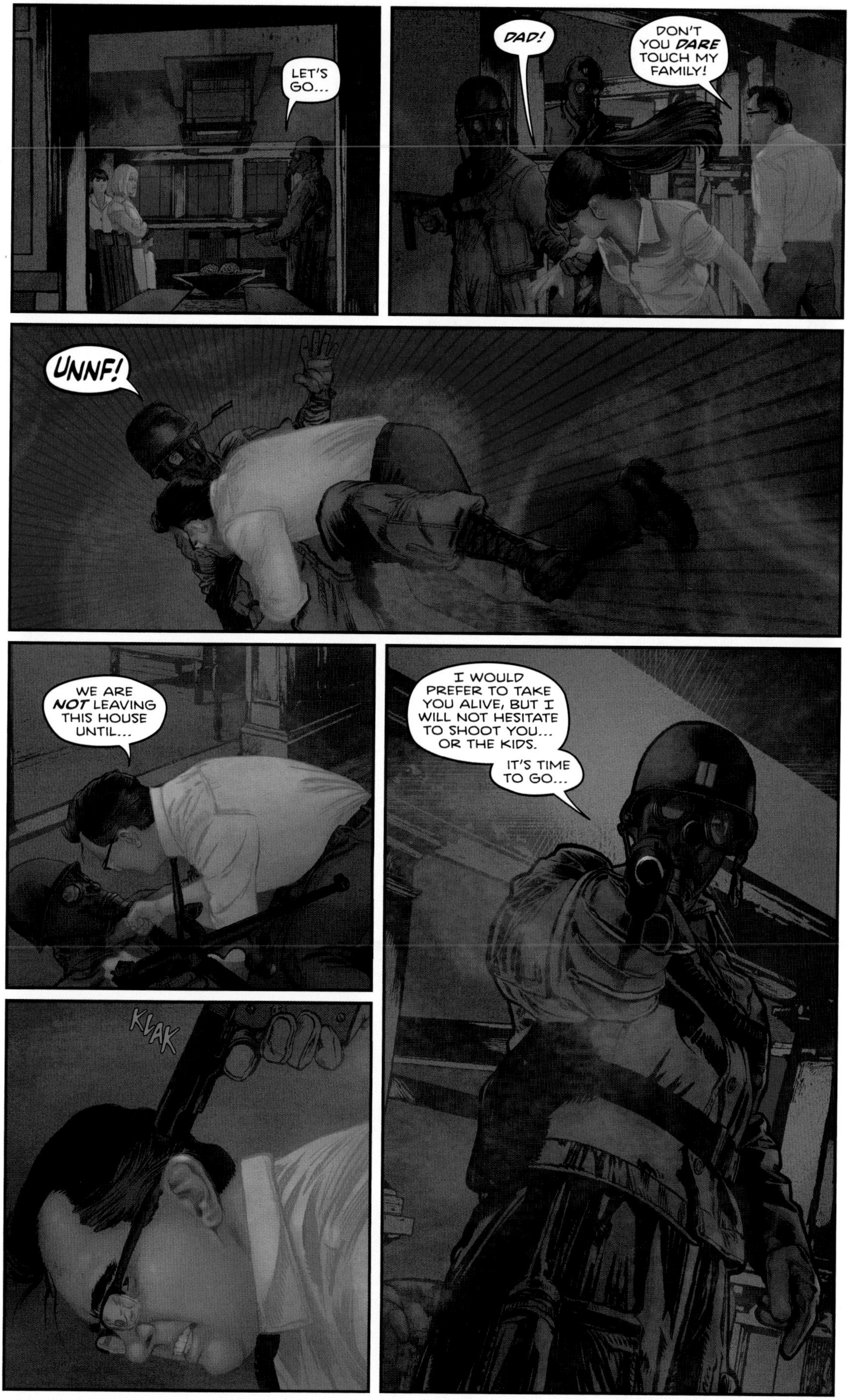
LET'S GO...
DAD!
DON'T YOU DARE TOUCH MY FAMILY!
UNNF!
WE ARE NOT LEAVING THIS HOUSE UNTIL...
KLAK
I WOULD PREFER TO TAKE YOU ALIVE, BUT I WILL NOT HESITATE TO SHOOT YOU... OR THE KIDS.
IT'S TIME TO GO...

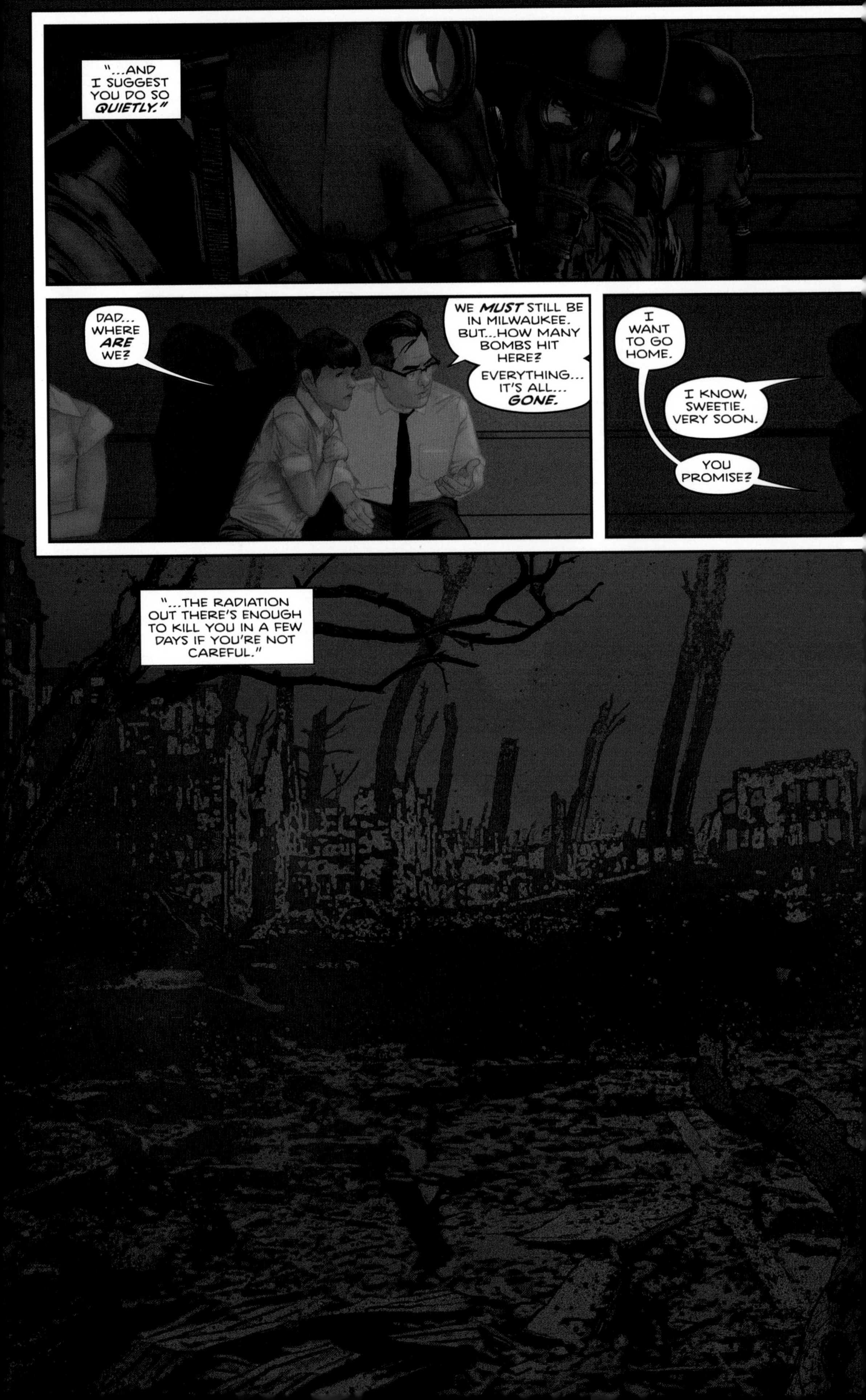
"...AND I SUGGEST YOU DO SO QUIETLY."
DAD... WHERE ARE WE?
WE MUST STILL BE IN MILWAUKEE. BUT...HOW MANY BOMBS HIT HERE?
EVERYTHING... IT'S ALL... GONE.
I WANT TO GO HOME.
I KNOW, SWEETIE. VERY SOON.
YOU PROMISE?
"...THE RADIATION OUT THERE'S ENOUGH TO KILL YOU IN A FEW DAYS IF YOU'RE NOT CAREFUL."

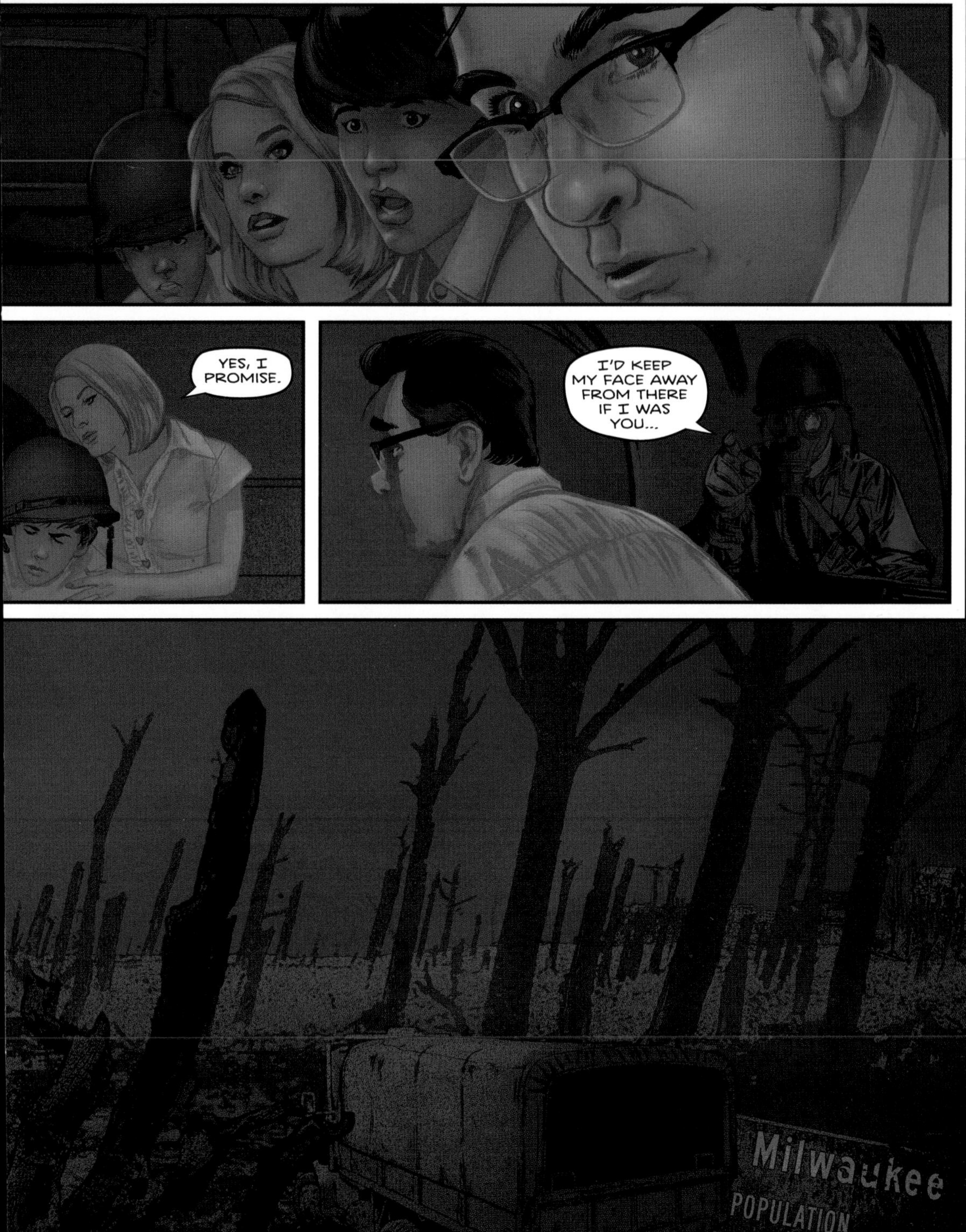
YES, I PROMISE.
I'D KEEP MY FACE AWAY FROM THERE IF I WAS YOU...
Milwaukee
POPULATION

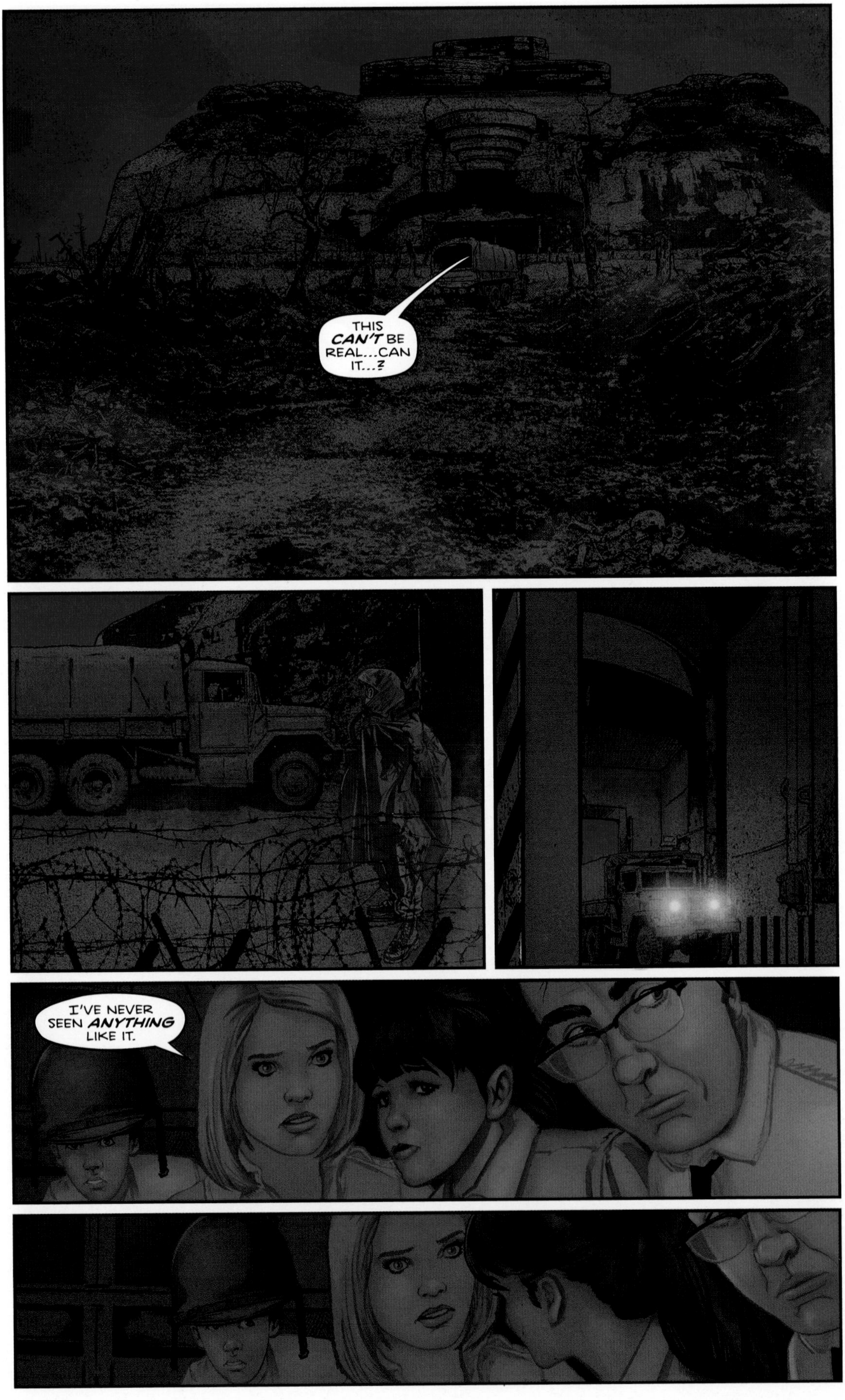
THIS CAN'T BE REAL...CAN IT...?
I'VE NEVER SEEN ANYTHING LIKE IT.

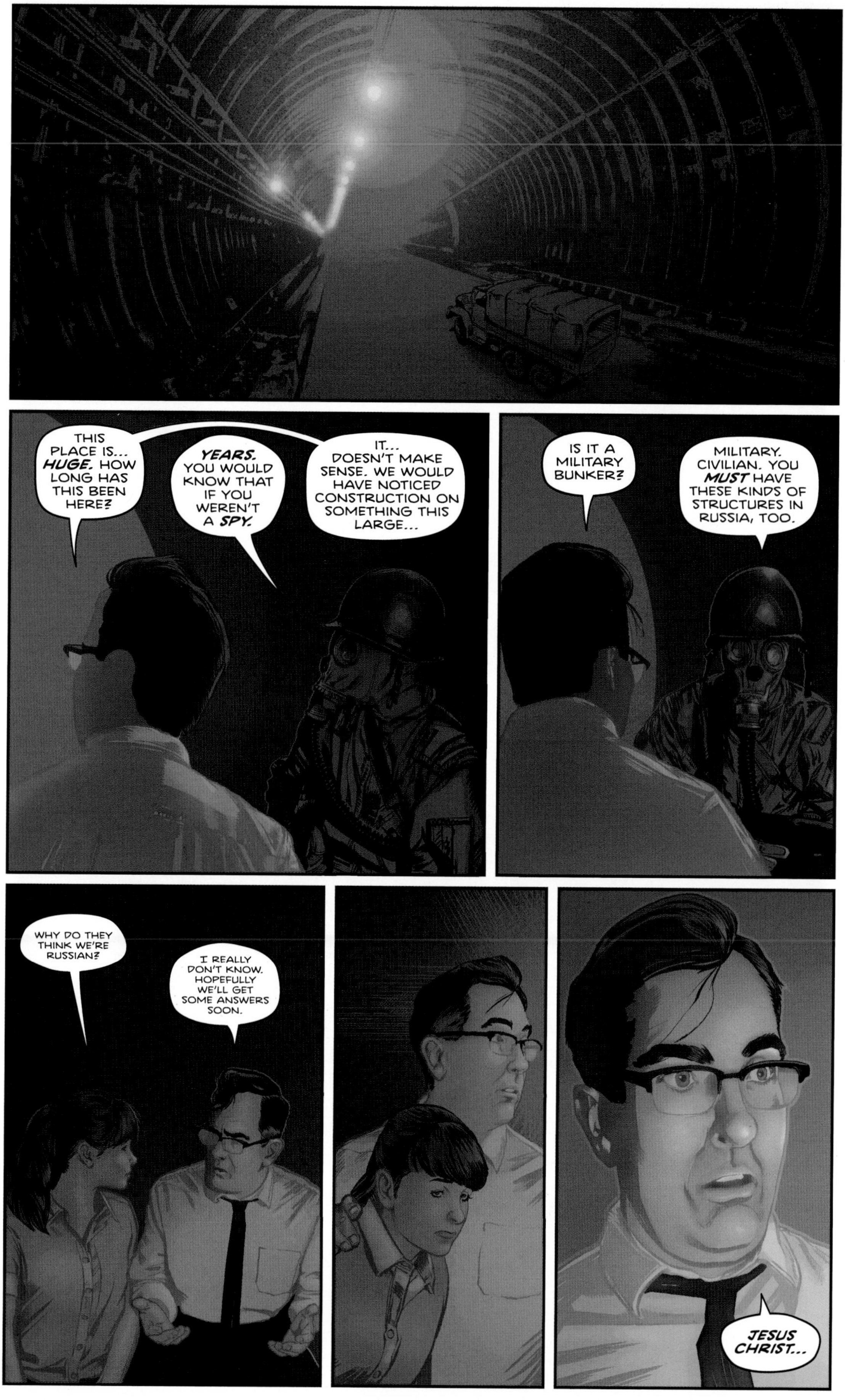
THIS PLACE IS... HUGE. HOW LONG HAS THIS BEEN HERE?
YEARS. YOU WOULD KNOW THAT IF YOU WEREN'T A SPY.
IT... DOESN'T MAKE SENSE. WE WOULD HAVE NOTICED CONSTRUCTION ON SOMETHING THIS LARGE...
IS IT A MILITARY BUNKER?
MILITARY. CIVILIAN. YOU MUST HAVE THESE KINDS OF STRUCTURES IN RUSSIA, TOO.
WHY DO THEY THINK WE'RE RUSSIAN?
I REALLY DON'T KNOW. HOPEFULLY WE'LL GET SOME ANSWERS SOON.
JESUS CHRIST...

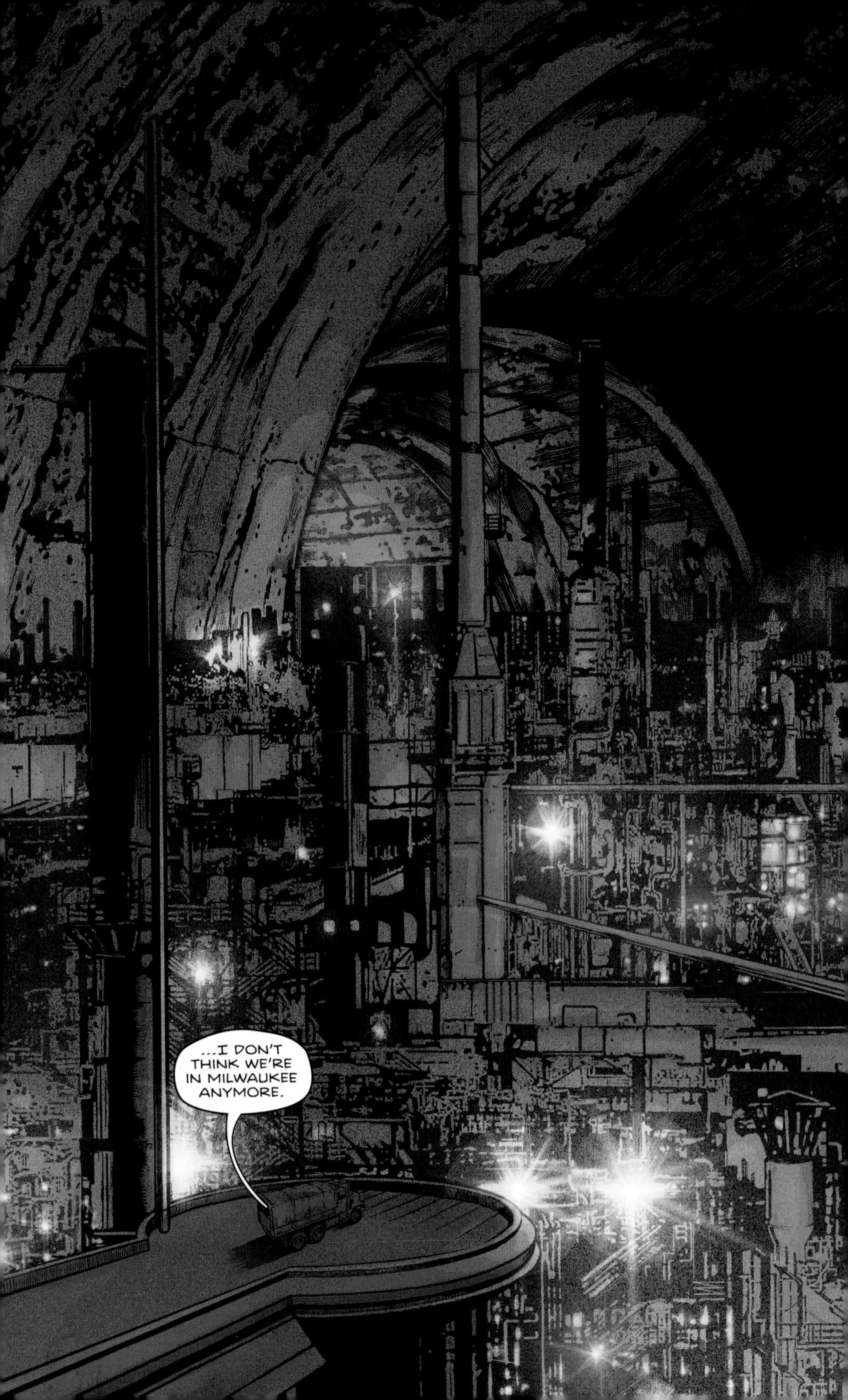
...I DON'T THINK WE'RE IN MILWAUKEE ANYMORE.

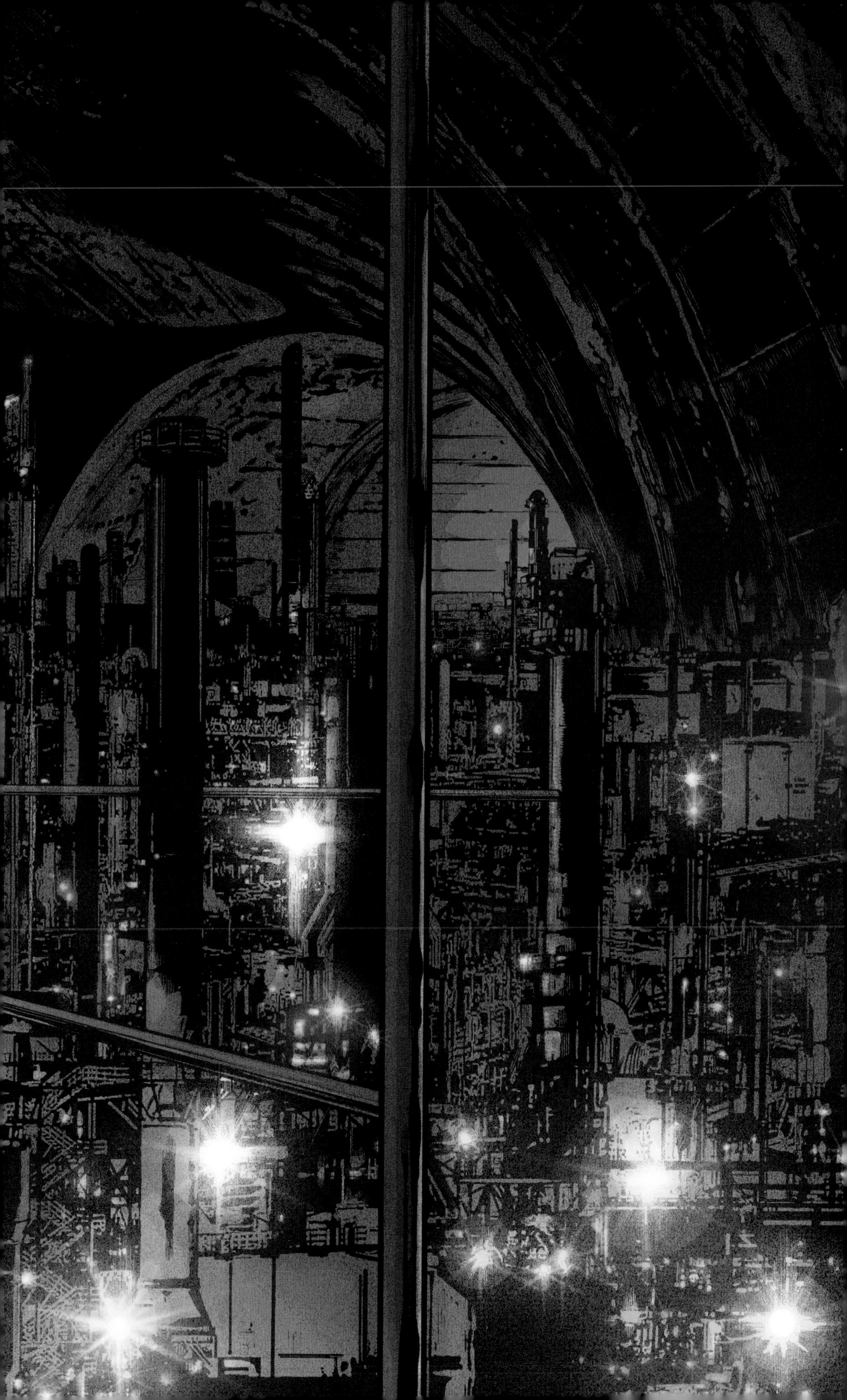

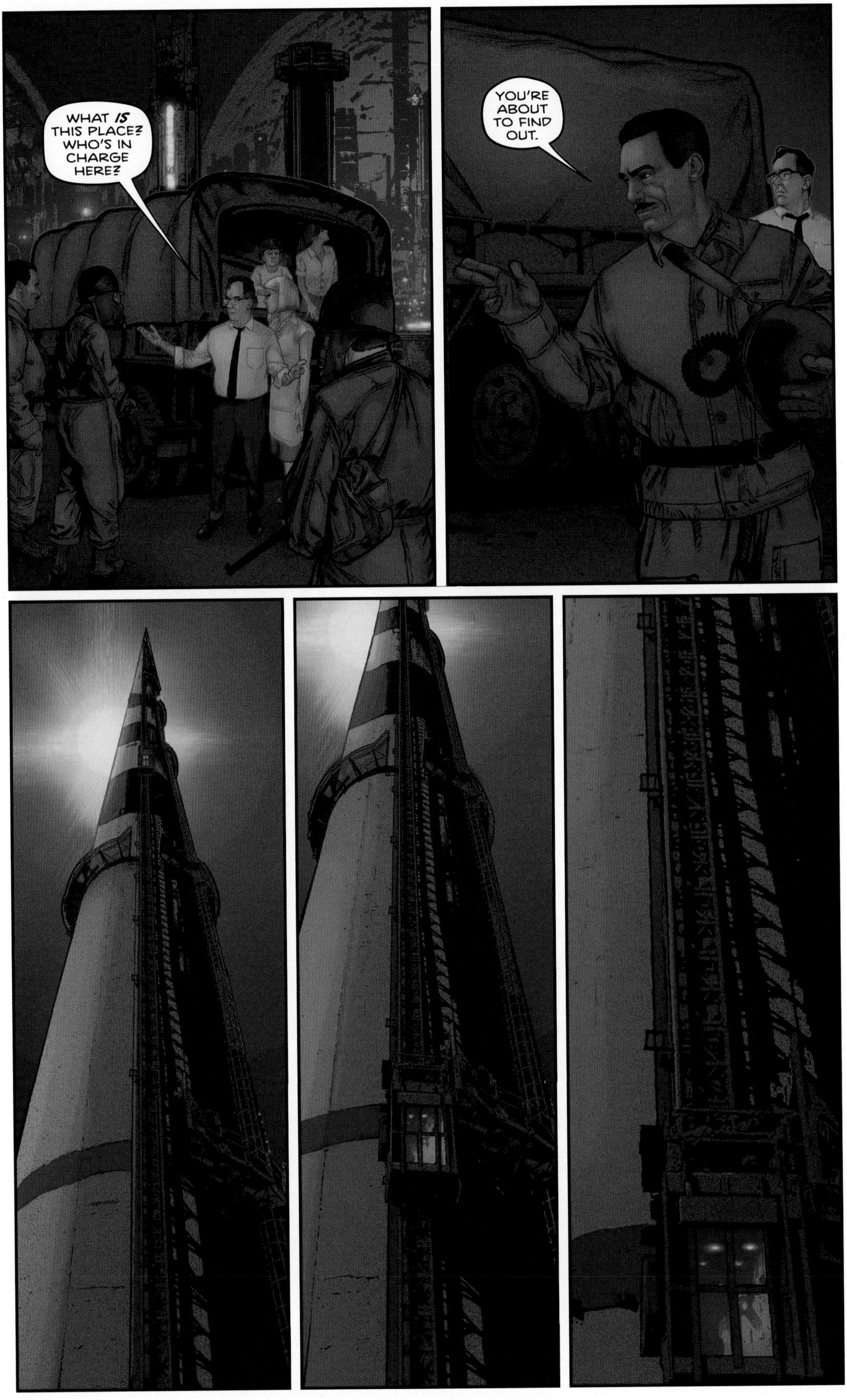
WHAT IS THIS PLACE? WHO'S IN CHARGE HERE?
YOU'RE ABOUT TO FIND OUT.

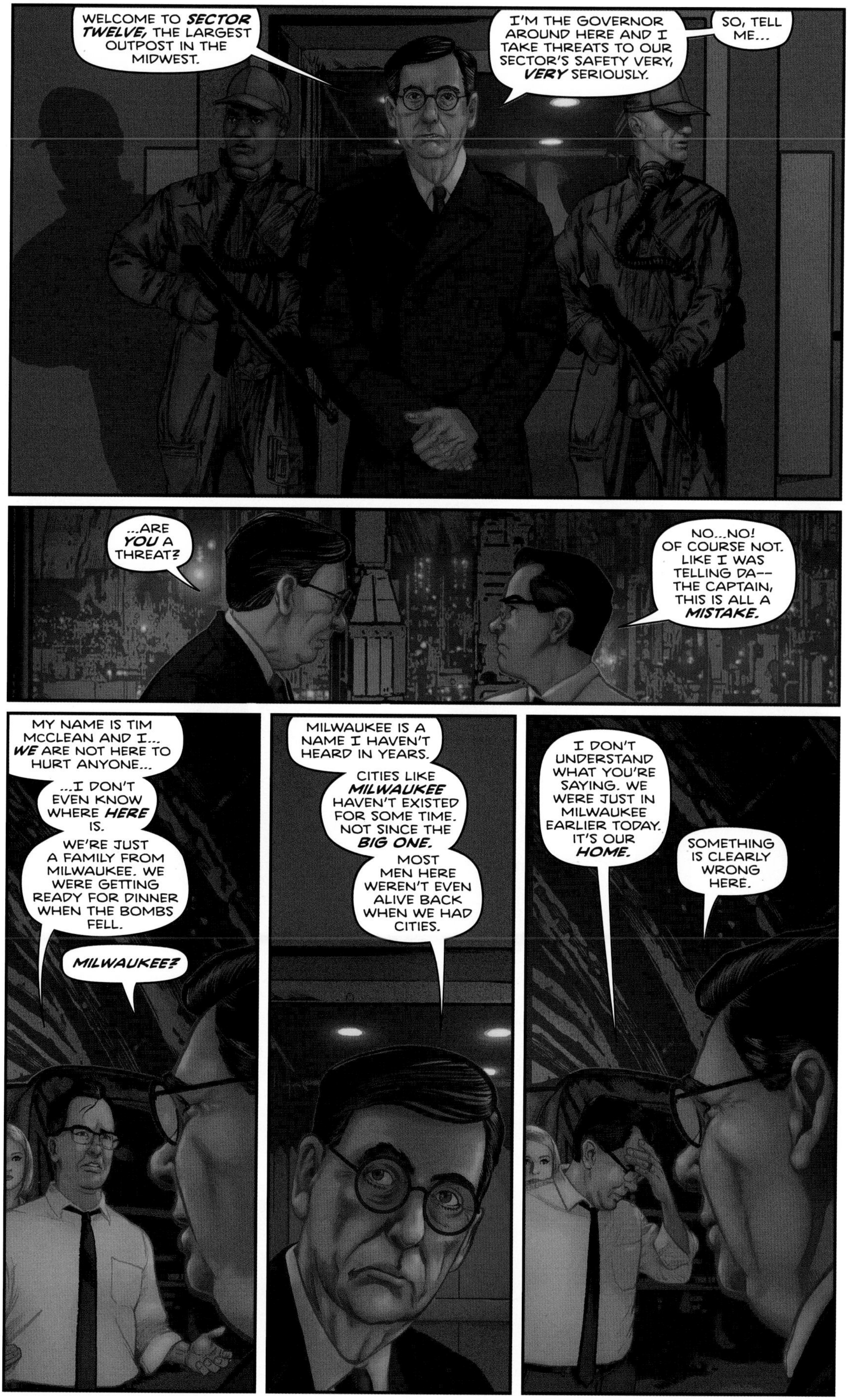
WELCOME TO SECTOR TWELVE, THE LARGEST OUTPOST IN THE MIDWEST.
I'M THE GOVERNOR AROUND HERE AND I TAKE THREATS TO OUR SECTOR'S SAFETY VERY, VERY SERIOUSLY.
SO, TELL ME...
...ARE YOU A THREAT?
NO...NO! OF COURSE NOT. LIKE I WAS TELLING DA-- THE CAPTAIN, THIS IS ALL A MISTAKE.
MY NAME IS TIM McCLEAN AND I... WE ARE NOT HERE TO HURT ANYONE...
...I DON'T EVEN KNOW WHERE HERE IS.
WE'RE JUST A FAMILY FROM MILWAUKEE. WE WERE GETTING READY FOR DINNER WHEN THE BOMBS FELL.
MILWAUKEE?
MILWAUKEE IS A NAME I HAVEN'T HEARD IN YEARS.
CITIES LIKE MILWAUKEE HAVEN'T EXISTED FOR SOME TIME. NOT SINCE THE BIG ONE.
MOST MEN HERE WEREN'T EVEN ALIVE BACK WHEN WE HAD CITIES.
I DON'T UNDERSTAND WHAT YOU'RE SAYING. WE WERE JUST IN MILWAUKEE EARLIER TODAY. IT'S OUR HOME.
SOMETHING IS CLEARLY WRONG HERE.

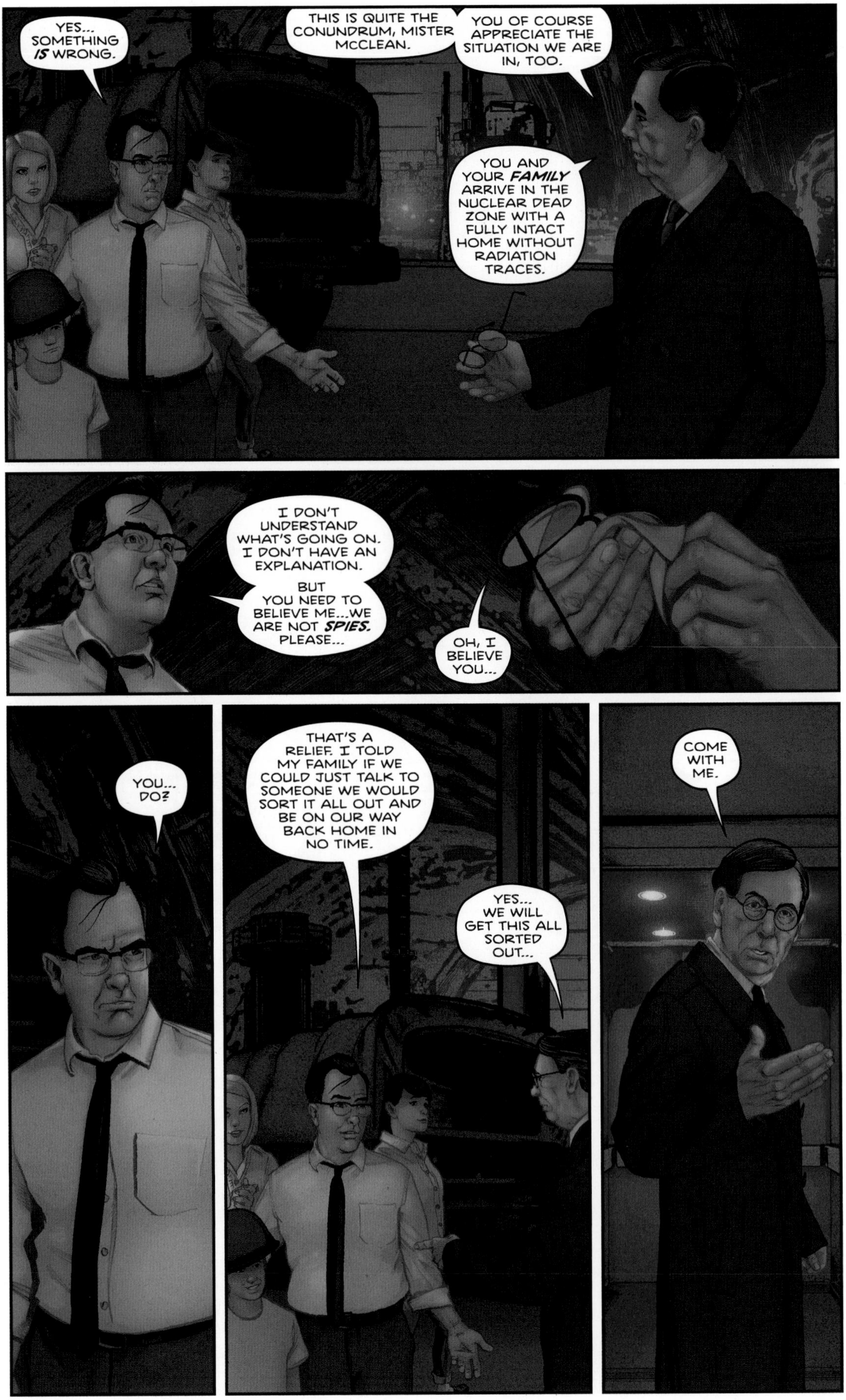
YES... SOMETHING IS WRONG.
THIS IS QUITE THE CONUNDRUM, MISTER McCLEAN.
YOU OF COURSE APPRECIATE THE SITUATION WE ARE IN, TOO.
YOU AND YOUR FAMILY ARRIVE IN THE NUCLEAR DEAD ZONE WITH A FULLY INTACT HOME WITHOUT RADIATION TRACES.
I DON'T UNDERSTAND WHAT'S GOING ON. I DON'T HAVE AN EXPLANATION.
BUT YOU NEED TO BELIEVE ME...WE ARE NOT SPIES. PLEASE...
OH, I BELIEVE YOU...
YOU... DO?
THAT'S A RELIEF. I TOLD MY FAMILY IF WE COULD JUST TALK TO SOMEONE WE WOULD SORT IT ALL OUT AND BE ON OUR WAY BACK HOME IN NO TIME.
YES... WE WILL GET THIS ALL SORTED OUT...
COME WITH ME.

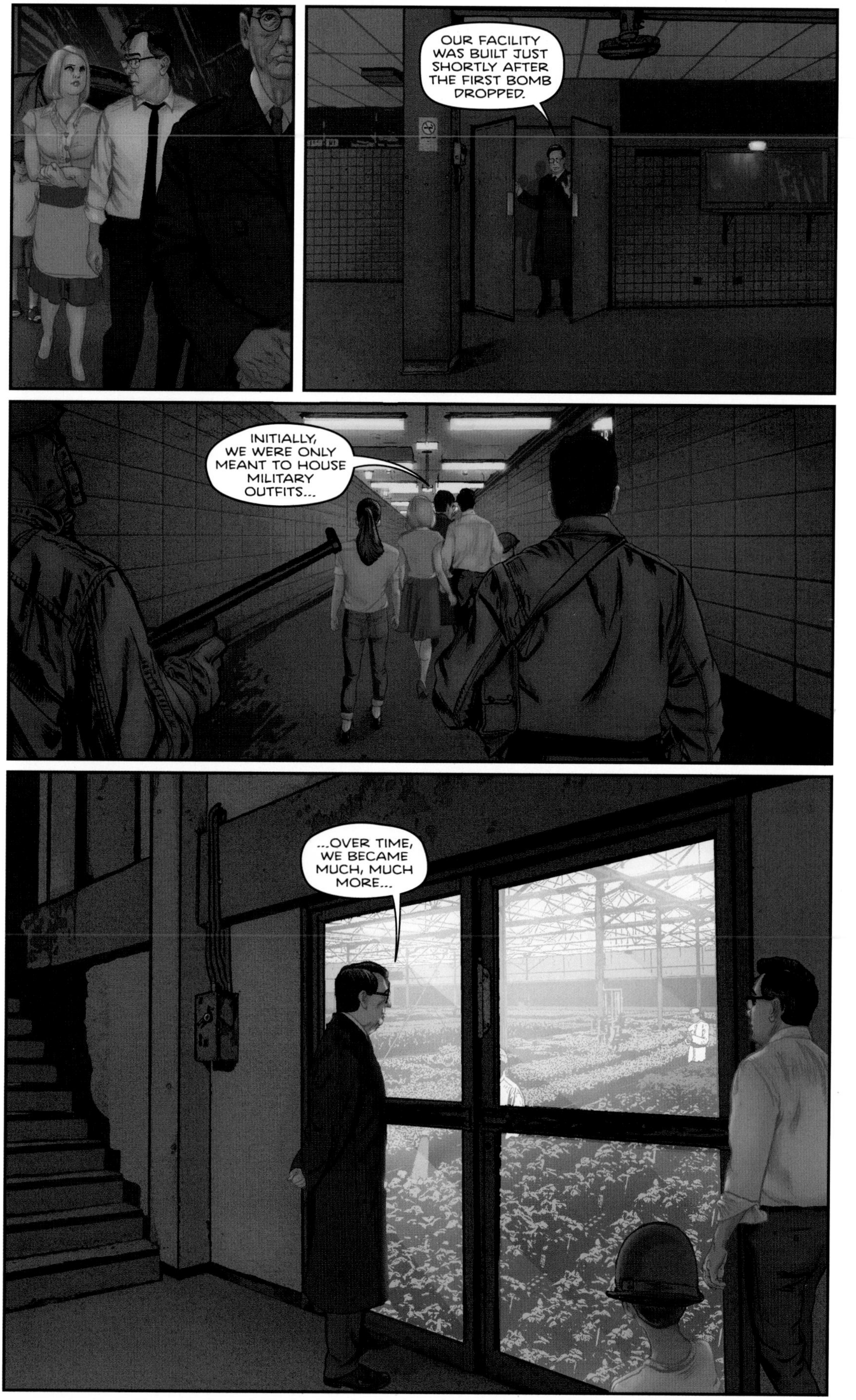
OUR FACILITY WAS BUILT JUST SHORTLY AFTER THE FIRST BOMB DROPPED.
INITIALLY, WE WERE ONLY MEANT TO HOUSE MILITARY OUTFITS...
...OVER TIME, WE BECAME MUCH, MUCH MORE...

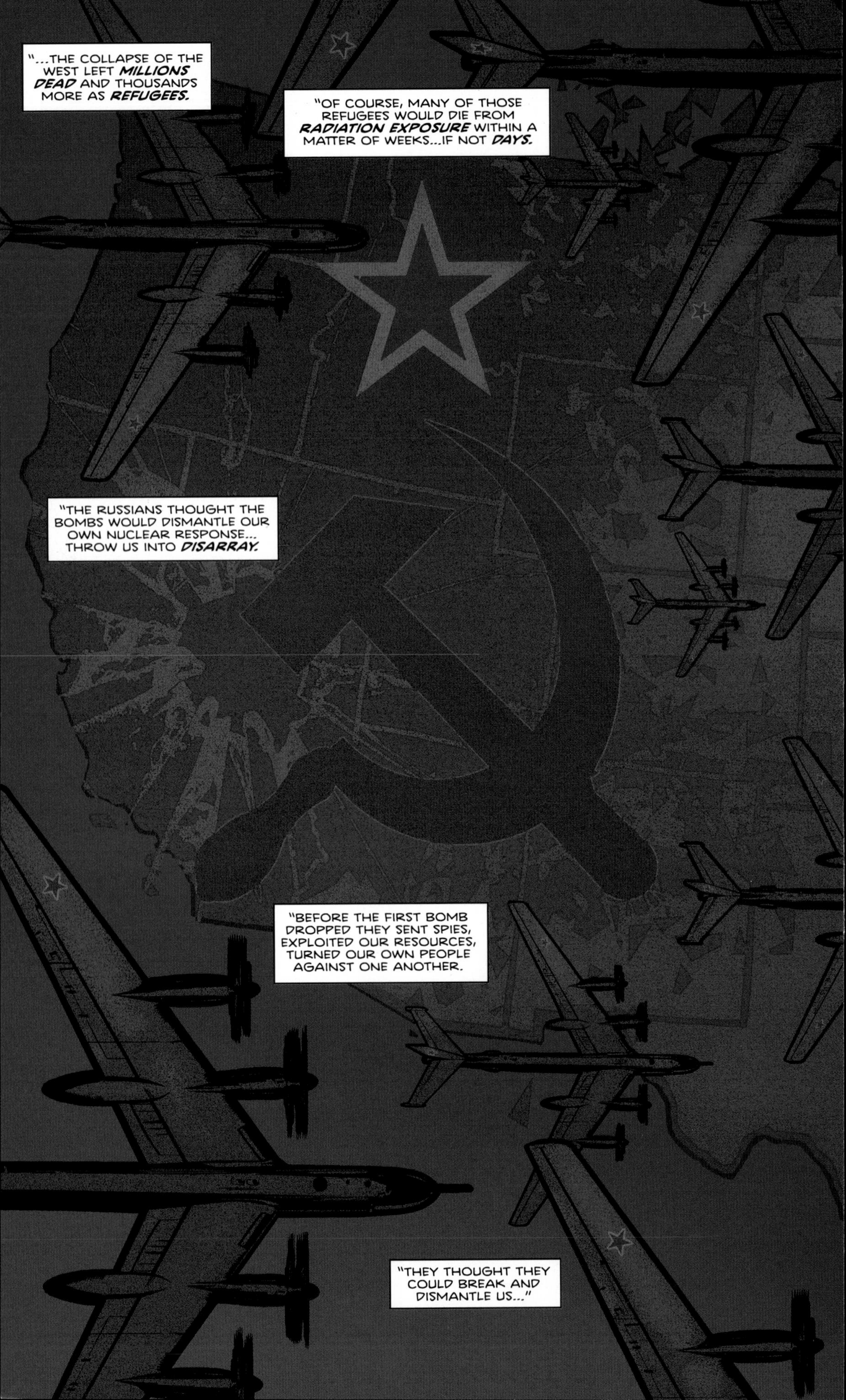
"...THE COLLAPSE OF THE WEST LEFT ***MILLIONS DEAD*** AND THOUSANDS MORE AS ***REFUGEES.***
"OF COURSE, MANY OF THOSE REFUGEES WOULD DIE FROM ***RADIATION EXPOSURE*** WITHIN A MATTER OF WEEKS...IF NOT ***DAYS.***
"THE RUSSIANS THOUGHT THE BOMBS WOULD DISMANTLE OUR OWN NUCLEAR RESPONSE... THROW US INTO ***DISARRAY.***
"BEFORE THE FIRST BOMB DROPPED THEY SENT SPIES, EXPLOITED OUR RESOURCES, TURNED OUR OWN PEOPLE AGAINST ONE ANOTHER.
"THEY THOUGHT THEY COULD BREAK AND DISMANTLE US..."

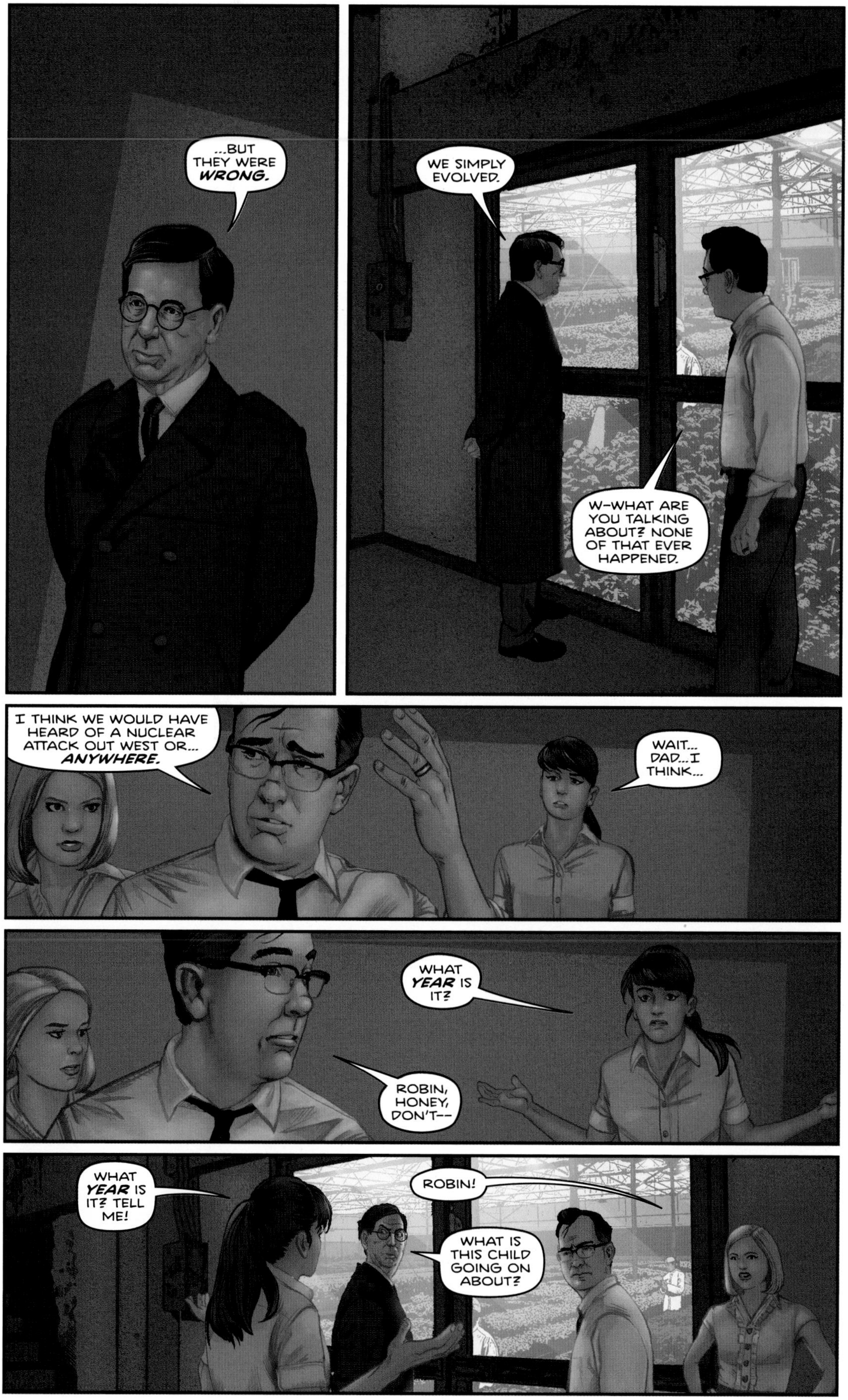
...BUT THEY WERE *WRONG.*
WE SIMPLY EVOLVED.
W-WHAT ARE YOU TALKING ABOUT? NONE OF THAT EVER HAPPENED.
I THINK WE WOULD HAVE HEARD OF A NUCLEAR ATTACK OUT WEST OR... *ANYWHERE.*
WAIT... DAD...I THINK...
WHAT *YEAR* IS IT?
ROBIN, HONEY, DON'T--
WHAT *YEAR* IS IT? TELL ME!
ROBIN!
WHAT IS THIS CHILD GOING ON ABOUT?

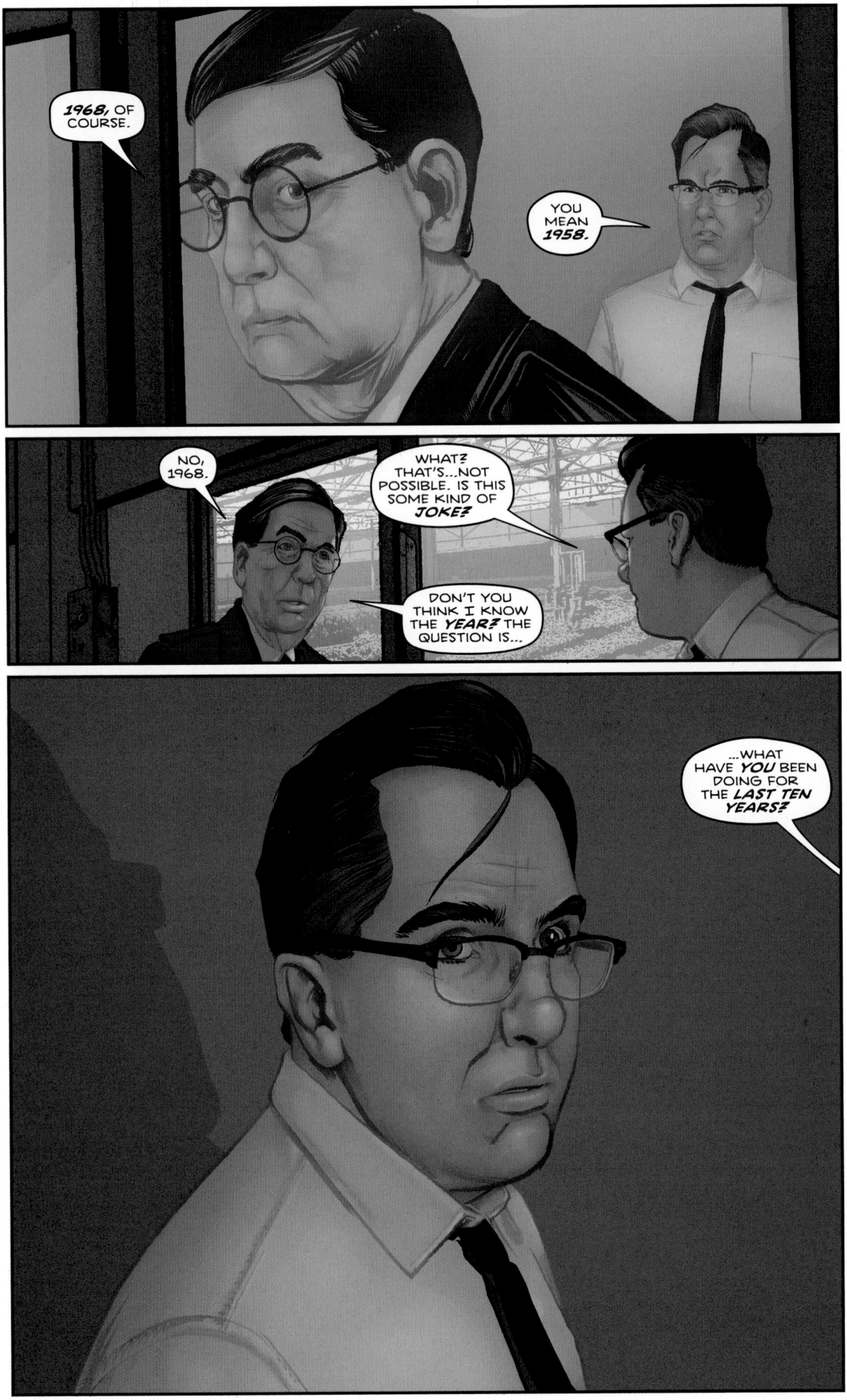
1968, OF COURSE.
YOU MEAN 1958.
NO, 1968.
WHAT? THAT'S...NOT POSSIBLE. IS THIS SOME KIND OF JOKE?
DON'T YOU THINK I KNOW THE YEAR? THE QUESTION IS...
...WHAT HAVE YOU BEEN DOING FOR THE LAST TEN YEARS?

3
PROTECT OUR LIBERTY
BUY WAR BONDS
UP WITH THE STATIC

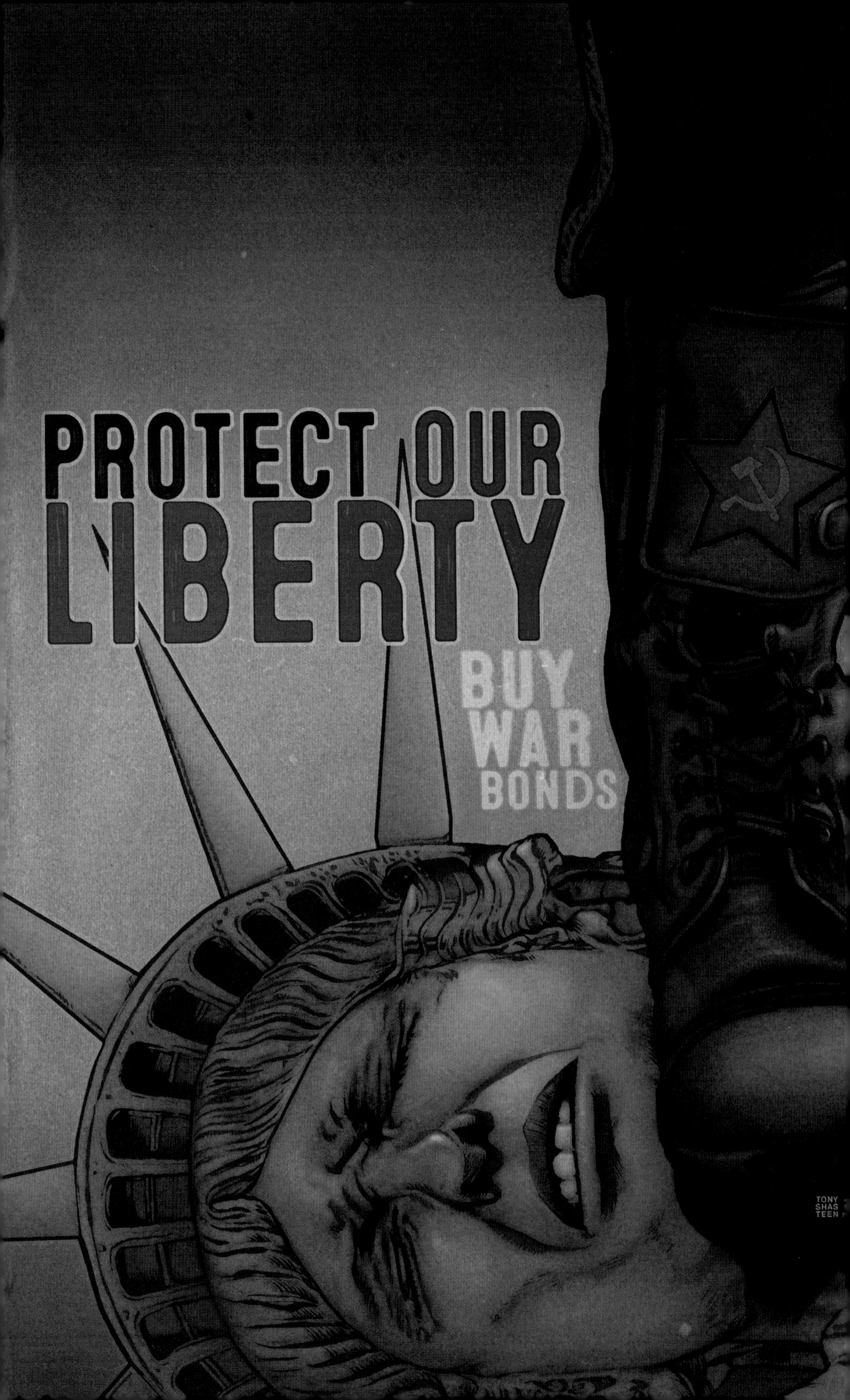
PROTECT OUR LIBERTY
BUY WAR BONDS
TONY SHASTEEN

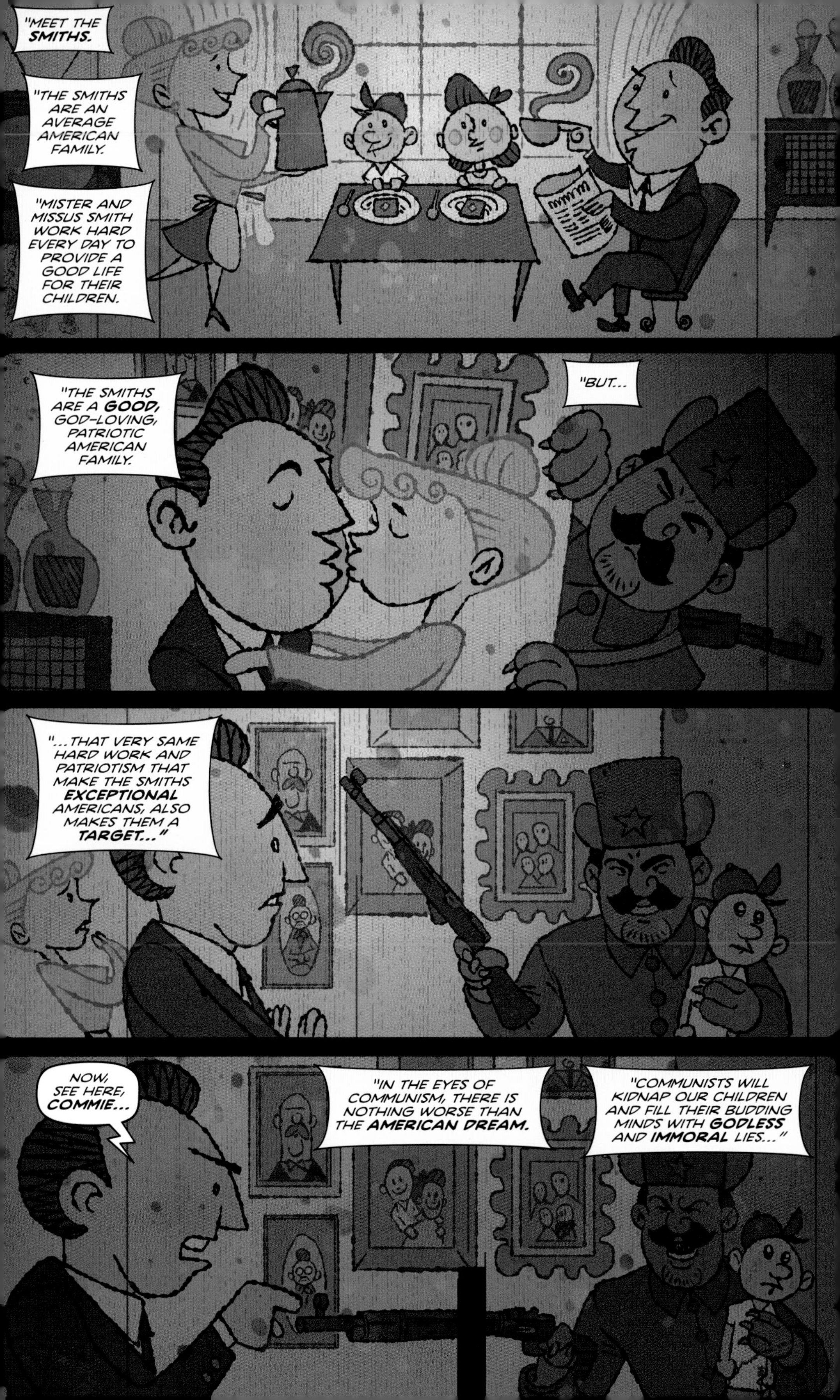
"MEET THE **SMITHS.**
"THE SMITHS ARE AN AVERAGE AMERICAN FAMILY.
"MISTER AND MISSUS SMITH WORK HARD EVERY DAY TO PROVIDE A GOOD LIFE FOR THEIR CHILDREN.
"THE SMITHS ARE A **GOOD,** GOD-LOVING, PATRIOTIC AMERICAN FAMILY.
"BUT...
"...THAT VERY SAME HARD WORK AND PATRIOTISM THAT MAKE THE SMITHS **EXCEPTIONAL** AMERICANS, ALSO MAKES THEM A **TARGET...**"
NOW, SEE HERE, **COMMIE...**
"IN THE EYES OF COMMUNISM, THERE IS NOTHING WORSE THAN THE **AMERICAN DREAM.**
"COMMUNISTS WILL KIDNAP OUR CHILDREN AND FILL THEIR BUDDING MINDS WITH **GODLESS** AND **IMMORAL** LIES..."

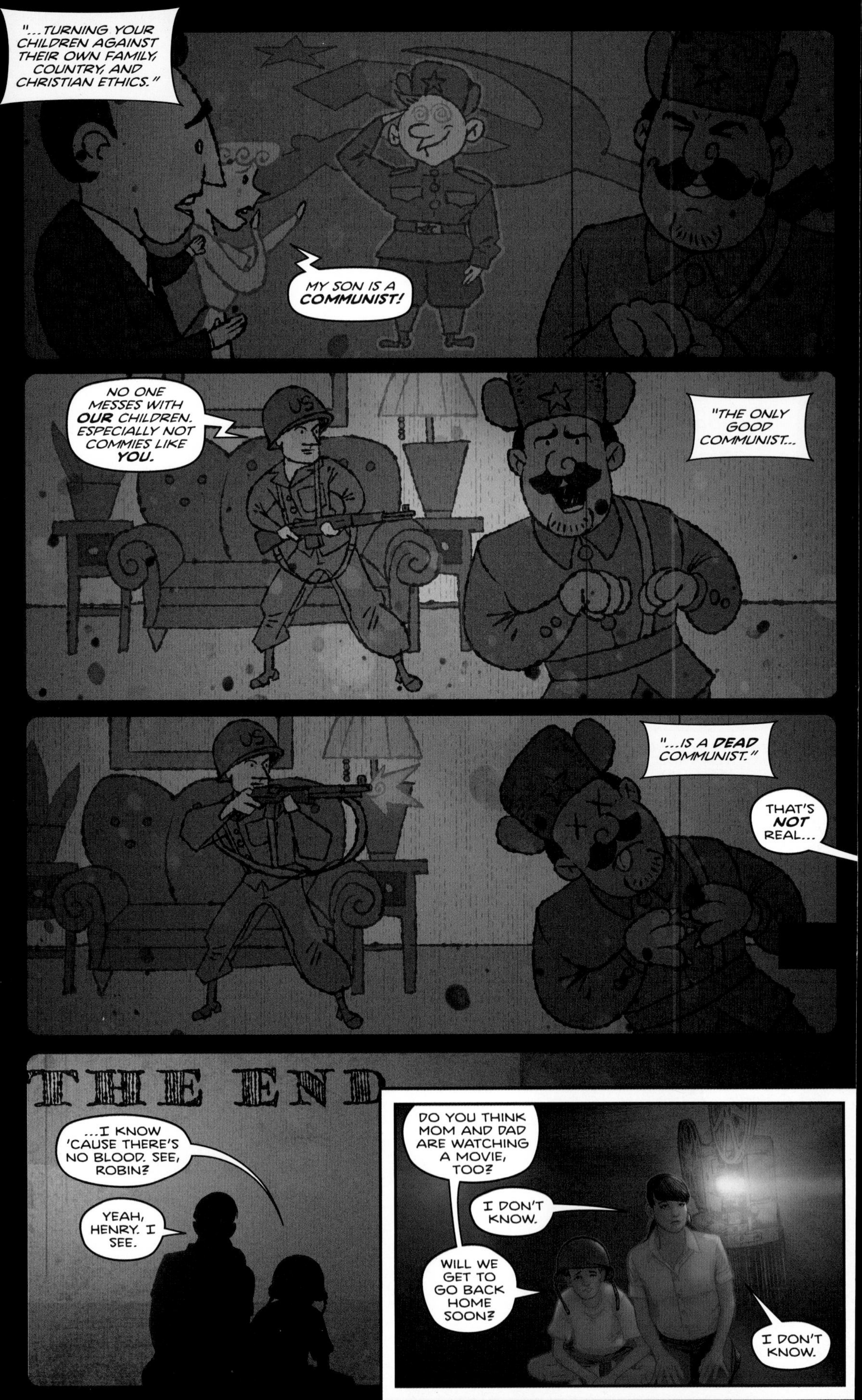

"...TURNING YOUR CHILDREN AGAINST THEIR OWN FAMILY, COUNTRY, AND CHRISTIAN ETHICS."
MY SON IS A COMMUNIST!
NO ONE MESSES WITH OUR CHILDREN. ESPECIALLY NOT COMMIES LIKE YOU.
"THE ONLY GOOD COMMUNIST...
"...IS A DEAD COMMUNIST."
THAT'S NOT REAL...
THE END
...I KNOW 'CAUSE THERE'S NO BLOOD. SEE, ROBIN?
YEAH, HENRY. I SEE.
DO YOU THINK MOM AND DAD ARE WATCHING A MOVIE, TOO?
I DON'T KNOW.
WILL WE GET TO GO BACK HOME SOON?
I DON'T KNOW.

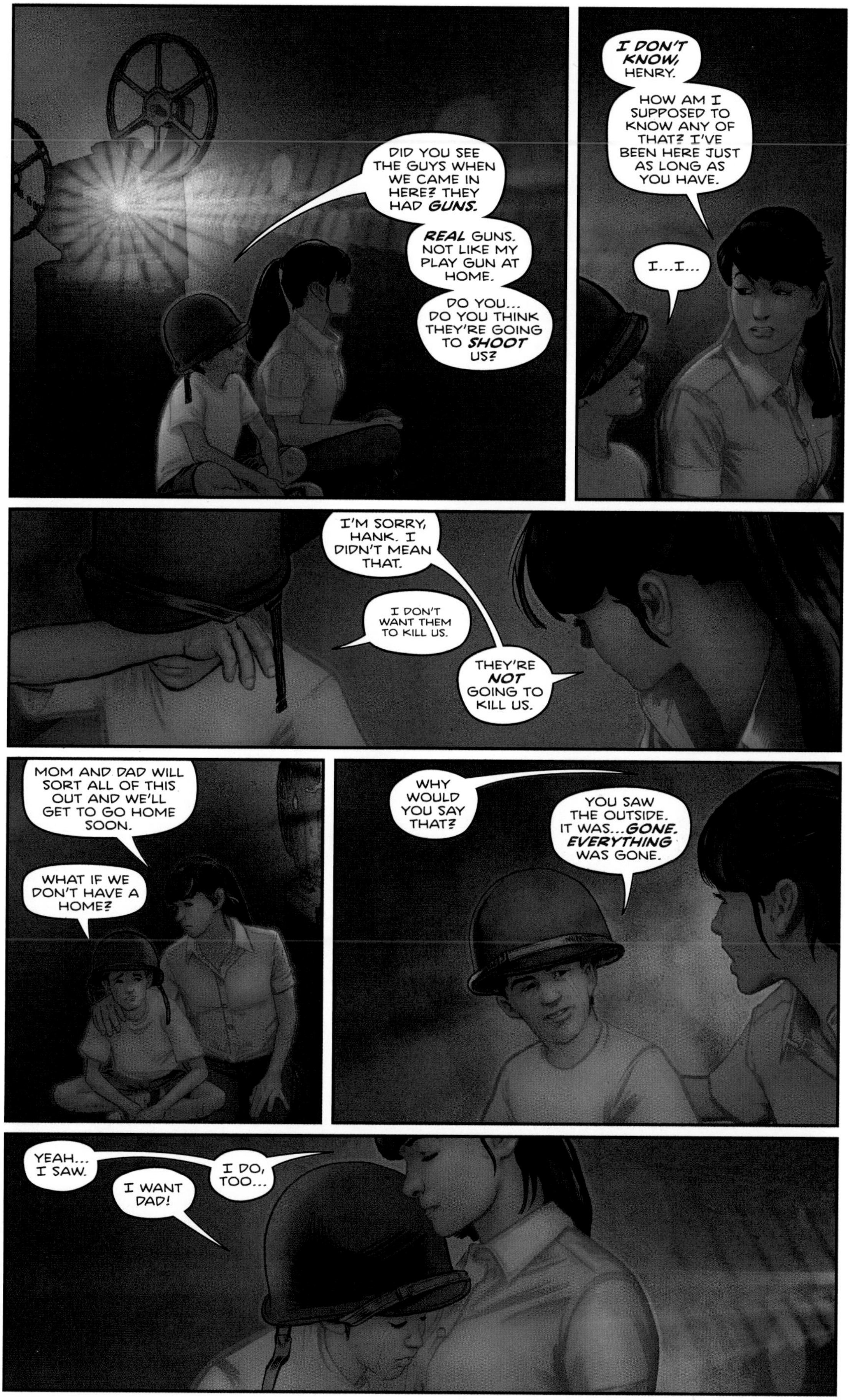
DID YOU SEE THE GUYS WHEN WE CAME IN HERE? THEY HAD GUNS.
REAL GUNS. NOT LIKE MY PLAY GUN AT HOME.
DO YOU... DO YOU THINK THEY'RE GOING TO SHOOT US?
I DON'T KNOW, HENRY.
HOW AM I SUPPOSED TO KNOW ANY OF THAT? I'VE BEEN HERE JUST AS LONG AS YOU HAVE.
I...I...
I'M SORRY, HANK. I DIDN'T MEAN THAT.
I DON'T WANT THEM TO KILL US.
THEY'RE NOT GOING TO KILL US.
MOM AND DAD WILL SORT ALL OF THIS OUT AND WE'LL GET TO GO HOME SOON.
WHAT IF WE DON'T HAVE A HOME?
WHY WOULD YOU SAY THAT?
YOU SAW THE OUTSIDE. IT WAS...GONE. EVERYTHING WAS GONE.
YEAH... I SAW.
I WANT DAD!
I DO, TOO...

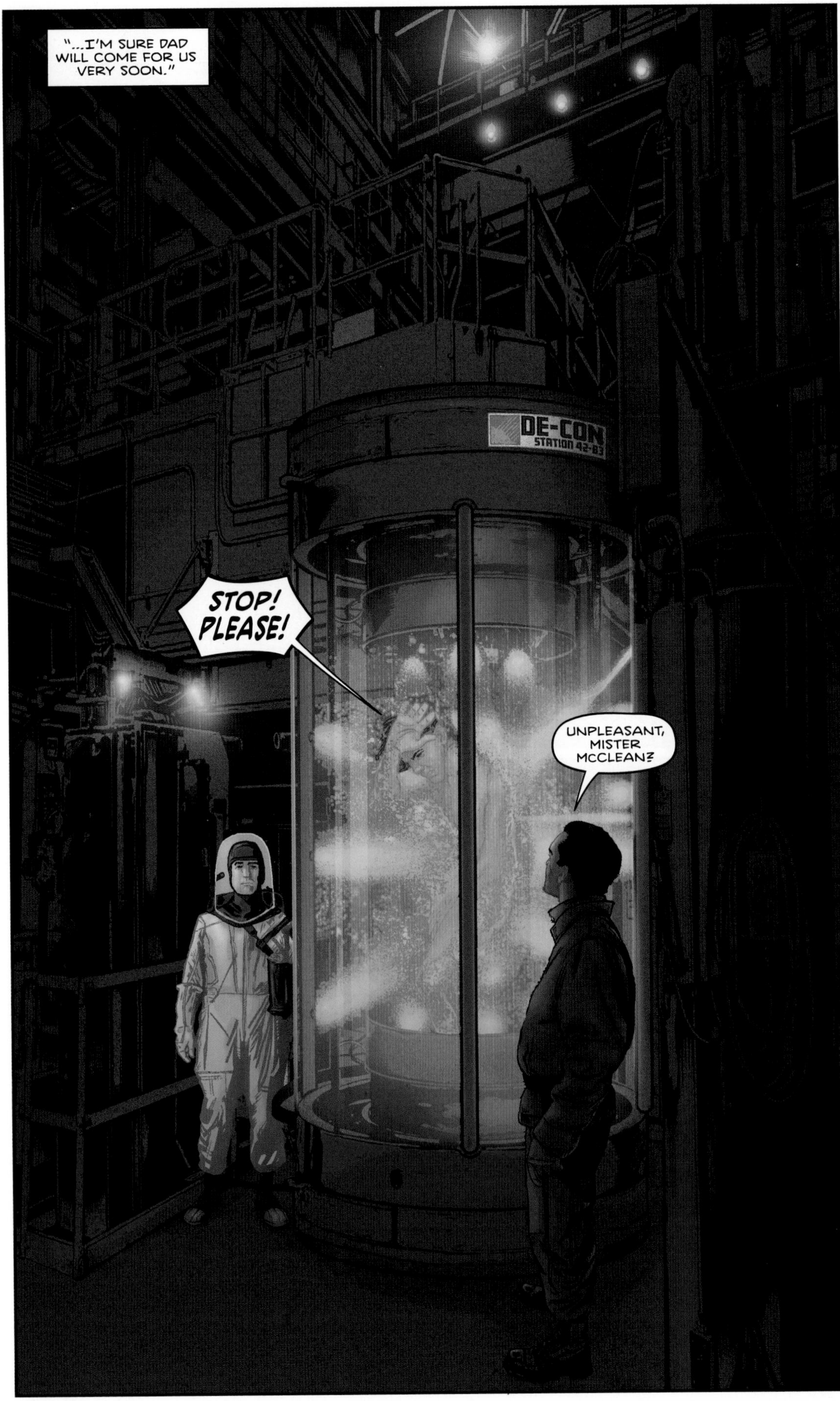
"...I'M SURE DAD WILL COME FOR US VERY SOON."
DE-CON STATION 42-83
STOP! PLEASE!
UNPLEASANT, MISTER MCCLEAN?

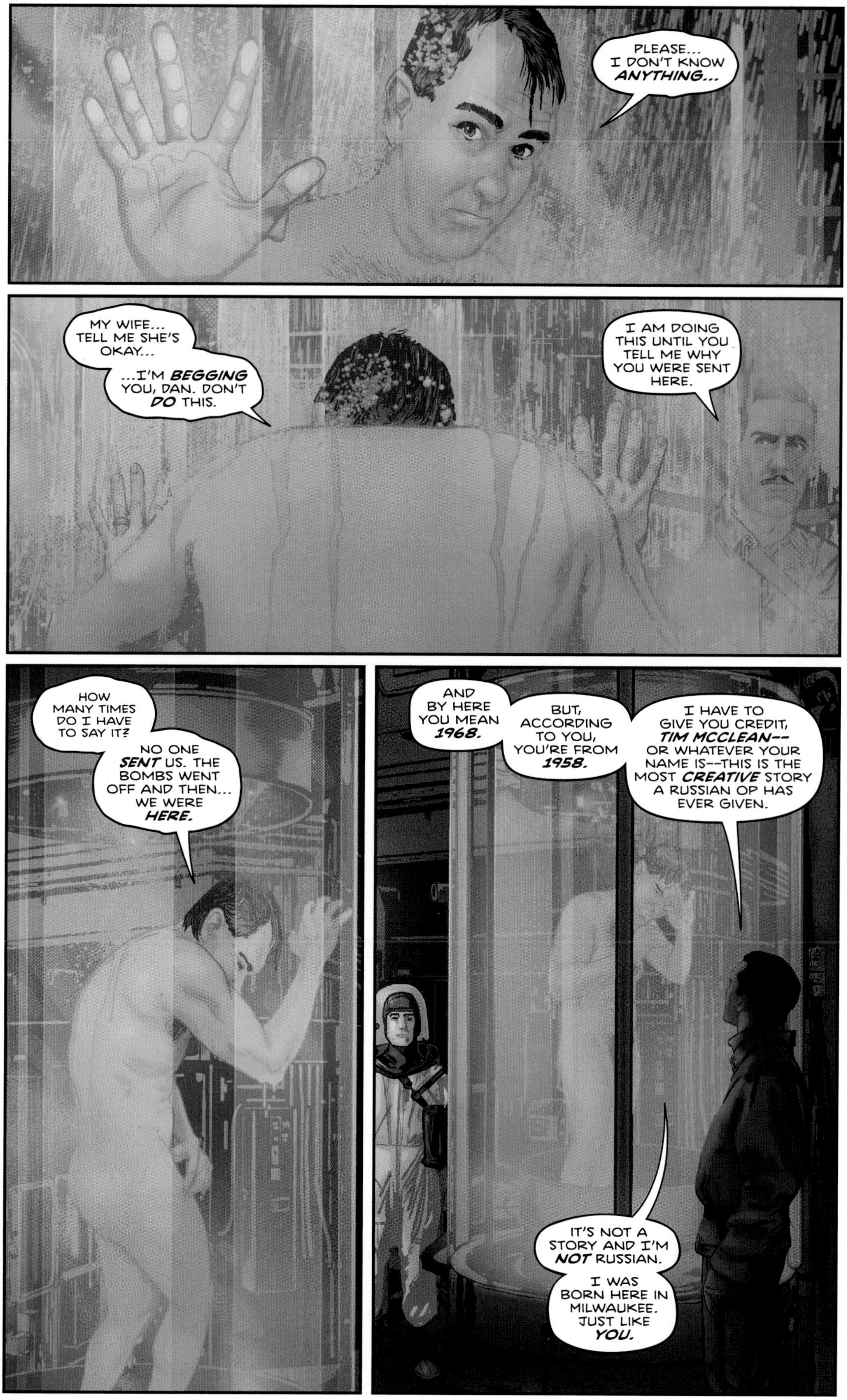
PLEASE... I DON'T KNOW ANYTHING...
MY WIFE... TELL ME SHE'S OKAY...
...I'M BEGGING YOU, DAN. DON'T DO THIS.
I AM DOING THIS UNTIL YOU TELL ME WHY YOU WERE SENT HERE.
HOW MANY TIMES DO I HAVE TO SAY IT?
NO ONE SENT US. THE BOMBS WENT OFF AND THEN... WE WERE HERE.
AND BY HERE YOU MEAN 1968.
BUT, ACCORDING TO YOU, YOU'RE FROM 1958.
I HAVE TO GIVE YOU CREDIT, TIM MCCLEAN--OR WHATEVER YOUR NAME IS--THIS IS THE MOST CREATIVE STORY A RUSSIAN OP HAS EVER GIVEN.
IT'S NOT A STORY AND I'M NOT RUSSIAN.
I WAS BORN HERE IN MILWAUKEE. JUST LIKE YOU.

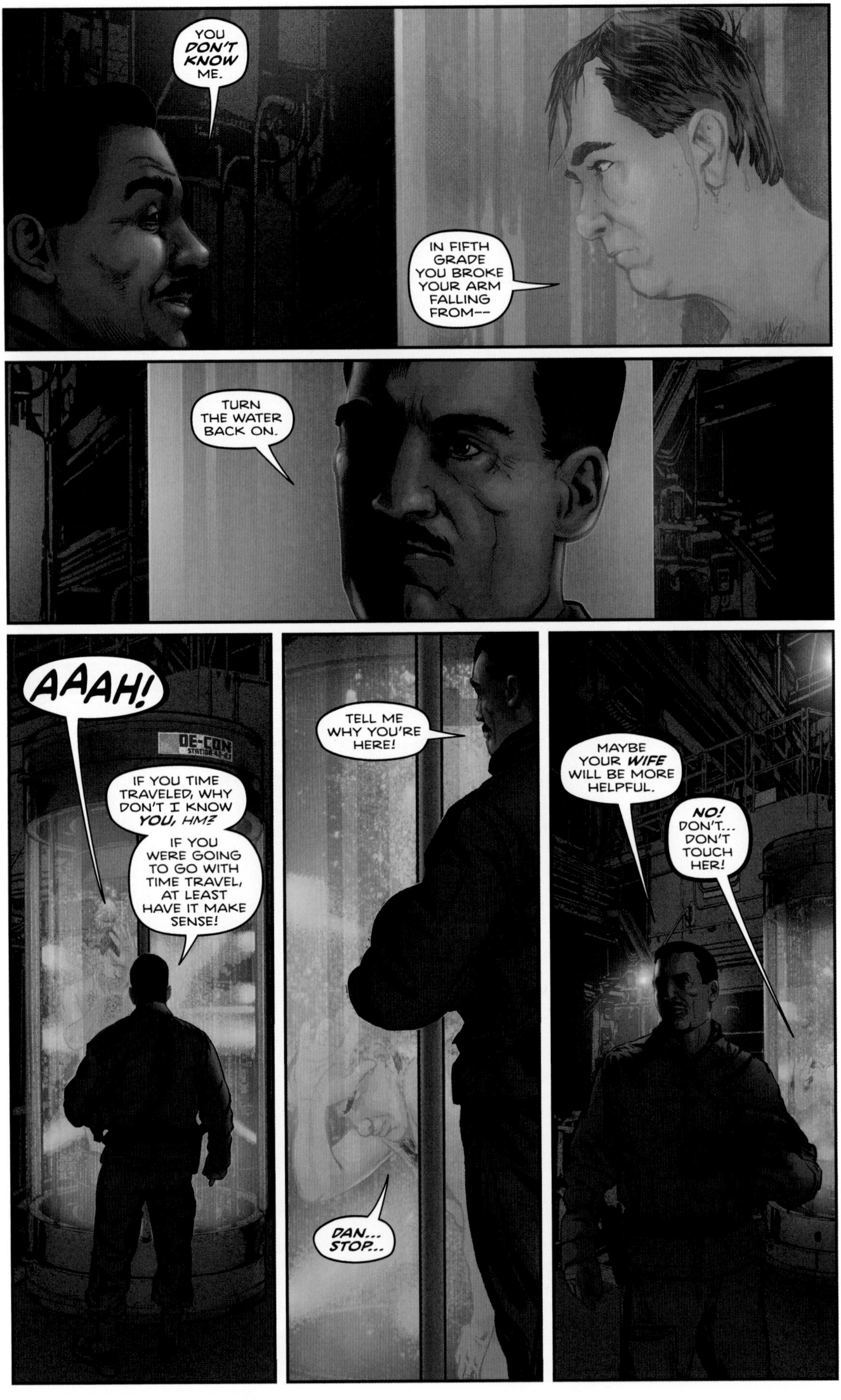

YOU *DON'T KNOW* ME.
IN FIFTH GRADE YOU BROKE YOUR ARM FALLING FROM--
TURN THE WATER BACK ON.
AAAH!
DE-CON
IF YOU TIME TRAVELED, WHY DON'T I KNOW *YOU, HM?*
IF YOU WERE GOING TO GO WITH TIME TRAVEL, AT LEAST HAVE IT MAKE SENSE!
TELL ME WHY YOU'RE HERE!
DAN... STOP...
MAYBE YOUR *WIFE* WILL BE MORE HELPFUL.
NO! DON'T... DON'T TOUCH HER!

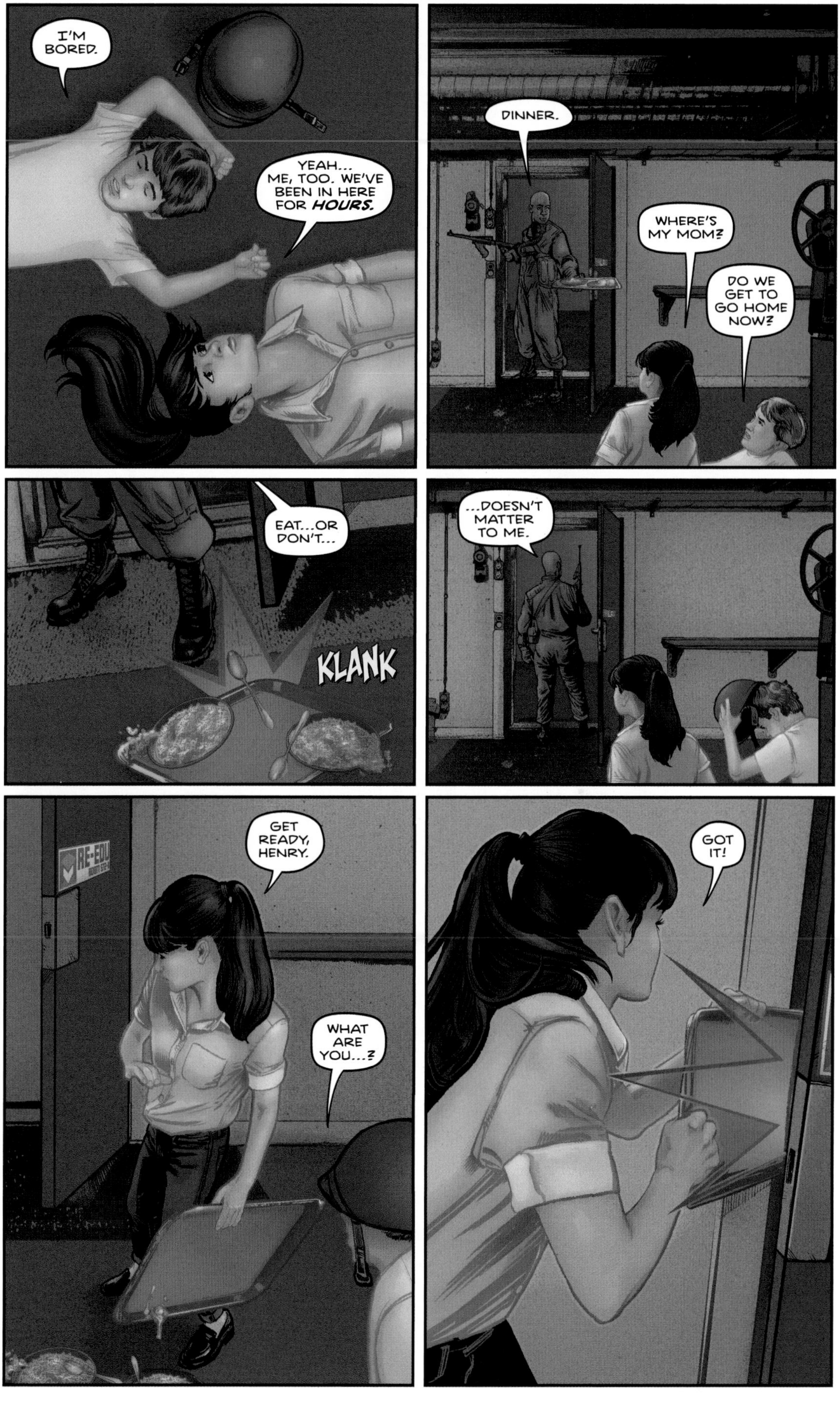
I'M BORED.
YEAH... ME, TOO. WE'VE BEEN IN HERE FOR HOURS.
DINNER.
WHERE'S MY MOM?
DO WE GET TO GO HOME NOW?
EAT...OR DON'T...
KLANK
...DOESN'T MATTER TO ME.
RE-EDU
GET READY, HENRY.
WHAT ARE YOU...?
GOT IT!

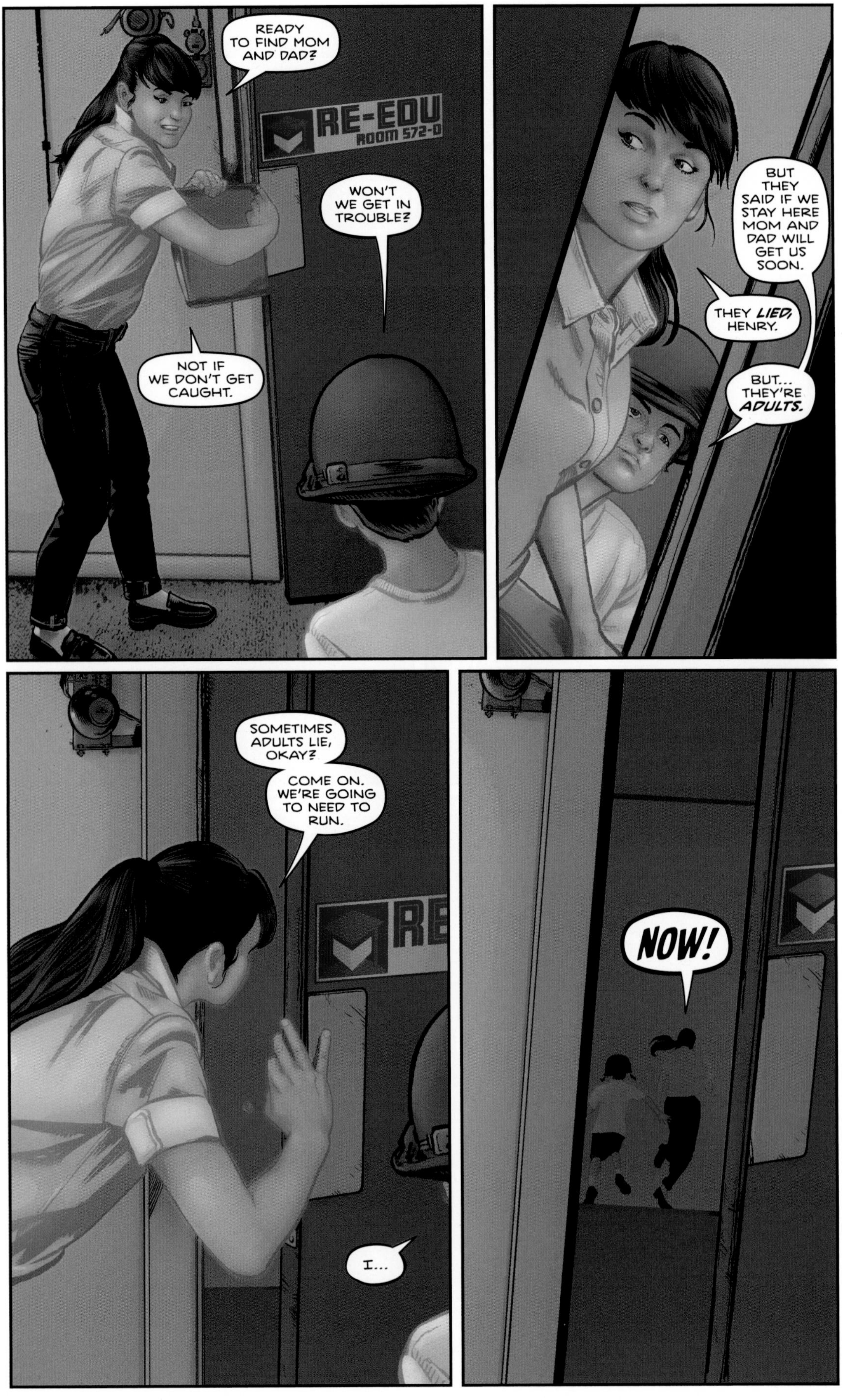
READY TO FIND MOM AND DAD?
RE-EDU
ROOM 572-D
WON'T WE GET IN TROUBLE?
NOT IF WE DON'T GET CAUGHT.
BUT THEY SAID IF WE STAY HERE MOM AND DAD WILL GET US SOON.
THEY *LIED*, HENRY.
BUT... THEY'RE ***ADULTS.***
SOMETIMES ADULTS LIE, OKAY?
COME ON. WE'RE GOING TO NEED TO RUN.
RE
I...
NOW!

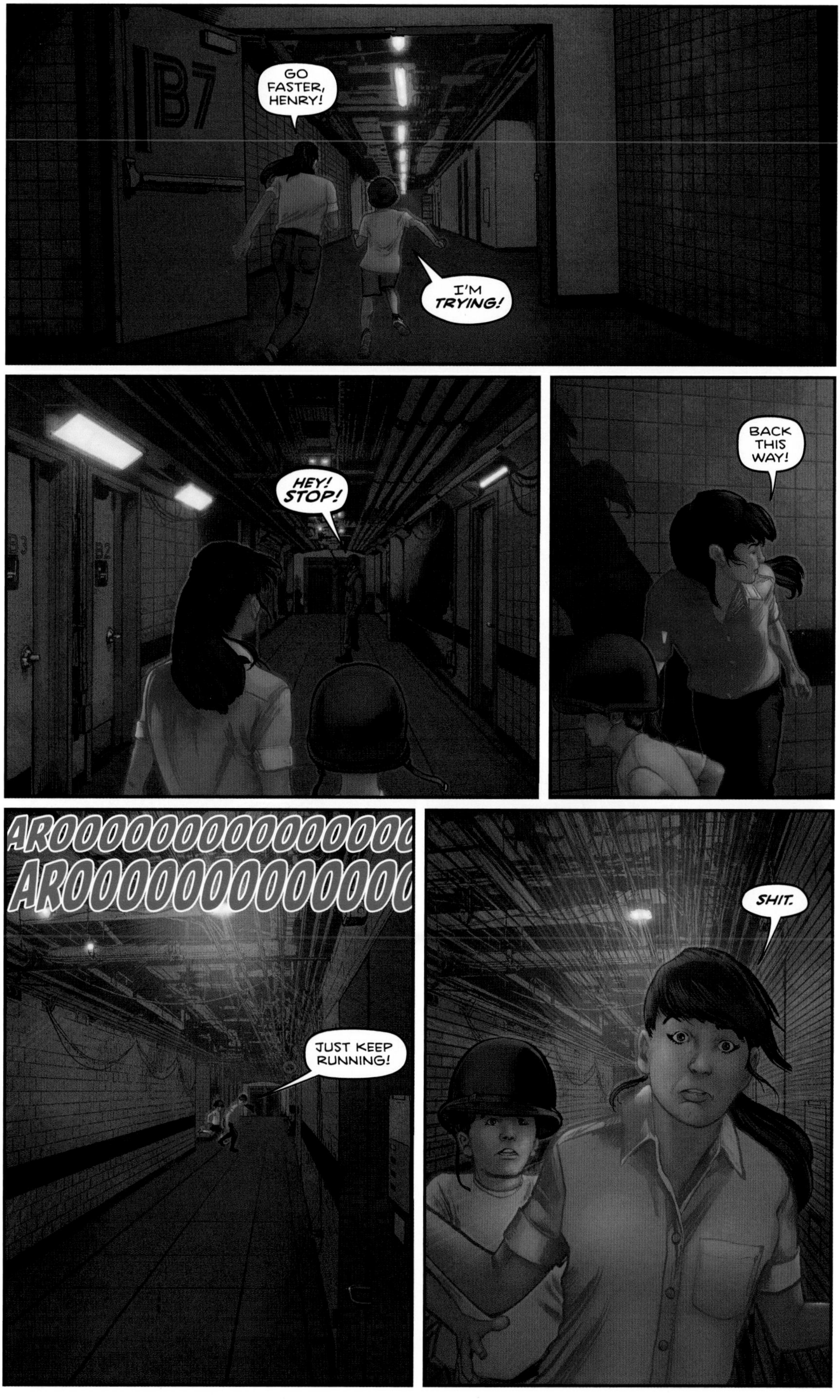
GO FASTER, HENRY!
I'M TRYING!
HEY! STOP!
BACK THIS WAY!
AROOOOOOOOOOOOOOOO
AROOOOOOOOOOOOOO
JUST KEEP RUNNING!
SHIT.

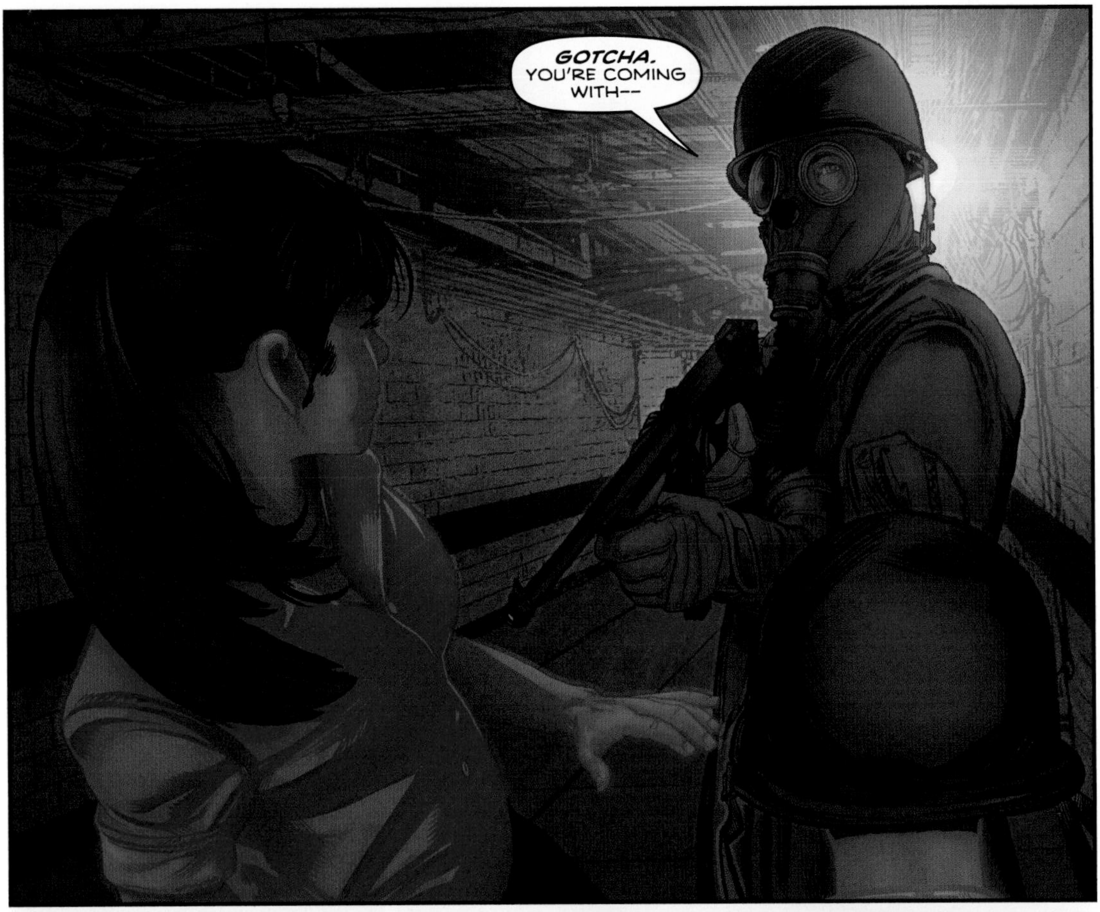
GOTCHA. YOU'RE COMING WITH--

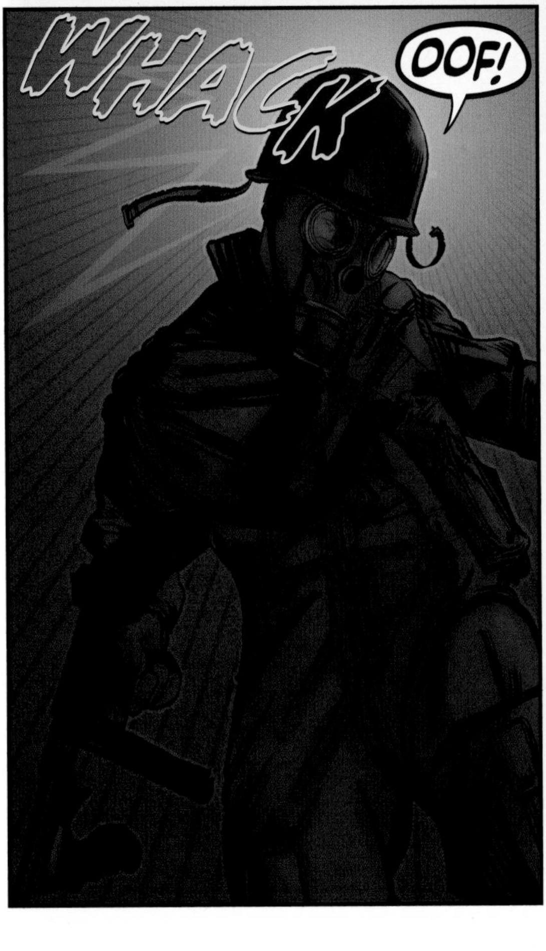
WHACK
OOF!

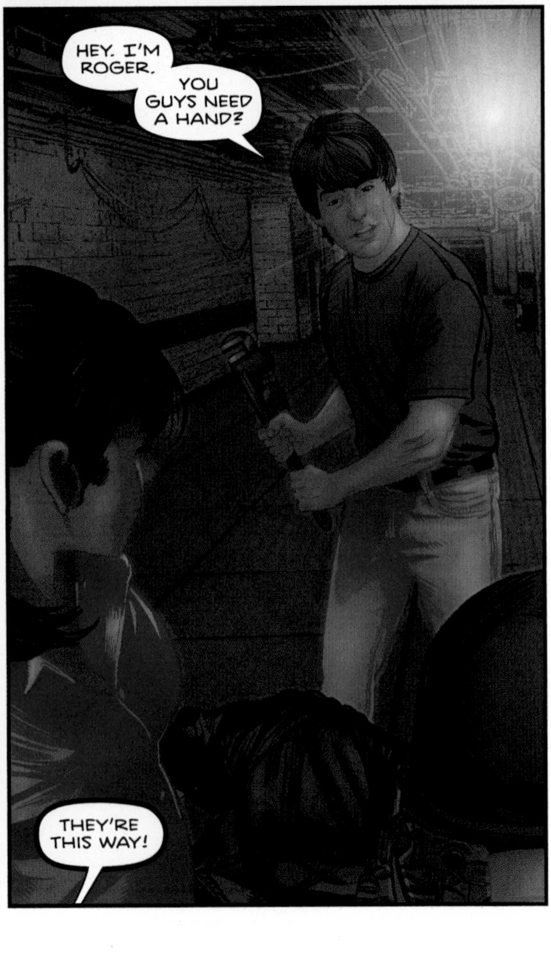
HEY. I'M ROGER.
YOU GUYS NEED A HAND?
THEY'RE THIS WAY!

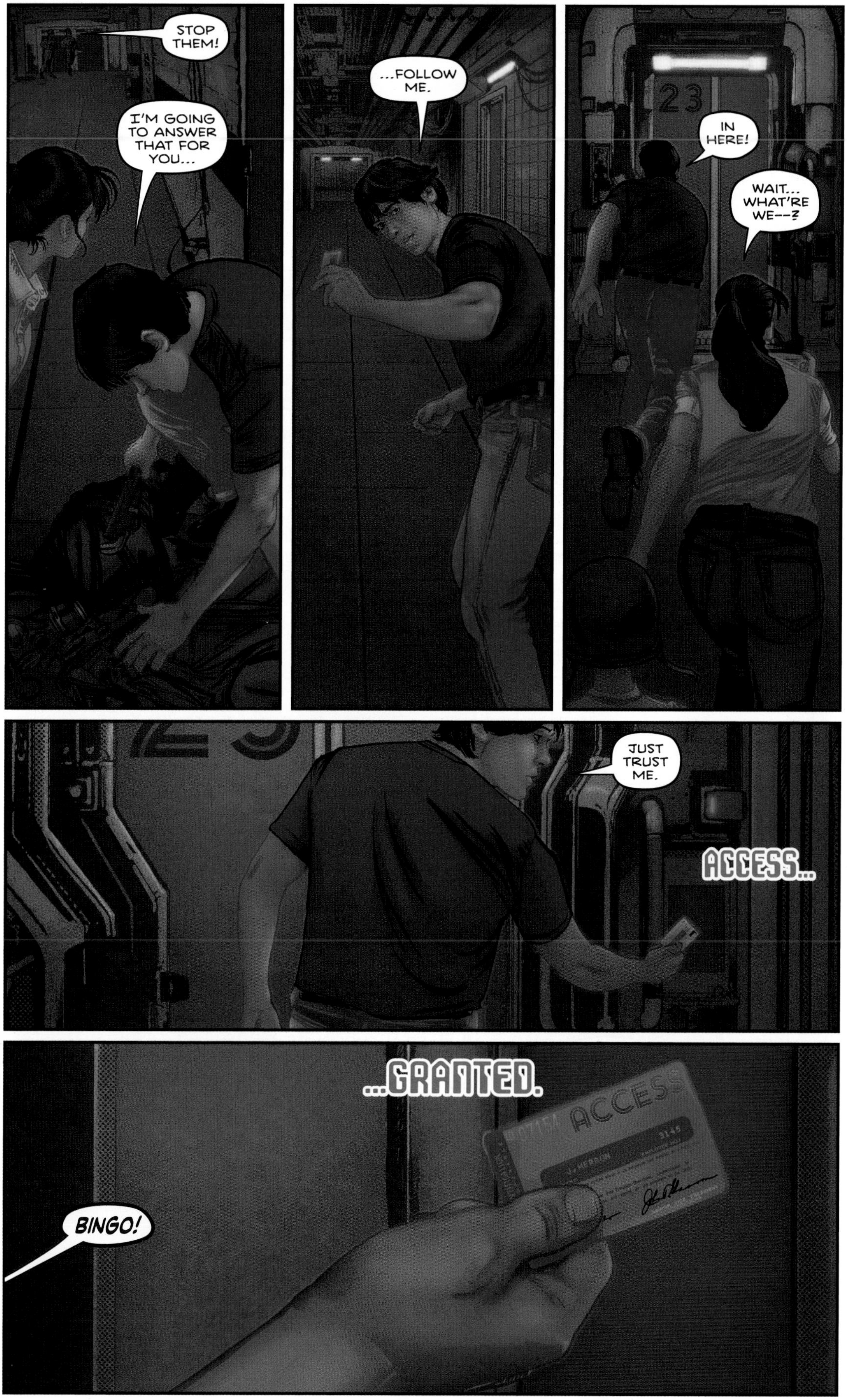
STOP THEM!
I'M GOING TO ANSWER THAT FOR YOU...
...FOLLOW ME.
IN HERE!
WAIT... WHAT'RE WE--?
JUST TRUST ME.
ACCESS...
...GRANTED.
ACCESS
BINGO!

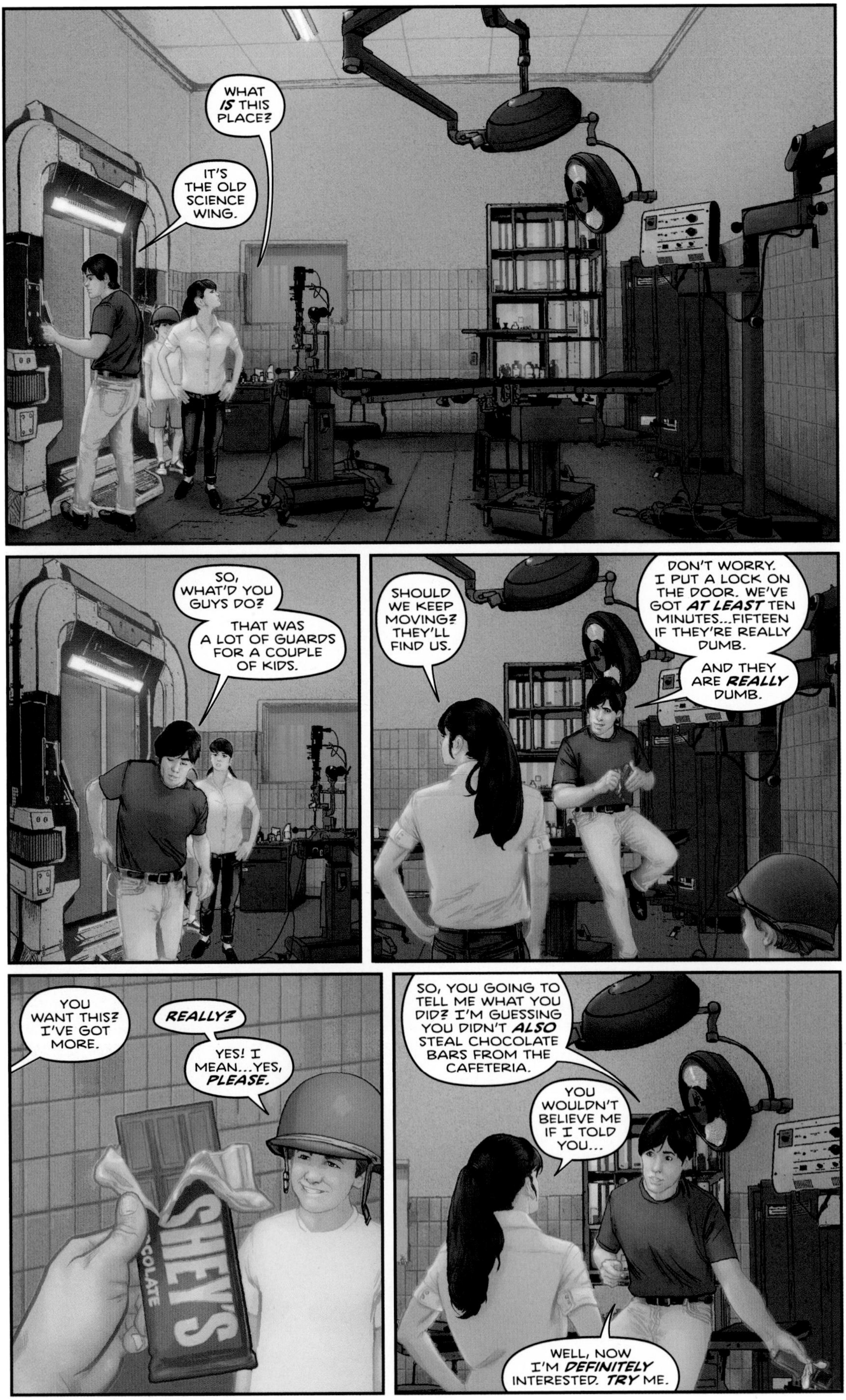
WHAT *IS* THIS PLACE?
IT'S THE OLD SCIENCE WING.
SO, WHAT'D YOU GUYS DO?
THAT WAS A LOT OF GUARDS FOR A COUPLE OF KIDS.
SHOULD WE KEEP MOVING? THEY'LL FIND US.
DON'T WORRY. I PUT A LOCK ON THE DOOR. WE'VE GOT *AT LEAST* TEN MINUTES...FIFTEEN IF THEY'RE REALLY DUMB.
AND THEY ARE *REALLY* DUMB.
YOU WANT THIS? I'VE GOT MORE.
REALLY?
YES! I MEAN...YES, *PLEASE.*
SHEY'S
COLATE
SO, YOU GOING TO TELL ME WHAT YOU DID? I'M GUESSING YOU DIDN'T *ALSO* STEAL CHOCOLATE BARS FROM THE CAFETERIA.
YOU WOULDN'T BELIEVE ME IF I TOLD YOU...
WELL, NOW I'M *DEFINITELY* INTERESTED. *TRY* ME.

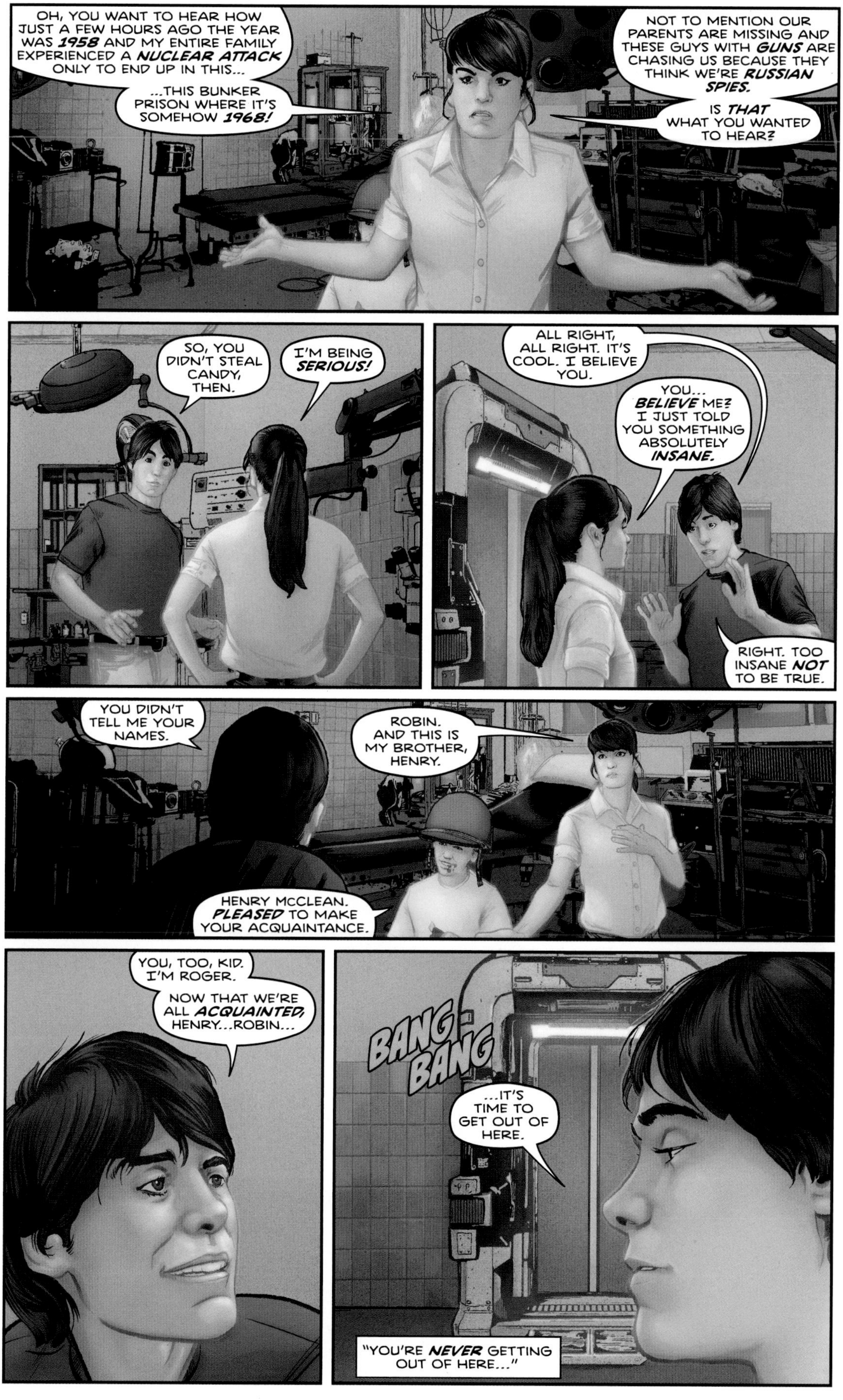
OH, YOU WANT TO HEAR HOW JUST A FEW HOURS AGO THE YEAR WAS 1958 AND MY ENTIRE FAMILY EXPERIENCED A NUCLEAR ATTACK ONLY TO END UP IN THIS...
...THIS BUNKER PRISON WHERE IT'S SOMEHOW 1968!
NOT TO MENTION OUR PARENTS ARE MISSING AND THESE GUYS WITH GUNS ARE CHASING US BECAUSE THEY THINK WE'RE RUSSIAN SPIES.
IS THAT WHAT YOU WANTED TO HEAR?
SO, YOU DIDN'T STEAL CANDY, THEN.
I'M BEING SERIOUS!
ALL RIGHT, ALL RIGHT. IT'S COOL. I BELIEVE YOU.
YOU... BELIEVE ME? I JUST TOLD YOU SOMETHING ABSOLUTELY INSANE.
RIGHT. TOO INSANE NOT TO BE TRUE.
YOU DIDN'T TELL ME YOUR NAMES.
ROBIN. AND THIS IS MY BROTHER, HENRY.
HENRY MCCLEAN. PLEASED TO MAKE YOUR ACQUAINTANCE.
YOU, TOO, KID. I'M ROGER.
NOW THAT WE'RE ALL ACQUAINTED, HENRY...ROBIN...
BANG-BANG
...IT'S TIME TO GET OUT OF HERE.
"YOU'RE NEVER GETTING OUT OF HERE..."

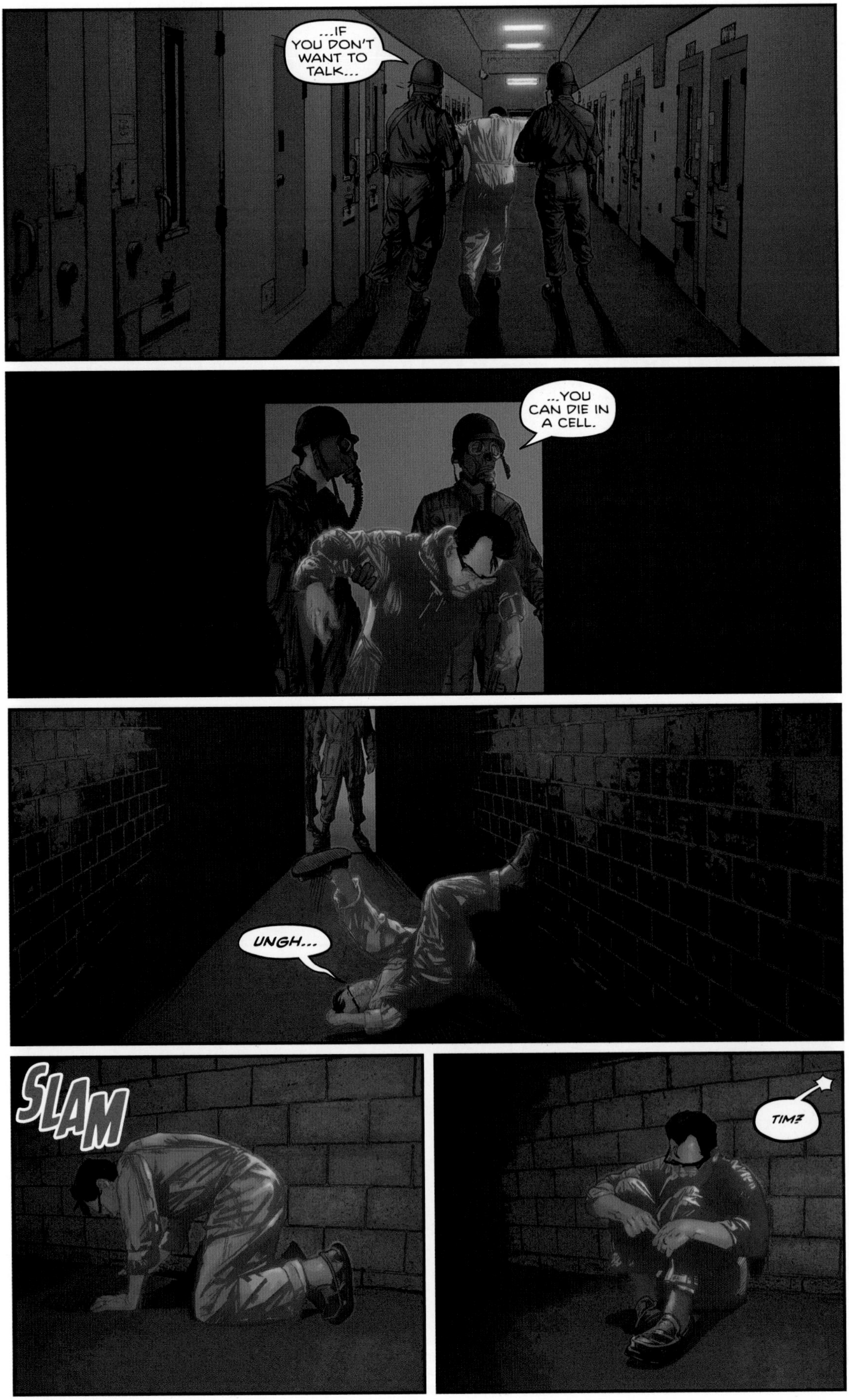
...IF YOU DON'T WANT TO TALK...
...YOU CAN DIE IN A CELL.
UNGH...
SLAM
TIM?

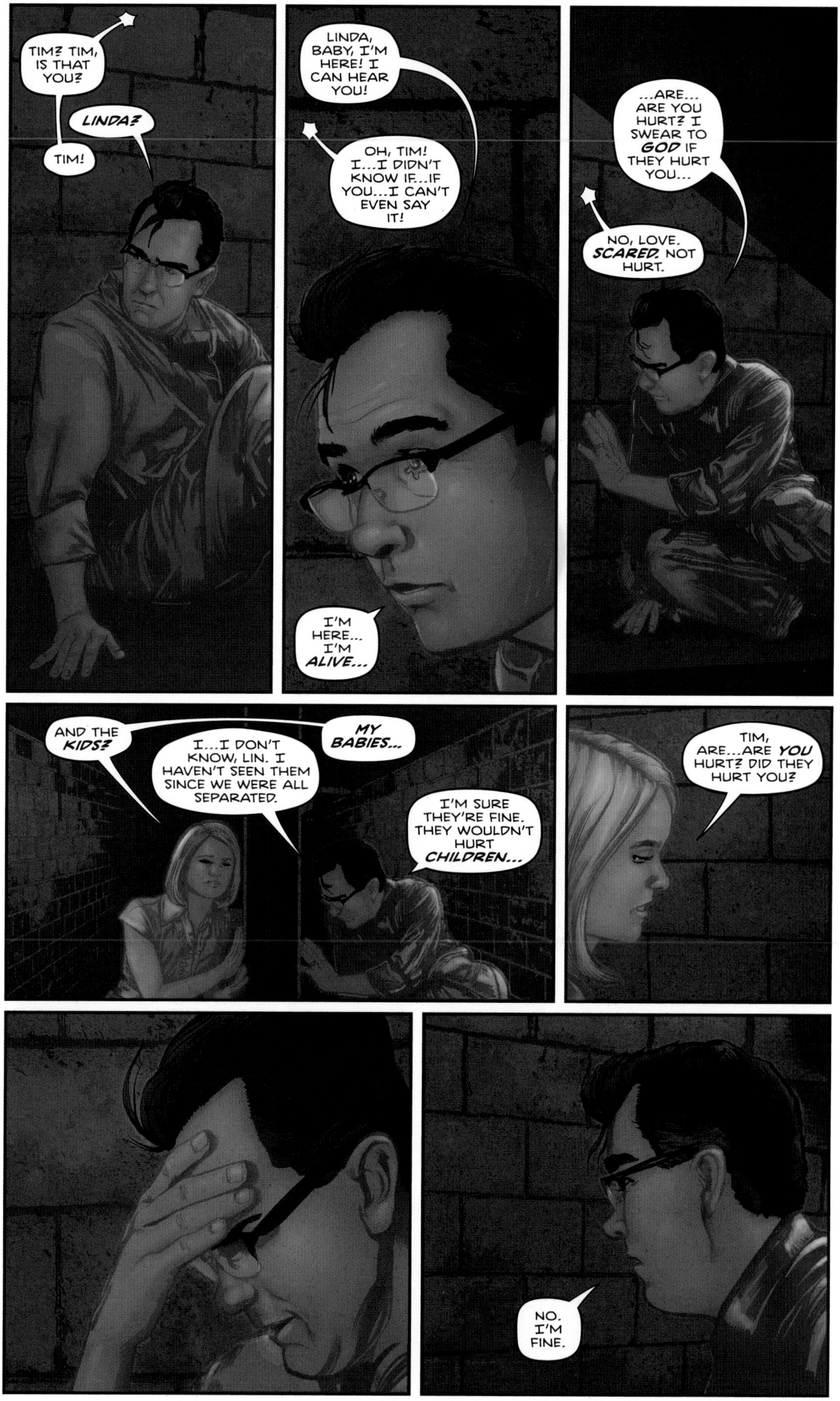
TIM? TIM, IS THAT YOU?
LINDA?
TIM!
LINDA, BABY, I'M HERE! I CAN HEAR YOU!
OH, TIM! I...I DIDN'T KNOW IF...IF YOU...I CAN'T EVEN SAY IT!
I'M HERE... I'M ALIVE...
...ARE... ARE YOU HURT? I SWEAR TO GOD IF THEY HURT YOU...
NO, LOVE. SCARED. NOT HURT.
AND THE KIDS?
MY BABIES...
I...I DON'T KNOW, LIN. I HAVEN'T SEEN THEM SINCE WE WERE ALL SEPARATED.
I'M SURE THEY'RE FINE. THEY WOULDN'T HURT CHILDREN...
TIM, ARE...ARE YOU HURT? DID THEY HURT YOU?
NO. I'M FINE.

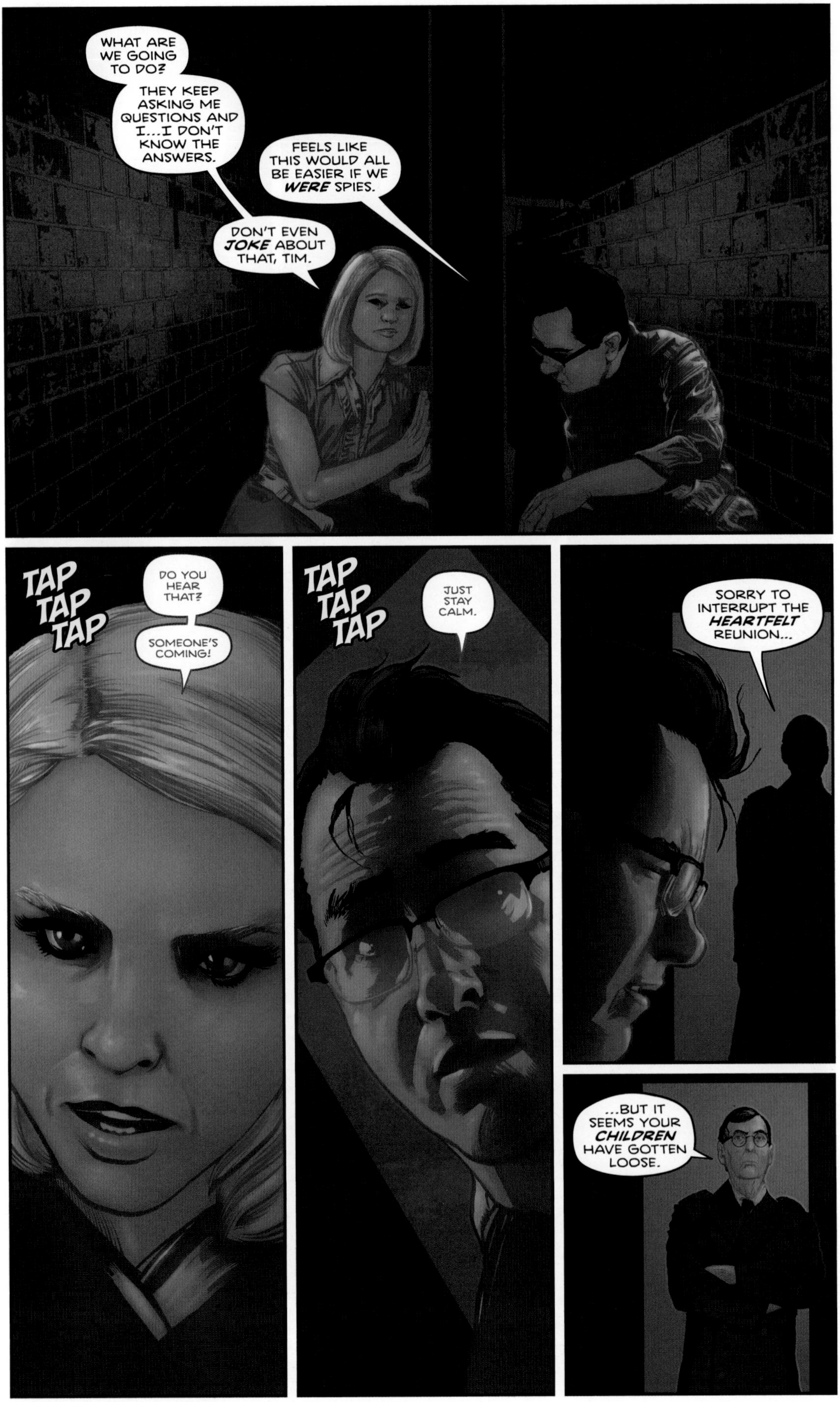
WHAT ARE WE GOING TO DO?
THEY KEEP ASKING ME QUESTIONS AND I...I DON'T KNOW THE ANSWERS.
FEELS LIKE THIS WOULD ALL BE EASIER IF WE *WERE* SPIES.
DON'T EVEN *JOKE* ABOUT THAT, TIM.
TAP TAP TAP
DO YOU HEAR THAT?
SOMEONE'S COMING!
TAP TAP TAP
JUST STAY CALM.
SORRY TO INTERRUPT THE *HEARTFELT* REUNION...
...BUT IT SEEMS YOUR *CHILDREN* HAVE GOTTEN LOOSE.

HURRY UP, ROGER.

I'VE GOT IT, JUST *RELAX.*

BANG

OPEN THIS DOOR!

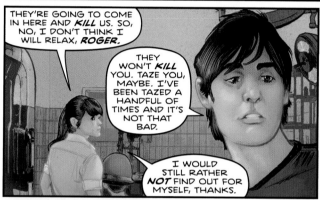

THEY'RE GOING TO COME IN HERE AND *KILL* US. SO, NO, I DON'T THINK I WILL RELAX, *ROGER.*

THEY WON'T *KILL* YOU. TAZE YOU, MAYBE. I'VE BEEN TAZED A HANDFUL OF TIMES AND IT'S NOT THAT BAD.

I WOULD STILL RATHER *NOT* FIND OUT FOR MYSELF, THANKS.

THEN, COULD I INTEREST YOU IN A NICE CRAWL THROUGH A VENTILATION SHAFT?

THERE'S NOT, LIKE...A *BACK DOOR,* MAYBE?

FINE.

TUNNEL OR TAZER. TAKE YOUR PICK.

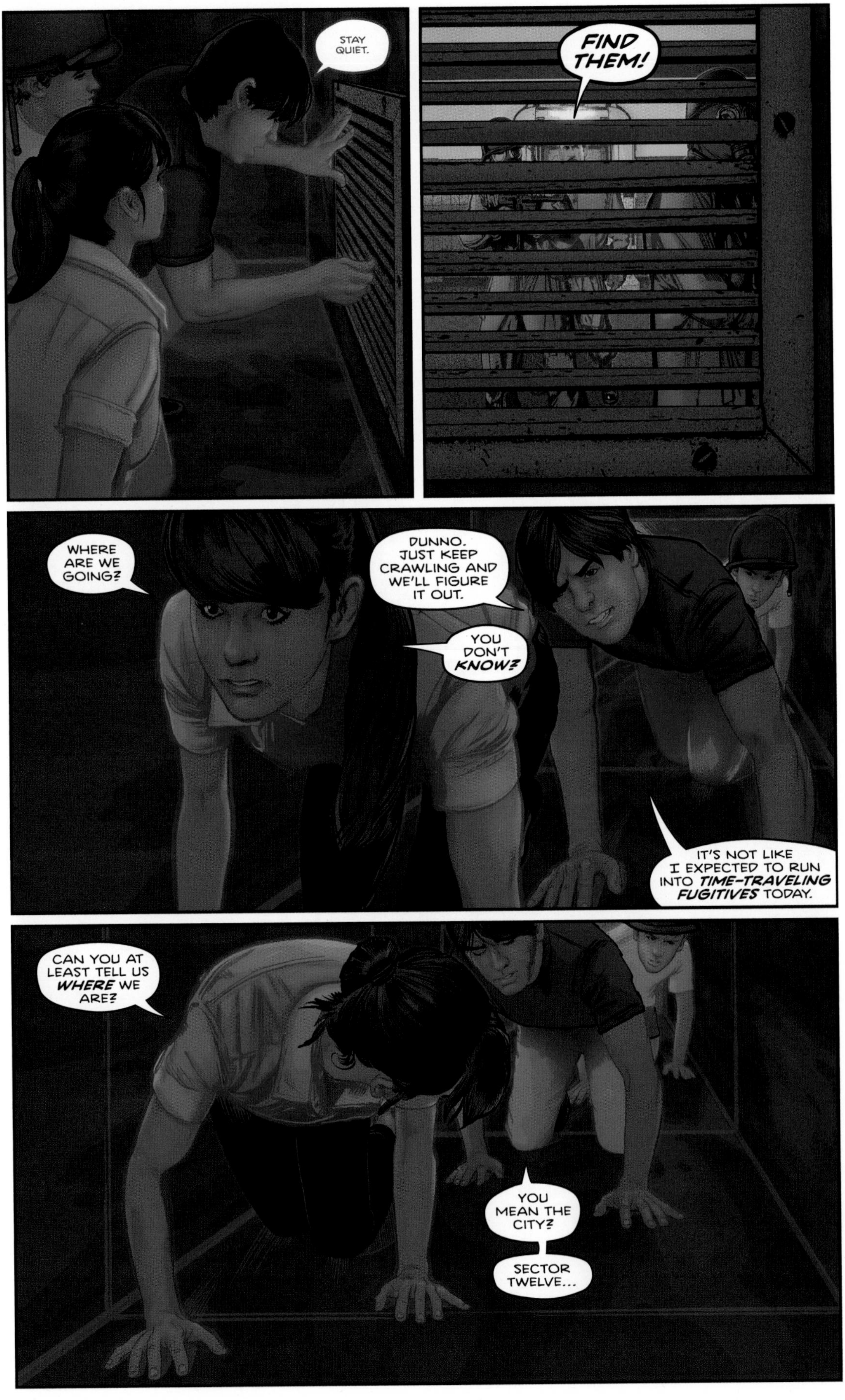
STAY QUIET.
FIND THEM!
WHERE ARE WE GOING?
DUNNO. JUST KEEP CRAWLING AND WE'LL FIGURE IT OUT.
YOU DON'T KNOW?
IT'S NOT LIKE I EXPECTED TO RUN INTO TIME-TRAVELING FUGITIVES TODAY.
CAN YOU AT LEAST TELL US WHERE WE ARE?
YOU MEAN THE CITY?
SECTOR TWELVE...

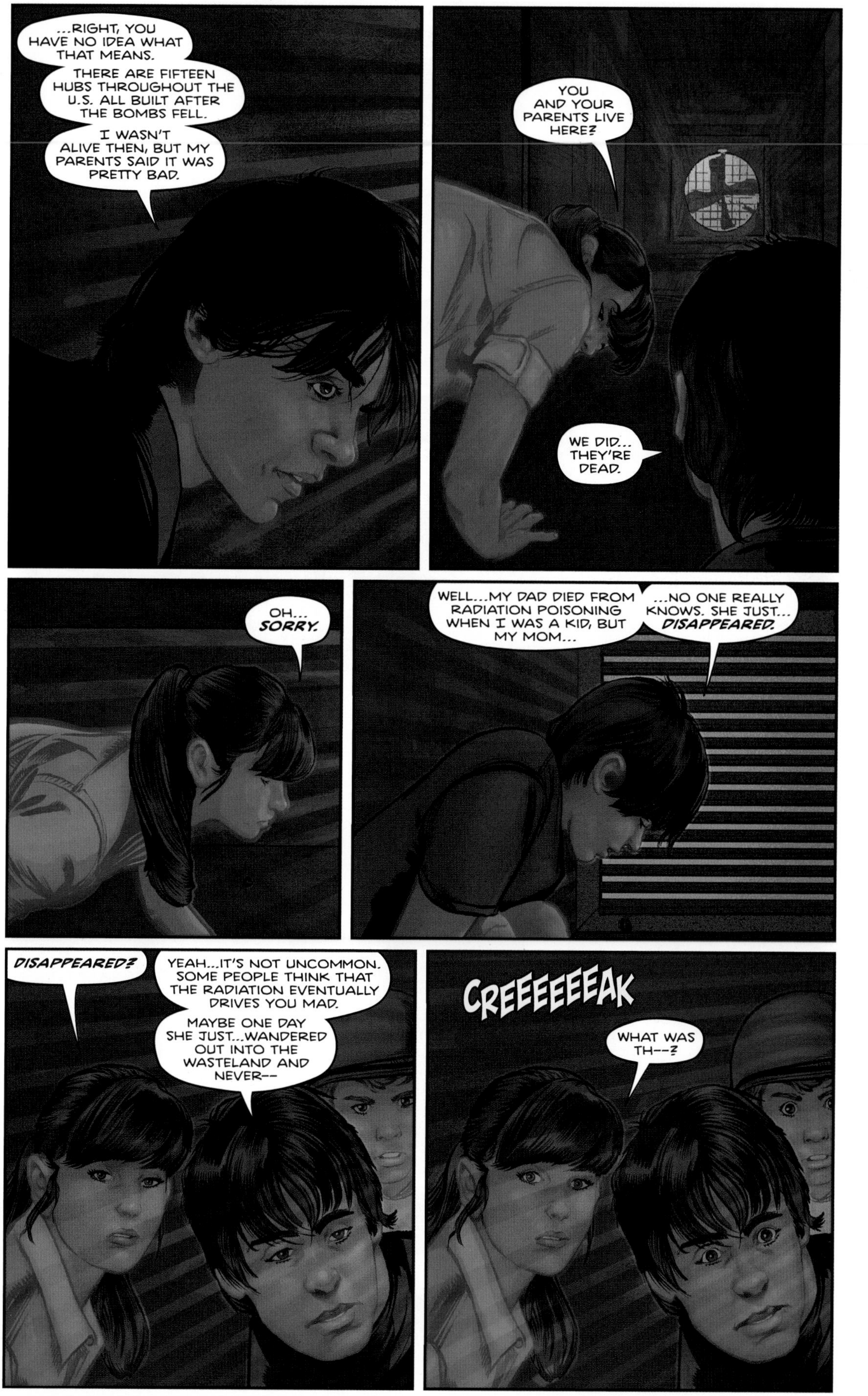
...RIGHT, YOU HAVE NO IDEA WHAT THAT MEANS.
THERE ARE FIFTEEN HUBS THROUGHOUT THE U.S. ALL BUILT AFTER THE BOMBS FELL.
I WASN'T ALIVE THEN, BUT MY PARENTS SAID IT WAS PRETTY BAD.
YOU AND YOUR PARENTS LIVE HERE?
WE DID... THEY'RE DEAD.
OH... *SORRY.*
WELL...MY DAD DIED FROM RADIATION POISONING WHEN I WAS A KID, BUT MY MOM...
...NO ONE REALLY KNOWS. SHE JUST... *DISAPPEARED.*
DISAPPEARED?
YEAH...IT'S NOT UNCOMMON. SOME PEOPLE THINK THAT THE RADIATION EVENTUALLY DRIVES YOU MAD.
MAYBE ONE DAY SHE JUST...WANDERED OUT INTO THE WASTELAND AND NEVER--
CREEEEEEAK
WHAT WAS TH--?

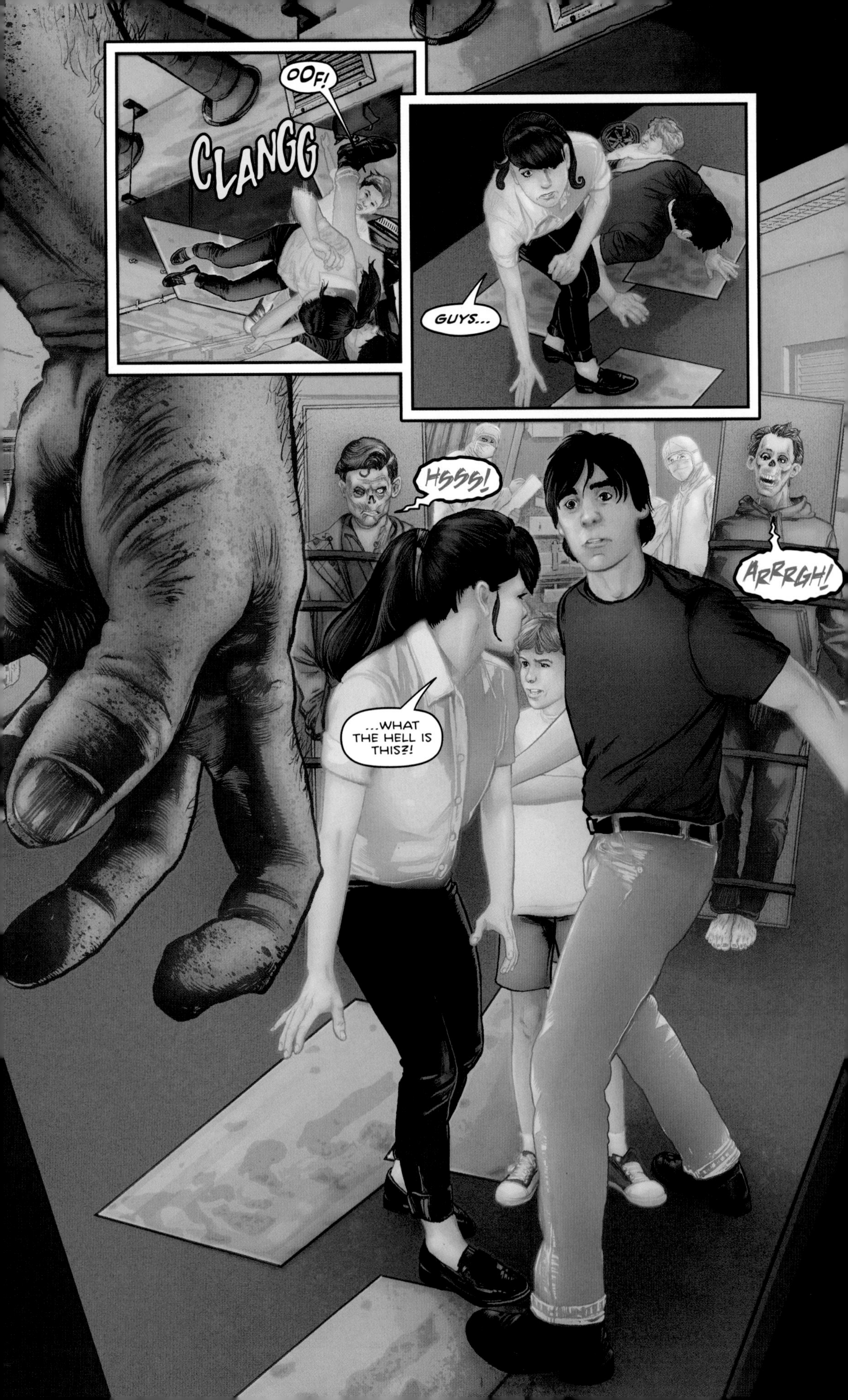
OOF!
CLANGG
GUYS...
HSSS!
ARRRGH!
...WHAT THE HELL IS THIS?!

4

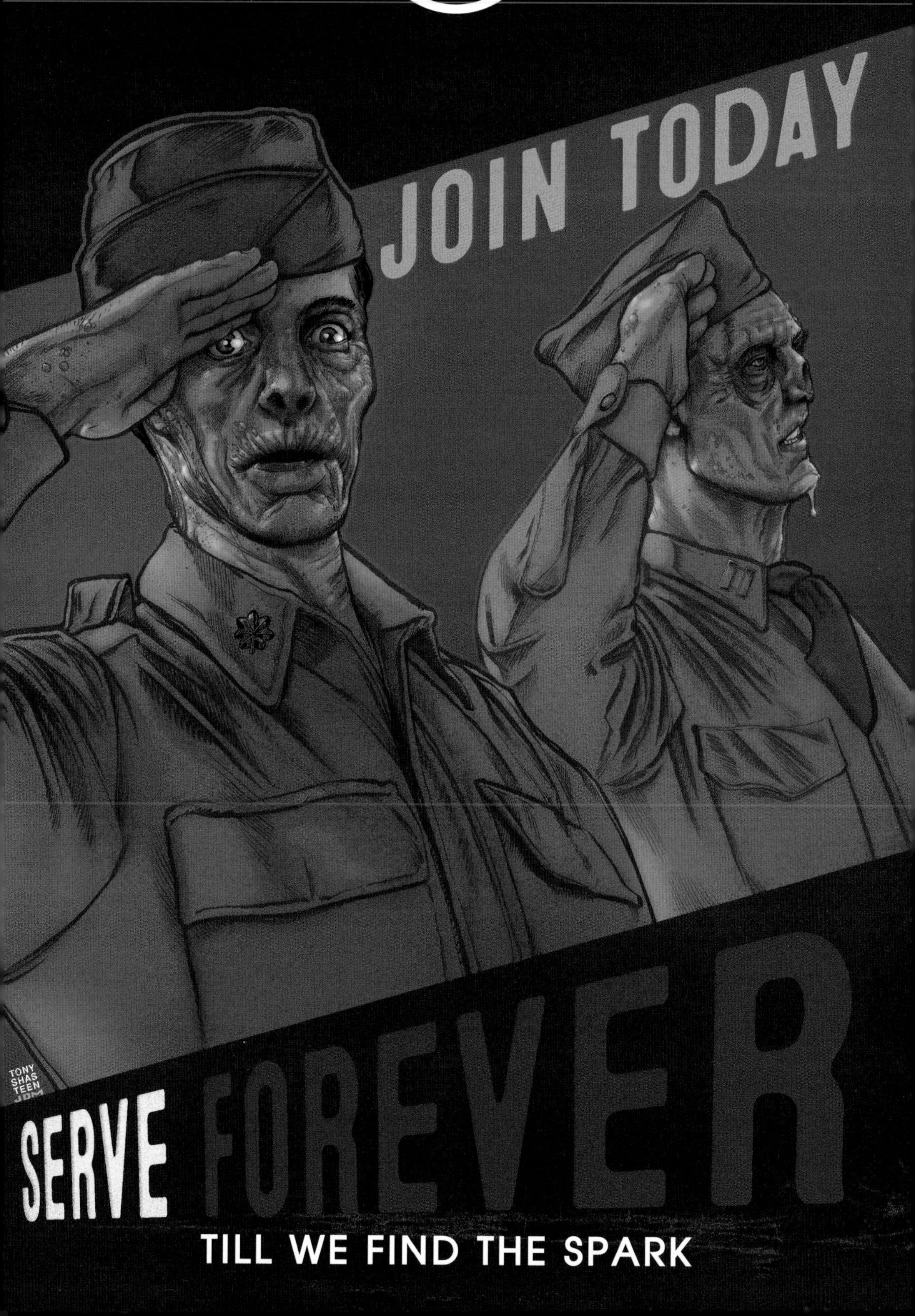
JOIN TODAY
TONY SHASTEEN
SERVE FOREVER
TILL WE FIND THE SPARK

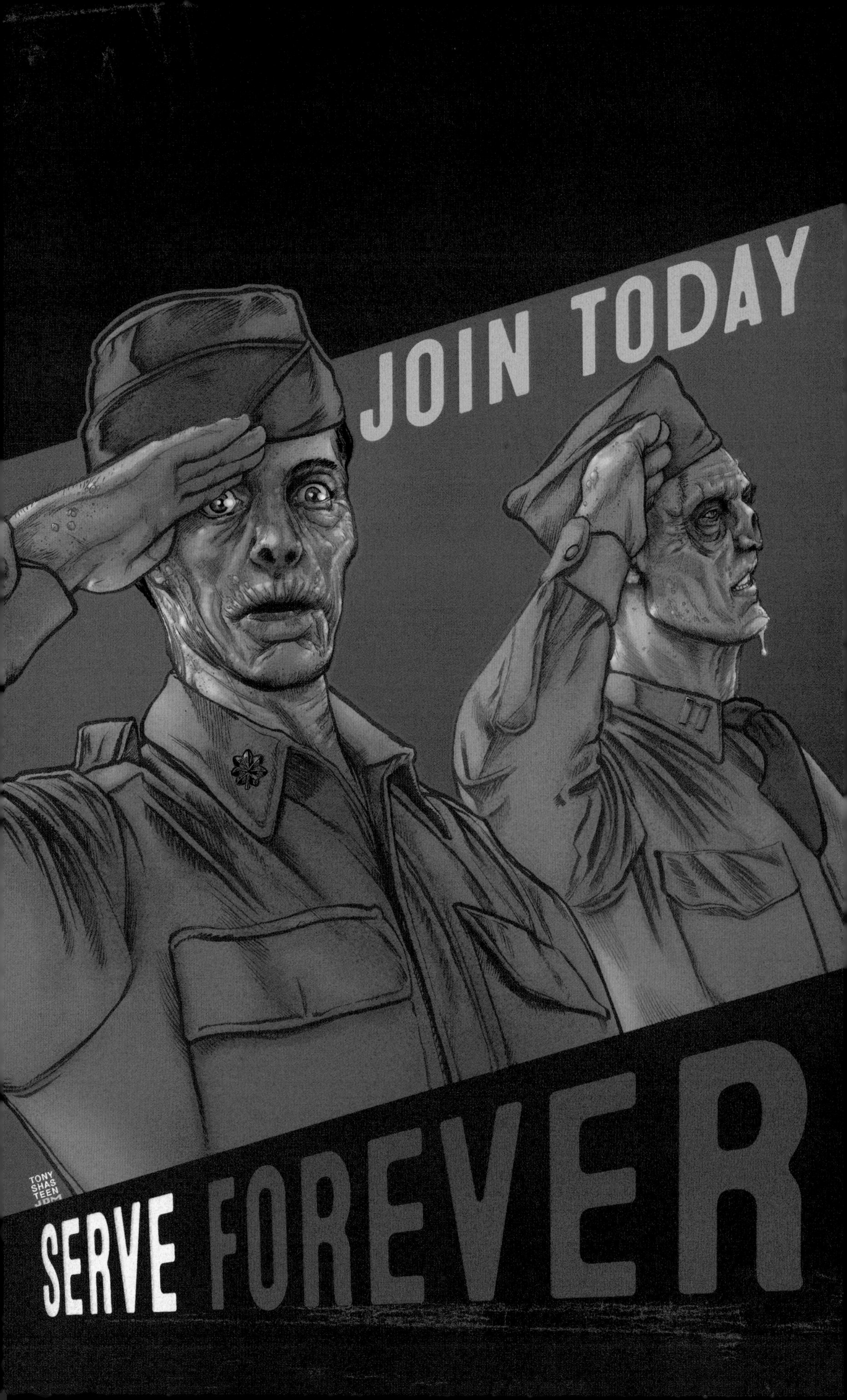
JOIN TODAY
TONY SHASTEEN
SERVE FOREVER

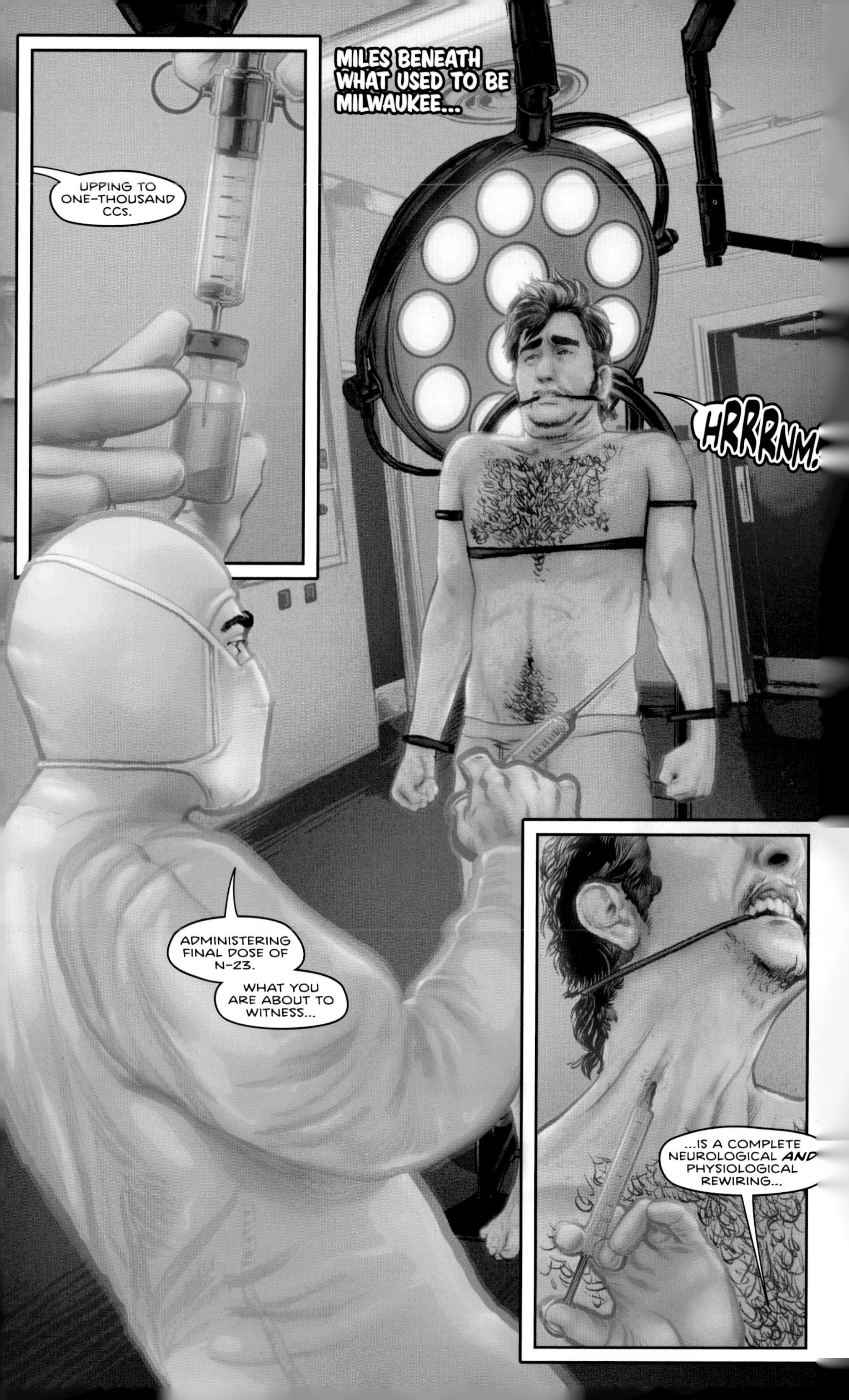

UPPING TO ONE-THOUSAND CCS.
MILES BENEATH WHAT USED TO BE MILWAUKEE...
HRRRNM!
ADMINISTERING FINAL DOSE OF N-23.
WHAT YOU ARE ABOUT TO WITNESS...
...IS A COMPLETE NEUROLOGICAL AND PHYSIOLOGICAL REWIRING...

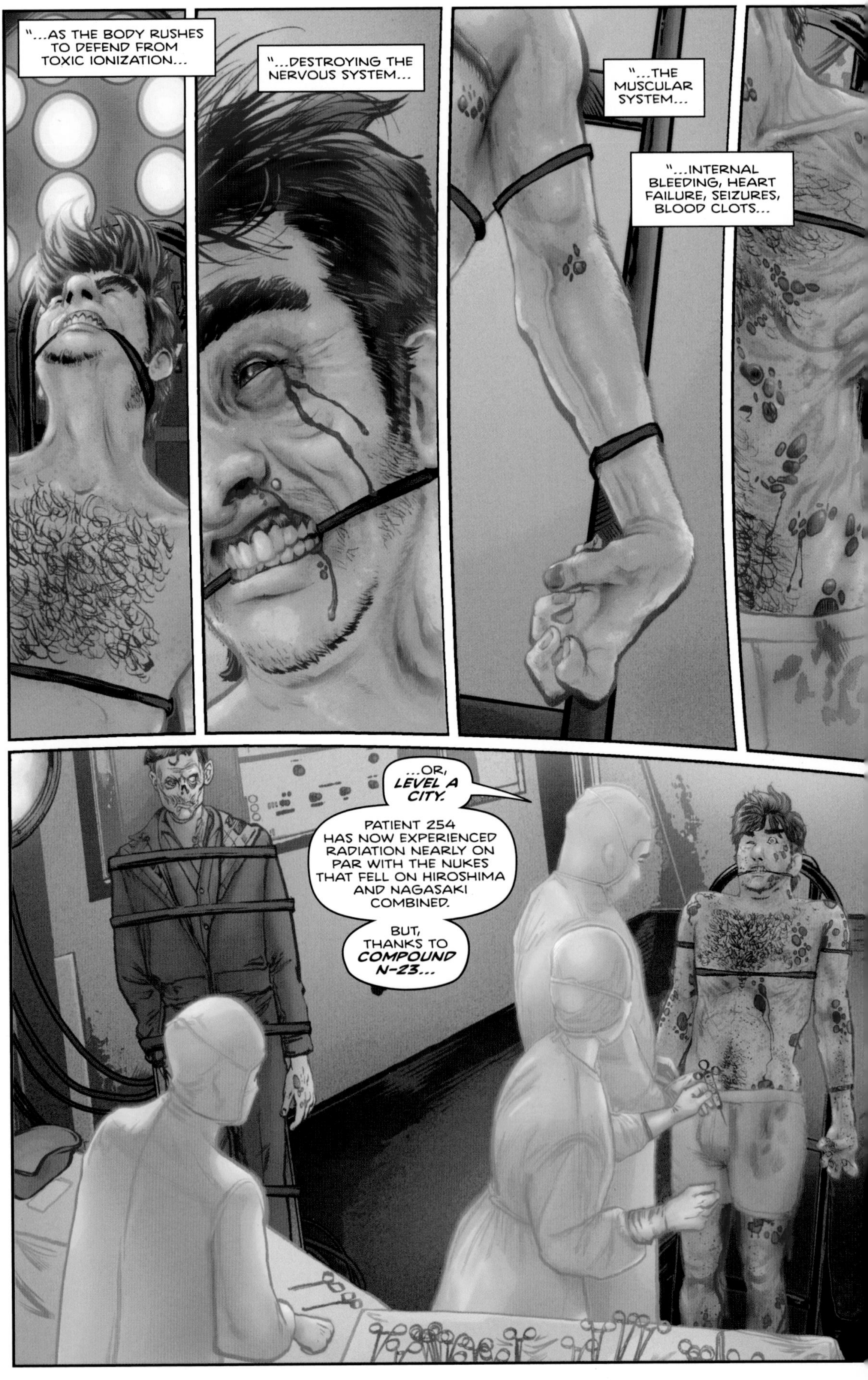
"...AS THE BODY RUSHES TO DEFEND FROM TOXIC IONIZATION...
"...DESTROYING THE NERVOUS SYSTEM...
"...THE MUSCULAR SYSTEM...
"...INTERNAL BLEEDING, HEART FAILURE, SEIZURES, BLOOD CLOTS...
...OR, LEVEL A CITY.
PATIENT 254 HAS NOW EXPERIENCED RADIATION NEARLY ON PAR WITH THE NUKES THAT FELL ON HIROSHIMA AND NAGASAKI COMBINED.
BUT, THANKS TO COMPOUND N-23...

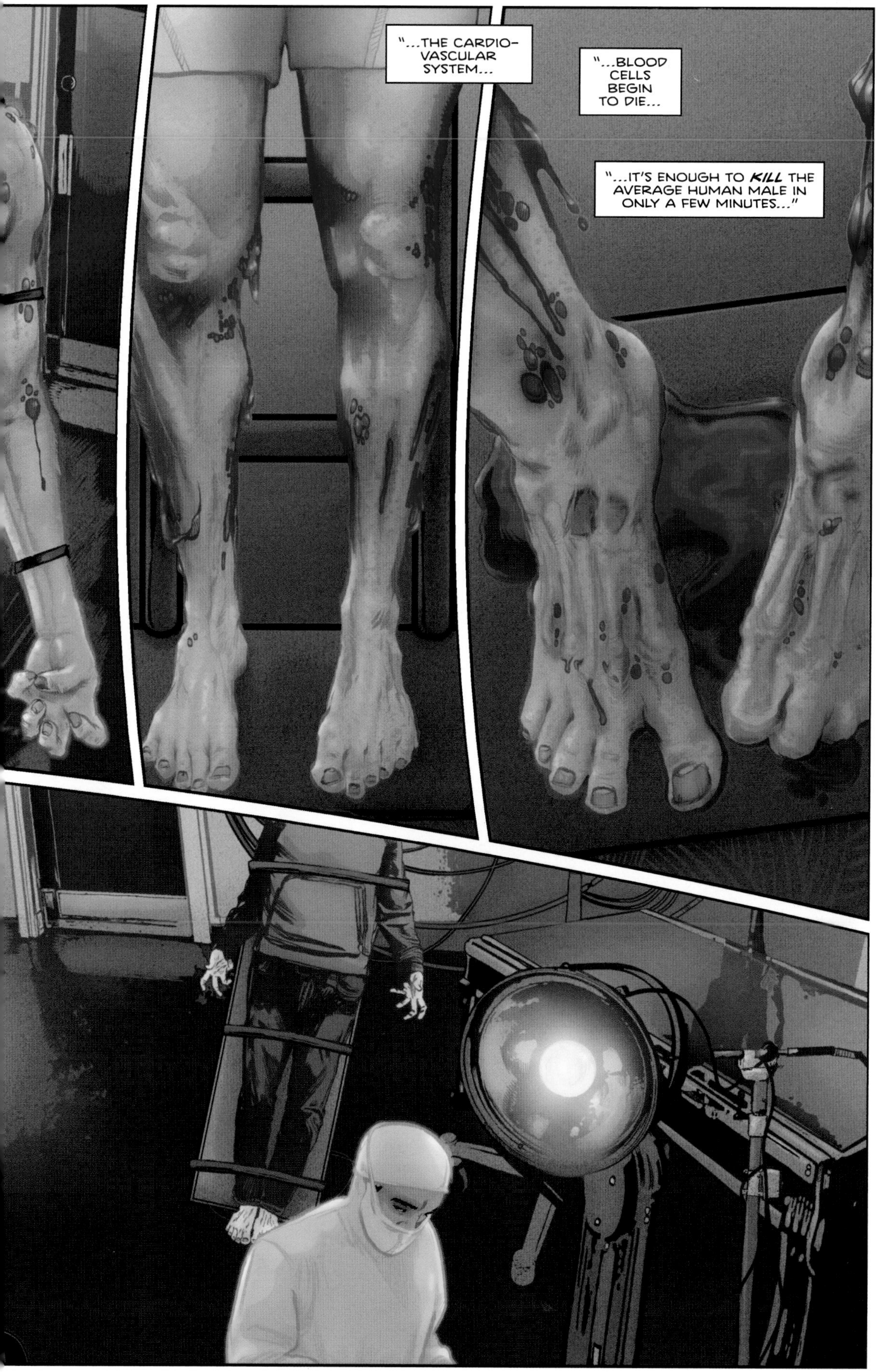
"...THE CARDIO-VASCULAR SYSTEM...
"...BLOOD CELLS BEGIN TO DIE...
"...IT'S ENOUGH TO KILL THE AVERAGE HUMAN MALE IN ONLY A FEW MINUTES..."

...WE CAN HALT THE MOMENT OF DEATH, CREATING A KIND OF STASIS FOR THE INTERNAL ORGANS TO...

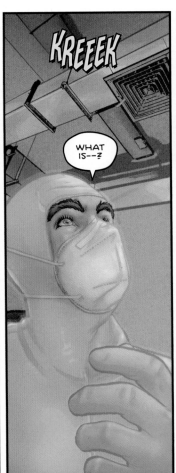

KREEEK

WHAT IS--?

AHH!

GUYS...

...WHAT THE HELL IS THIS?!

YOU SHOULD *NOT* BE HERE.

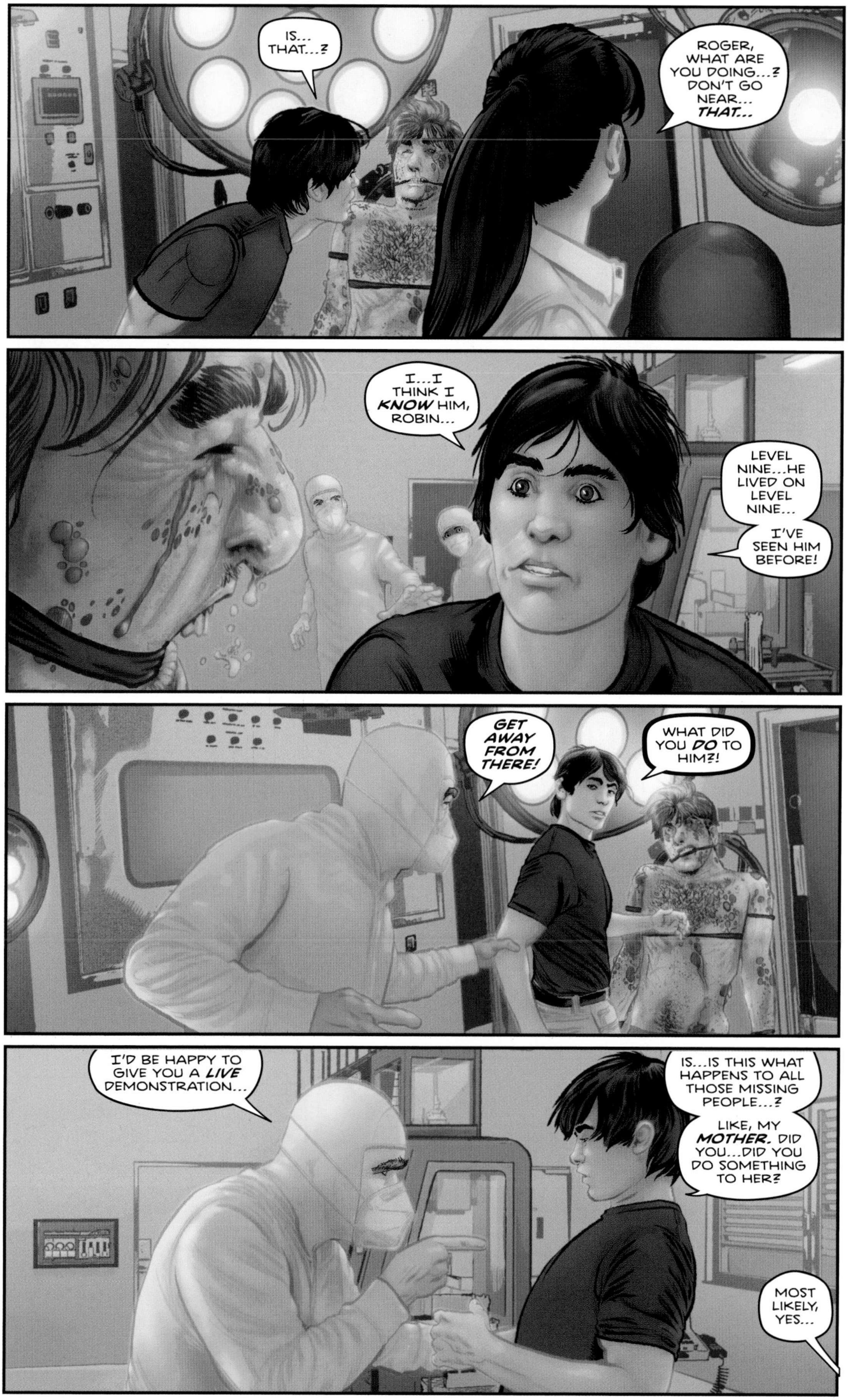

IS... THAT...?
ROGER, WHAT ARE YOU DOING...? DON'T GO NEAR... *THAT...*
I...I THINK I *KNOW* HIM, ROBIN...
LEVEL NINE...HE LIVED ON LEVEL NINE...
I'VE SEEN HIM BEFORE!
GET AWAY FROM THERE!
WHAT DID YOU *DO* TO HIM?!
I'D BE HAPPY TO GIVE YOU A *LIVE* DEMONSTRATION...
IS...IS THIS WHAT HAPPENS TO ALL THOSE MISSING PEOPLE...?
LIKE, MY *MOTHER.* DID YOU...DID YOU DO SOMETHING TO HER?
MOST LIKELY, YES...

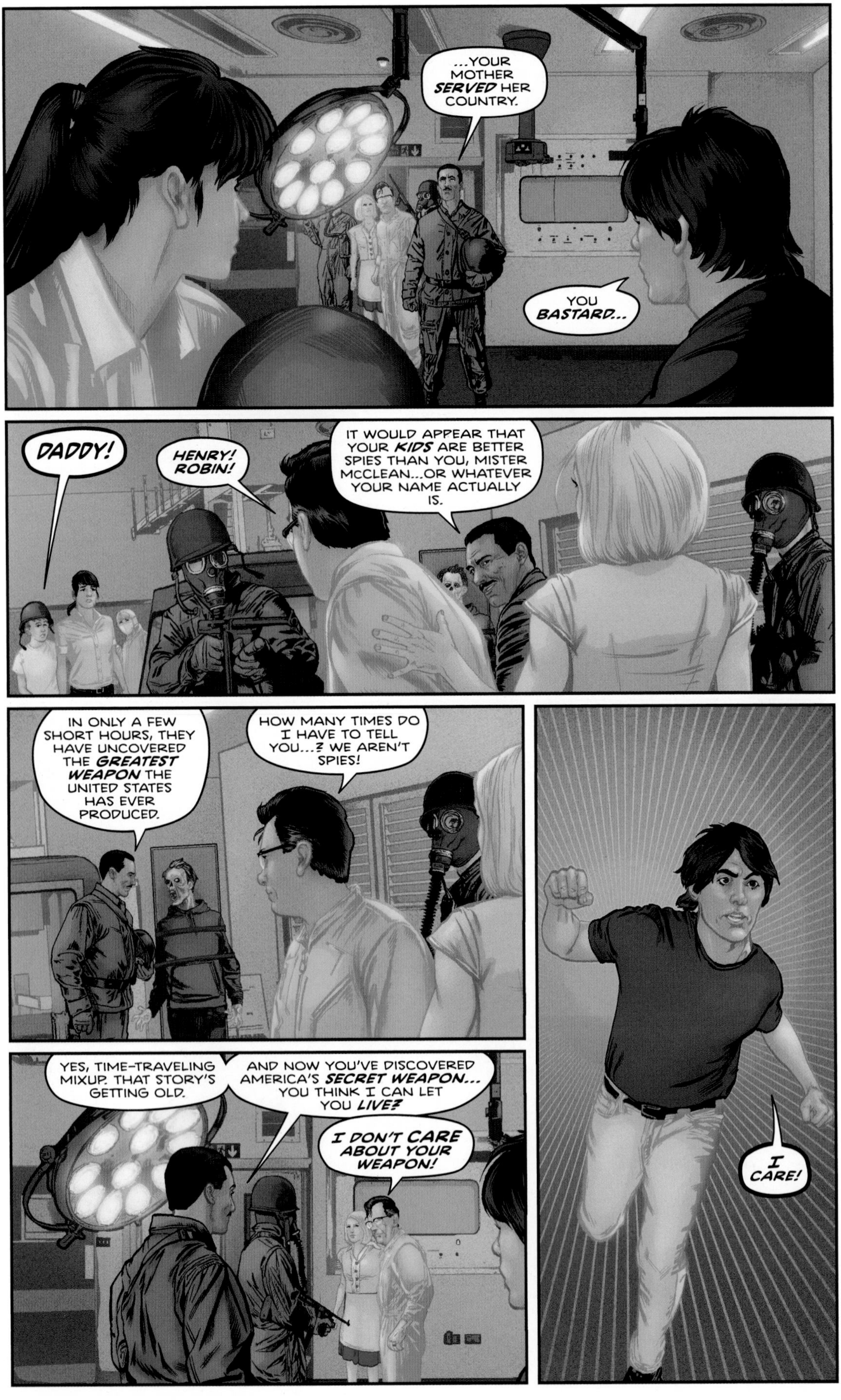
...YOUR MOTHER SERVED HER COUNTRY.
YOU BASTARD...
DADDY!
HENRY! ROBIN!
IT WOULD APPEAR THAT YOUR KIDS ARE BETTER SPIES THAN YOU, MISTER McCLEAN...OR WHATEVER YOUR NAME ACTUALLY IS.
IN ONLY A FEW SHORT HOURS, THEY HAVE UNCOVERED THE GREATEST WEAPON THE UNITED STATES HAS EVER PRODUCED.
HOW MANY TIMES DO I HAVE TO TELL YOU...? WE AREN'T SPIES!
YES, TIME-TRAVELING MIXUP. THAT STORY'S GETTING OLD.
AND NOW YOU'VE DISCOVERED AMERICA'S SECRET WEAPON... YOU THINK I CAN LET YOU LIVE?
I DON'T CARE ABOUT YOUR WEAPON!
I CARE!

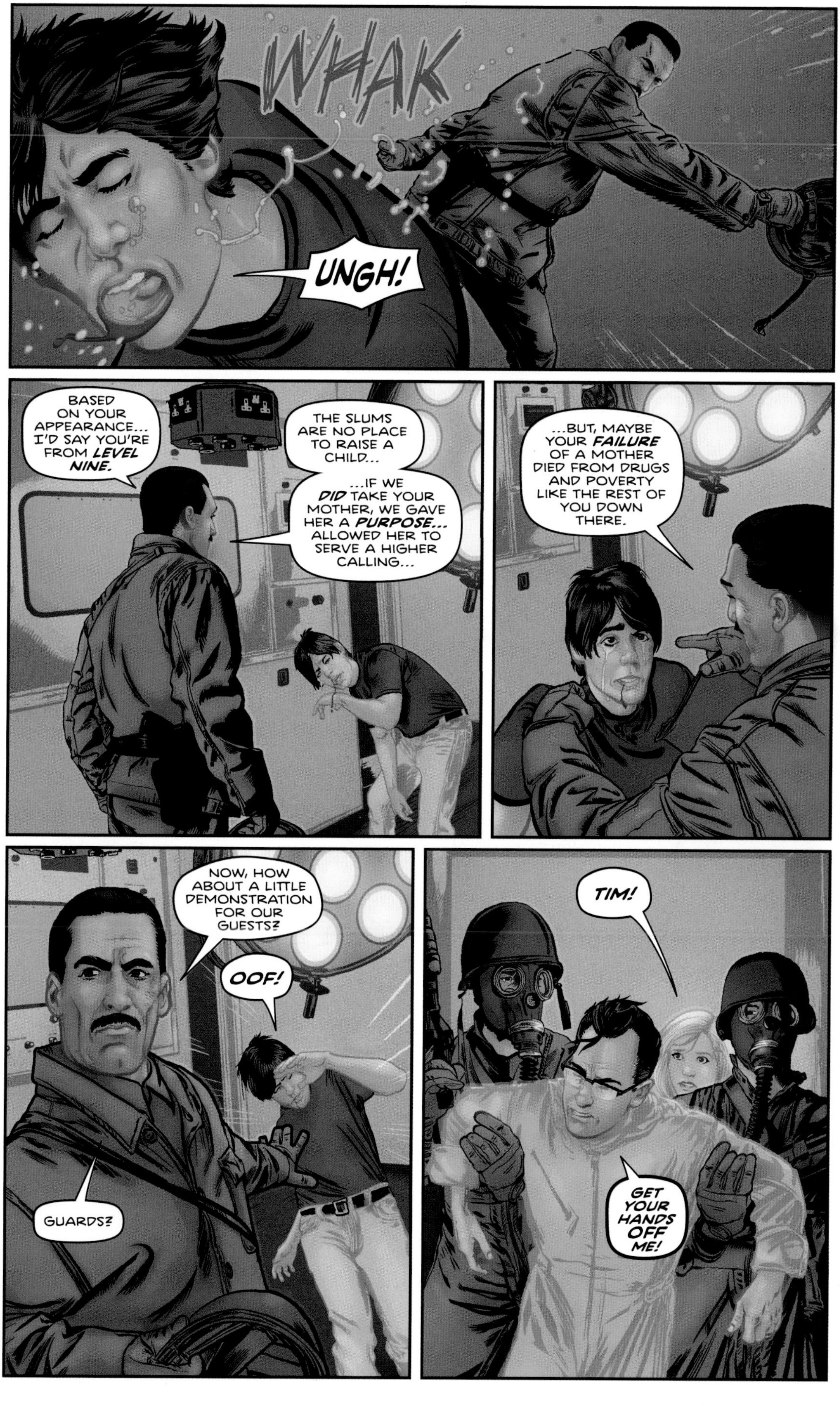
WHAK
UNGH!
BASED ON YOUR APPEARANCE... I'D SAY YOU'RE FROM LEVEL NINE.
THE SLUMS ARE NO PLACE TO RAISE A CHILD...
...IF WE DID TAKE YOUR MOTHER, WE GAVE HER A PURPOSE... ALLOWED HER TO SERVE A HIGHER CALLING...
...BUT, MAYBE YOUR FAILURE OF A MOTHER DIED FROM DRUGS AND POVERTY LIKE THE REST OF YOU DOWN THERE.
NOW, HOW ABOUT A LITTLE DEMONSTRATION FOR OUR GUESTS?
OOF!
GUARDS?
TIM!
GET YOUR HANDS OFF ME!

SEE, WHEN THE RUSSIANS DROVE US UNDERGROUND, WE REALIZED WE HAD TO RETHINK OUR ENTIRE APPROACH TO FIGHTING...

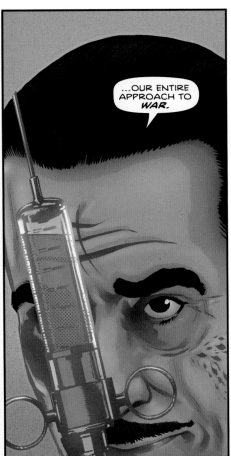

...OUR ENTIRE APPROACH TO *WAR.*

THE RADIATION POISONING WAS KILLING OUR TROOPS FASTER THAN ANY BOMB OR BULLET.

SO, WE *ADAPTED.*

LIKE THIS BUNKER, AMERICAN INGENUITY BUILT A NEW KIND OF SOLDIER...

...SOLDIERS RESISTANT TO RADIATION...

...BECAUSE THEY'RE *ALREADY DEAD.*

HRGNNN...

NO!

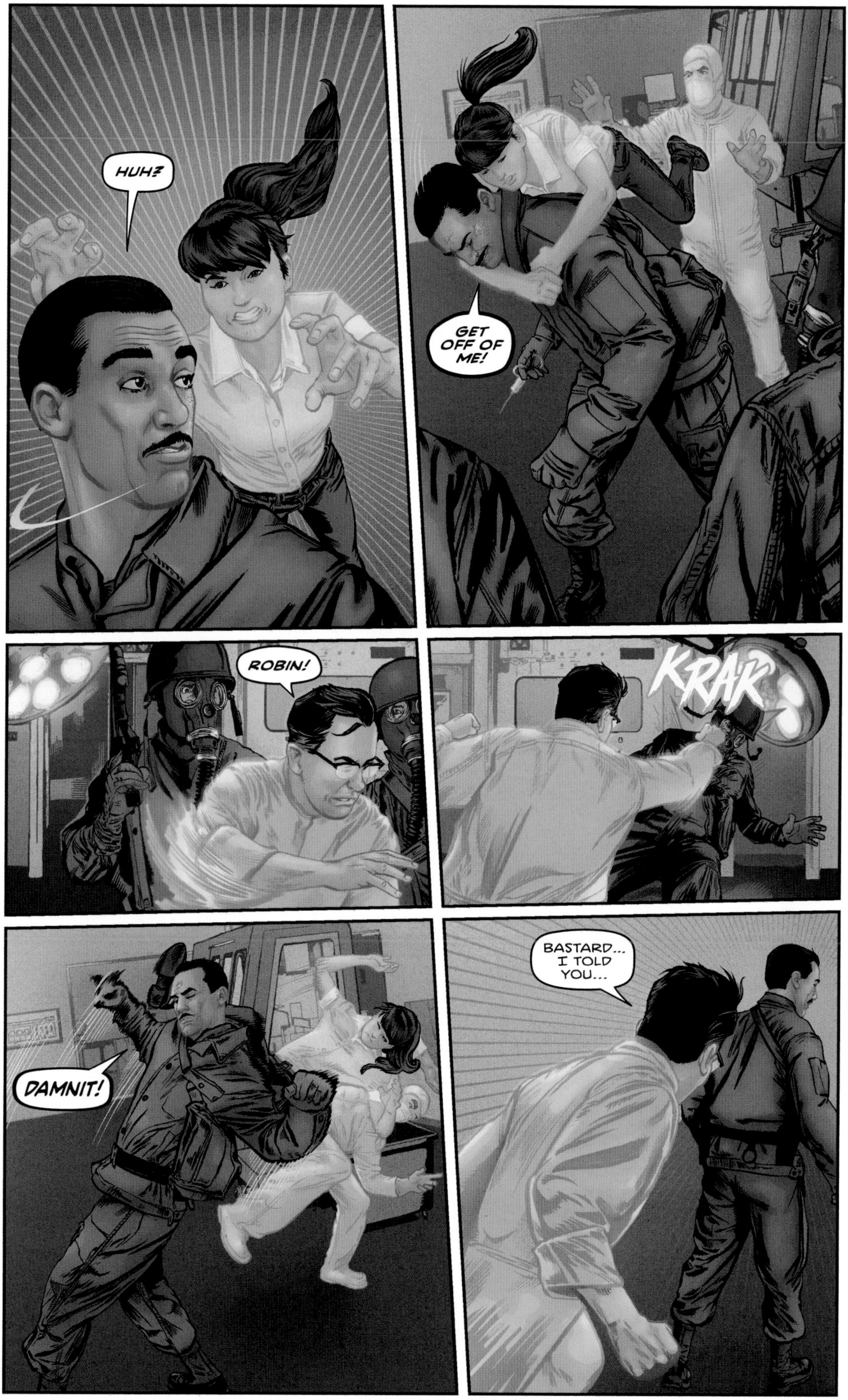
HUH?
GET OFF OF ME!
ROBIN!
KRAK
DAMNIT!
BASTARD... I TOLD YOU...

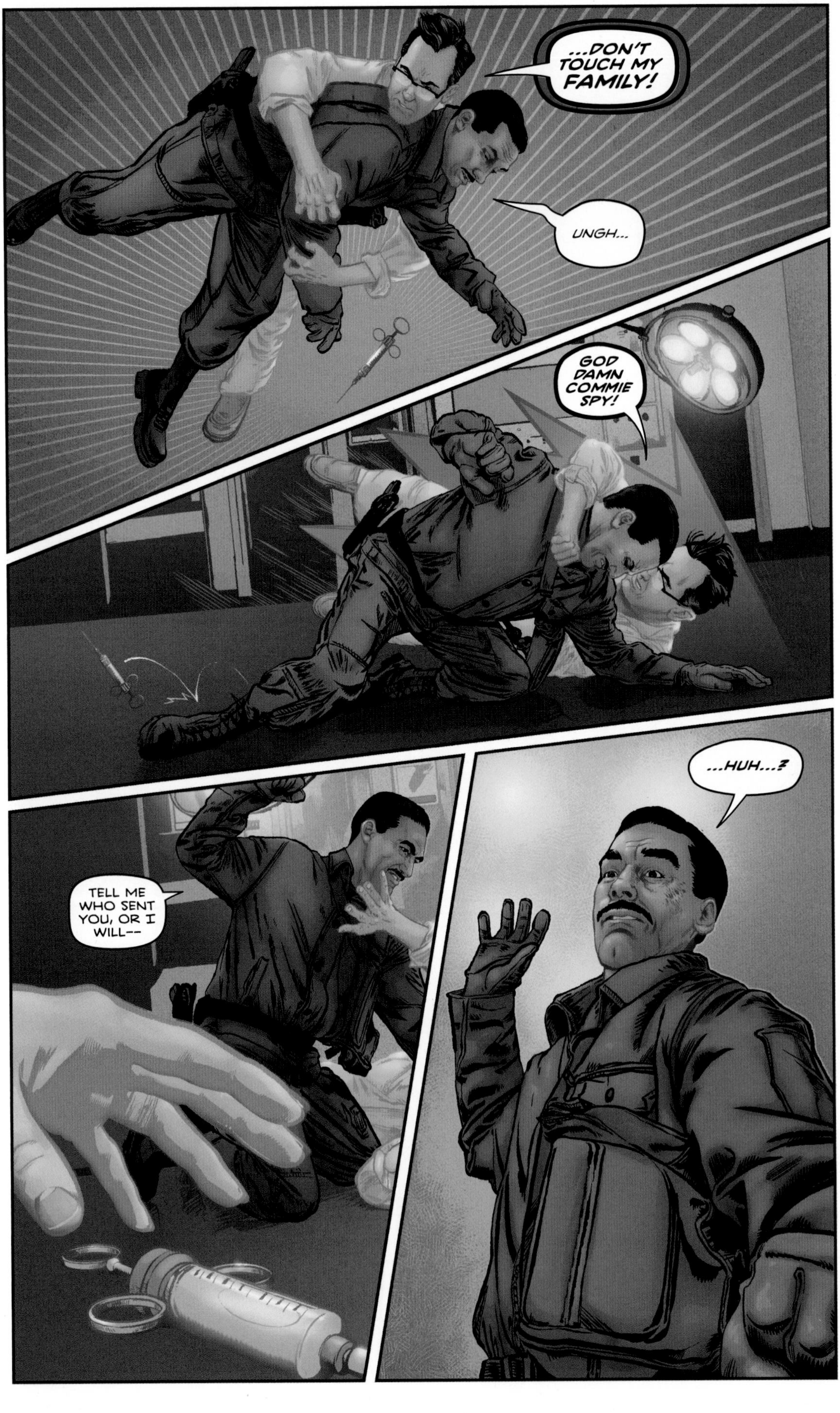
...DON'T TOUCH MY FAMILY!
UNGH...
GOD DAMN COMMIE SPY!
TELL ME WHO SENT YOU, OR I WILL--
...HUH...?

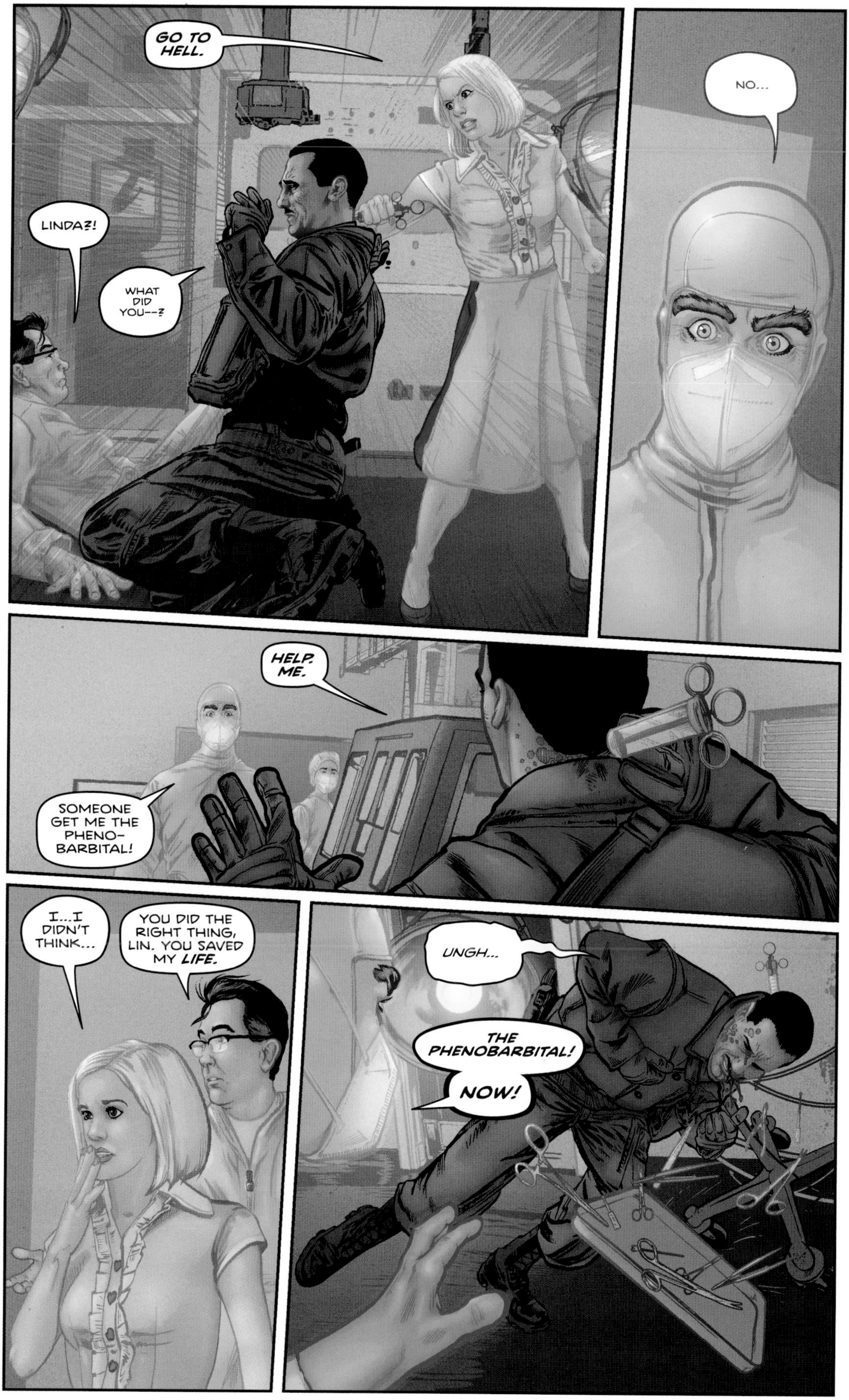
GO TO HELL.
LINDA?!
WHAT DID YOU--?
NO...
HELP. ME.
SOMEONE GET ME THE PHENO-BARBITAL!
I...I DIDN'T THINK...
YOU DID THE RIGHT THING, LIN. YOU SAVED MY LIFE.
UNGH...
THE PHENOBARBITAL!
NOW!

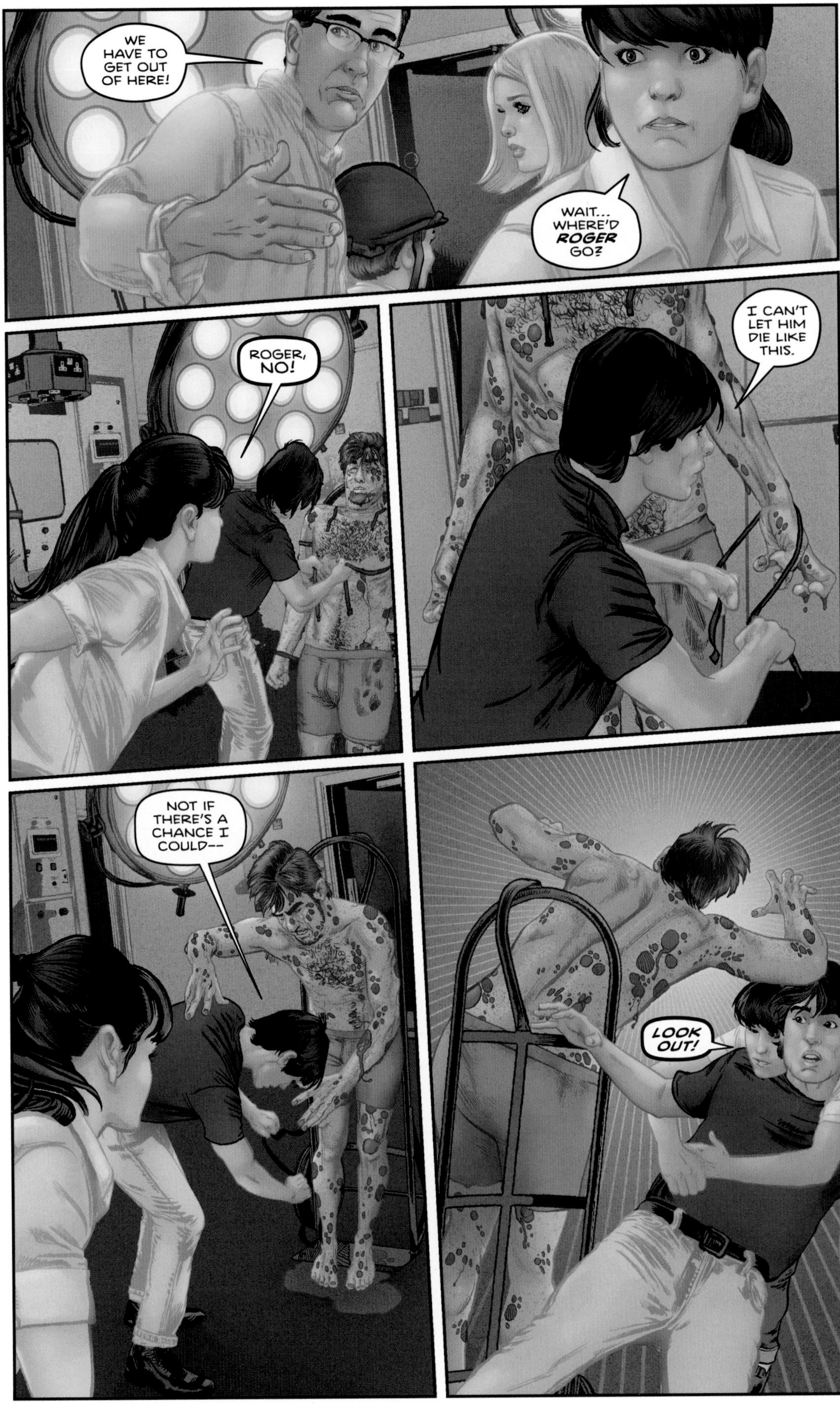
WE HAVE TO GET OUT OF HERE!
WAIT... WHERE'D ROGER GO?
ROGER, NO!
I CAN'T LET HIM DIE LIKE THIS.
NOT IF THERE'S A CHANCE I COULD--
LOOK OUT!

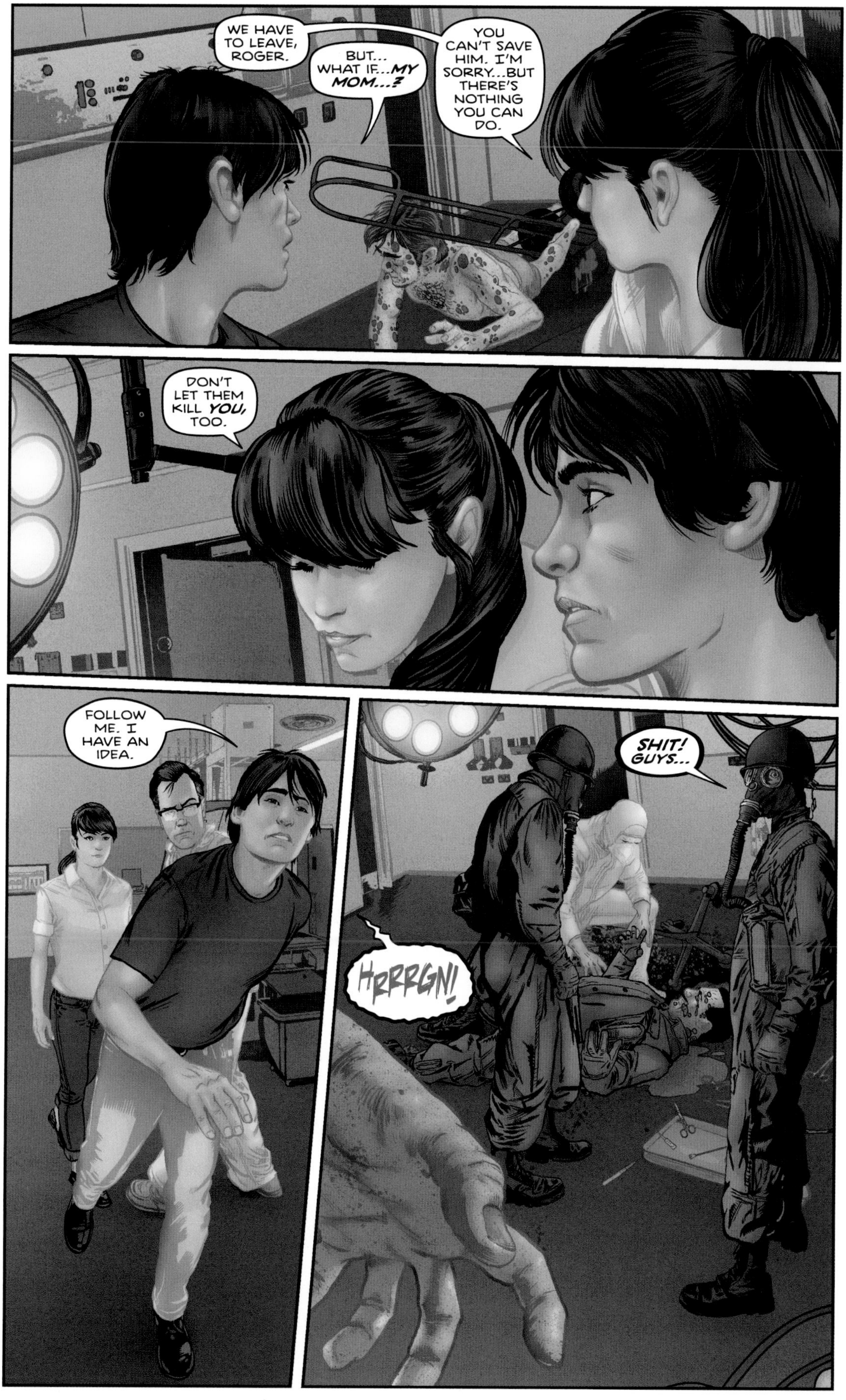
WE HAVE TO LEAVE, ROGER.
BUT... WHAT IF...MY MOM...?
YOU CAN'T SAVE HIM. I'M SORRY...BUT THERE'S NOTHING YOU CAN DO.
DON'T LET THEM KILL YOU, TOO.
FOLLOW ME. I HAVE AN IDEA.
SHIT! GUYS...
HRRRGN!

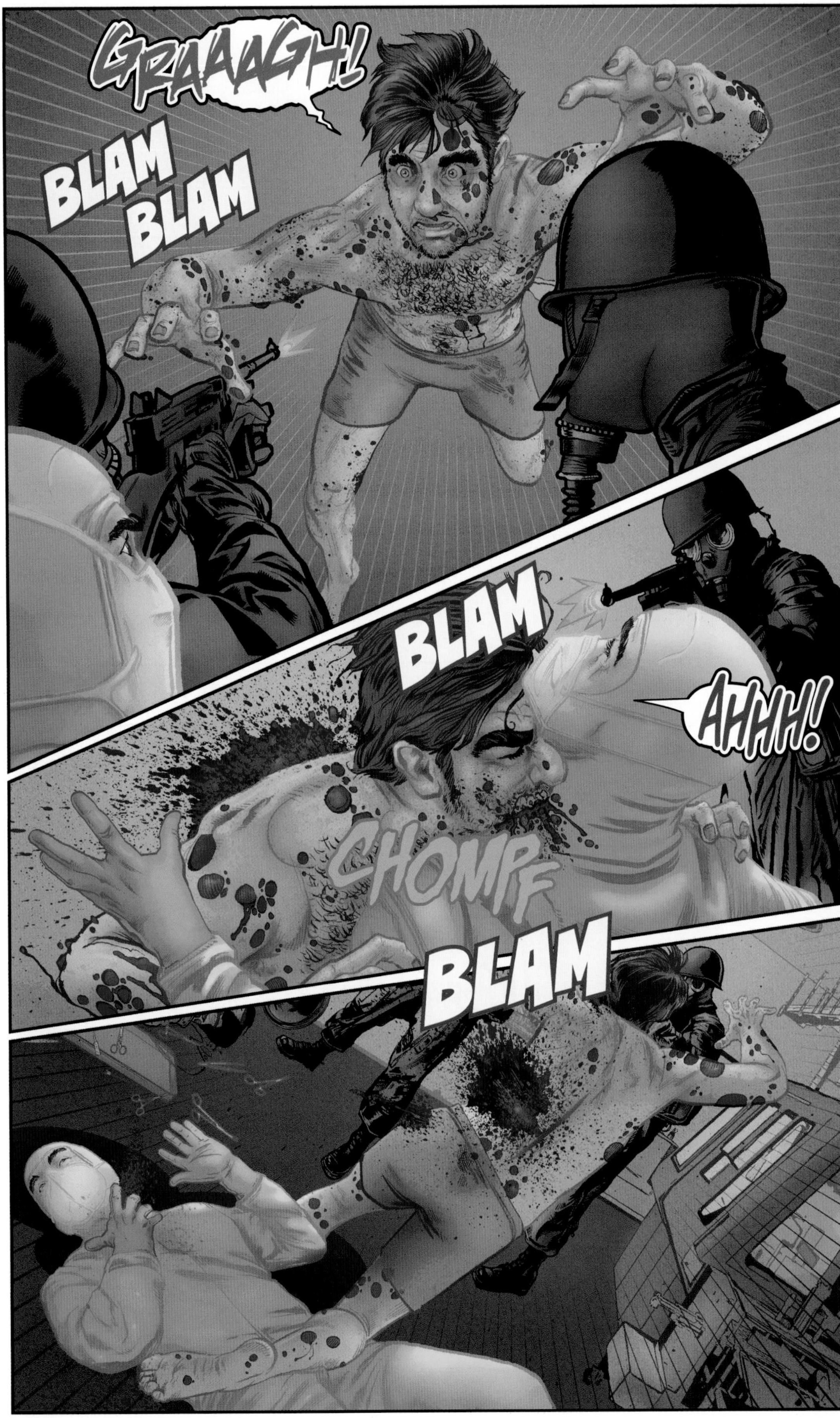
GRAAAGH!
BLAM
BLAM
BLAM
AHHH!
CHOMPF
BLAM

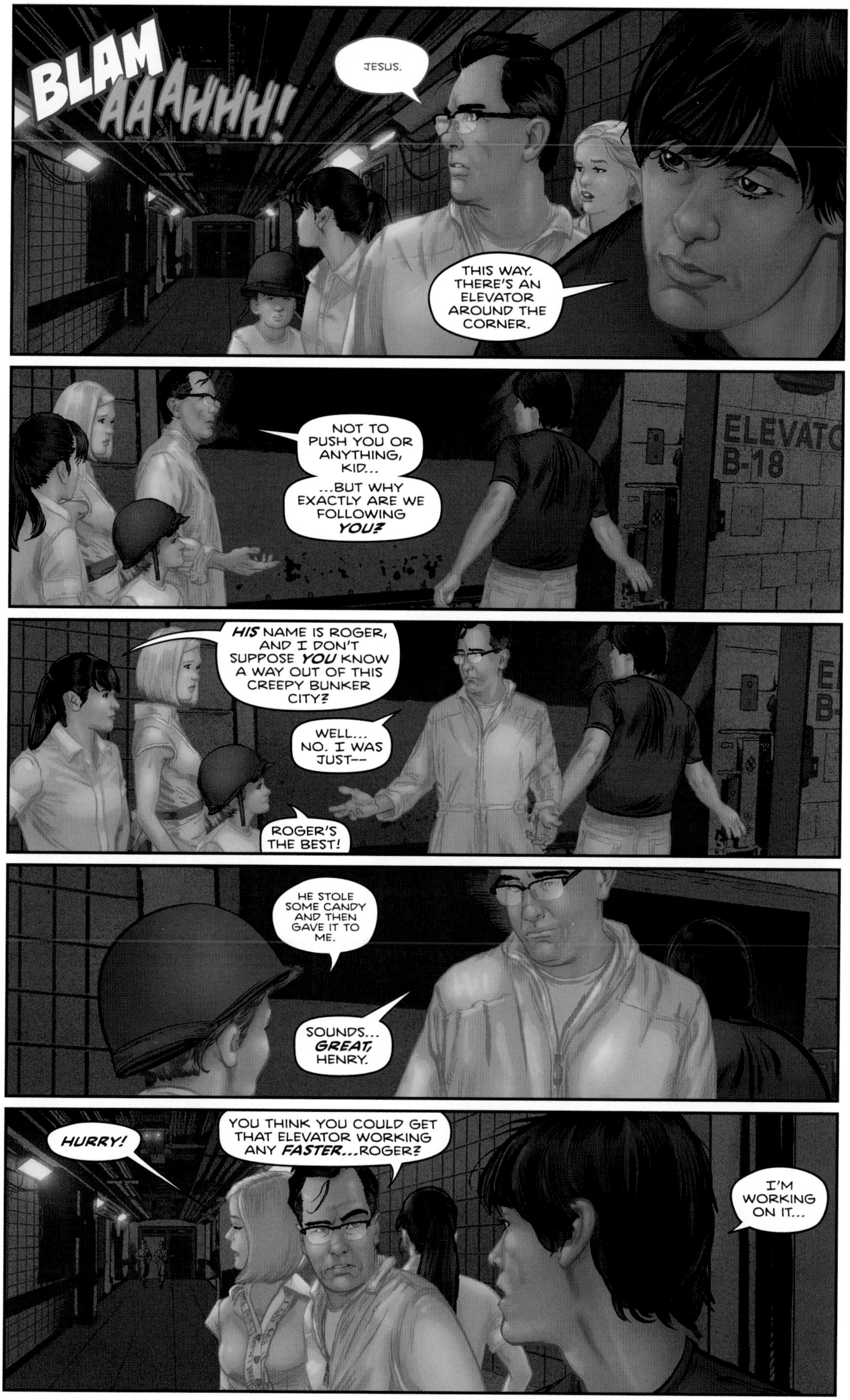
BLAM
AAAHHH!
JESUS.
THIS WAY. THERE'S AN ELEVATOR AROUND THE CORNER.
NOT TO PUSH YOU OR ANYTHING, KID...
...BUT WHY EXACTLY ARE WE FOLLOWING *YOU?*
ELEVATOR B-18
HIS NAME IS ROGER, AND I DON'T SUPPOSE *YOU* KNOW A WAY OUT OF THIS CREEPY BUNKER CITY?
WELL... NO. I WAS JUST--
ROGER'S THE BEST!
HE STOLE SOME CANDY AND THEN GAVE IT TO ME.
SOUNDS... *GREAT,* HENRY.
HURRY!
YOU THINK YOU COULD GET THAT ELEVATOR WORKING ANY *FASTER...*ROGER?
I'M WORKING ON IT...

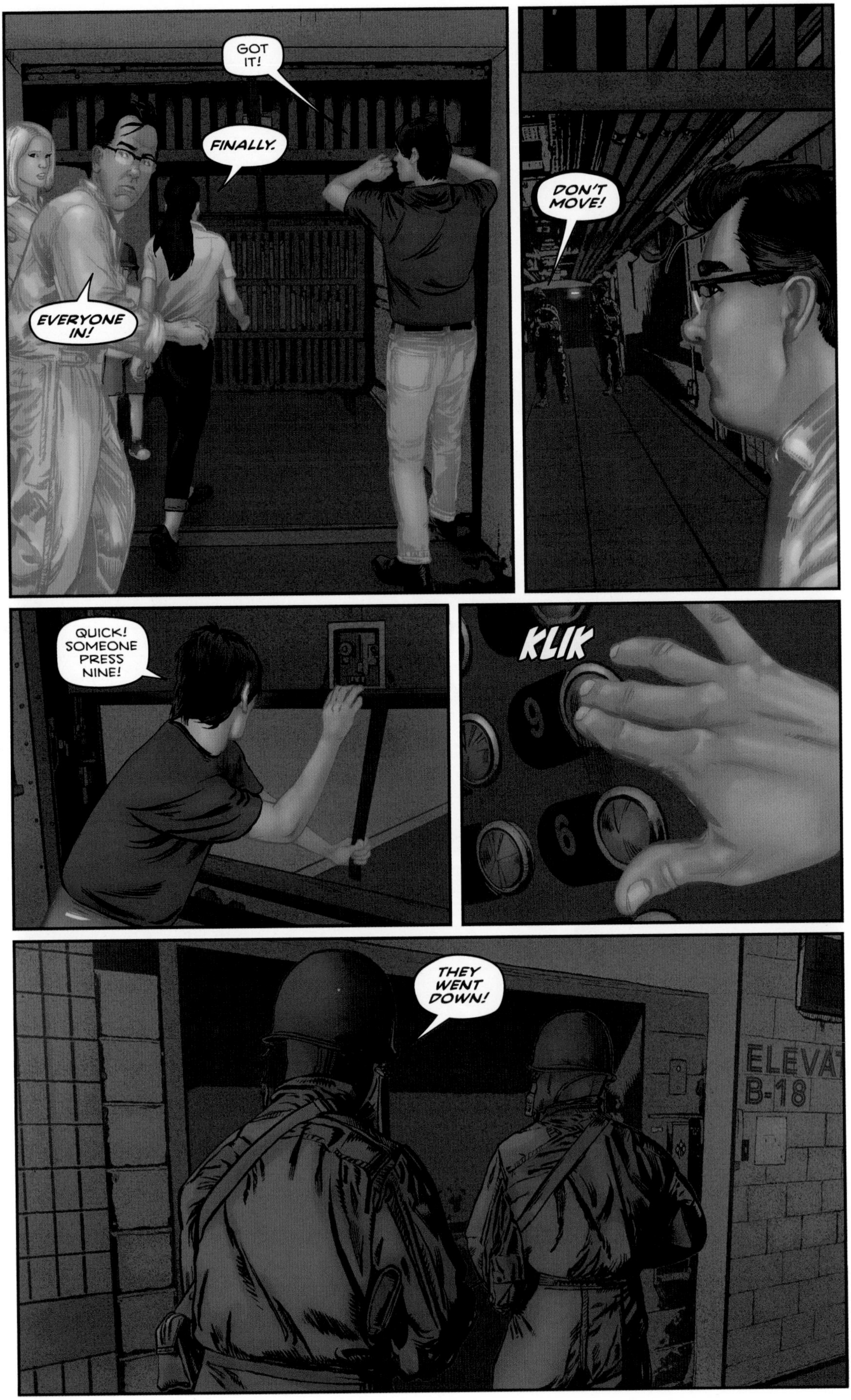
GOT IT!
FINALLY.
EVERYONE IN!
DON'T MOVE!
QUICK! SOMEONE PRESS NINE!
KLIK
THEY WENT DOWN!
ELEVAT
B-18

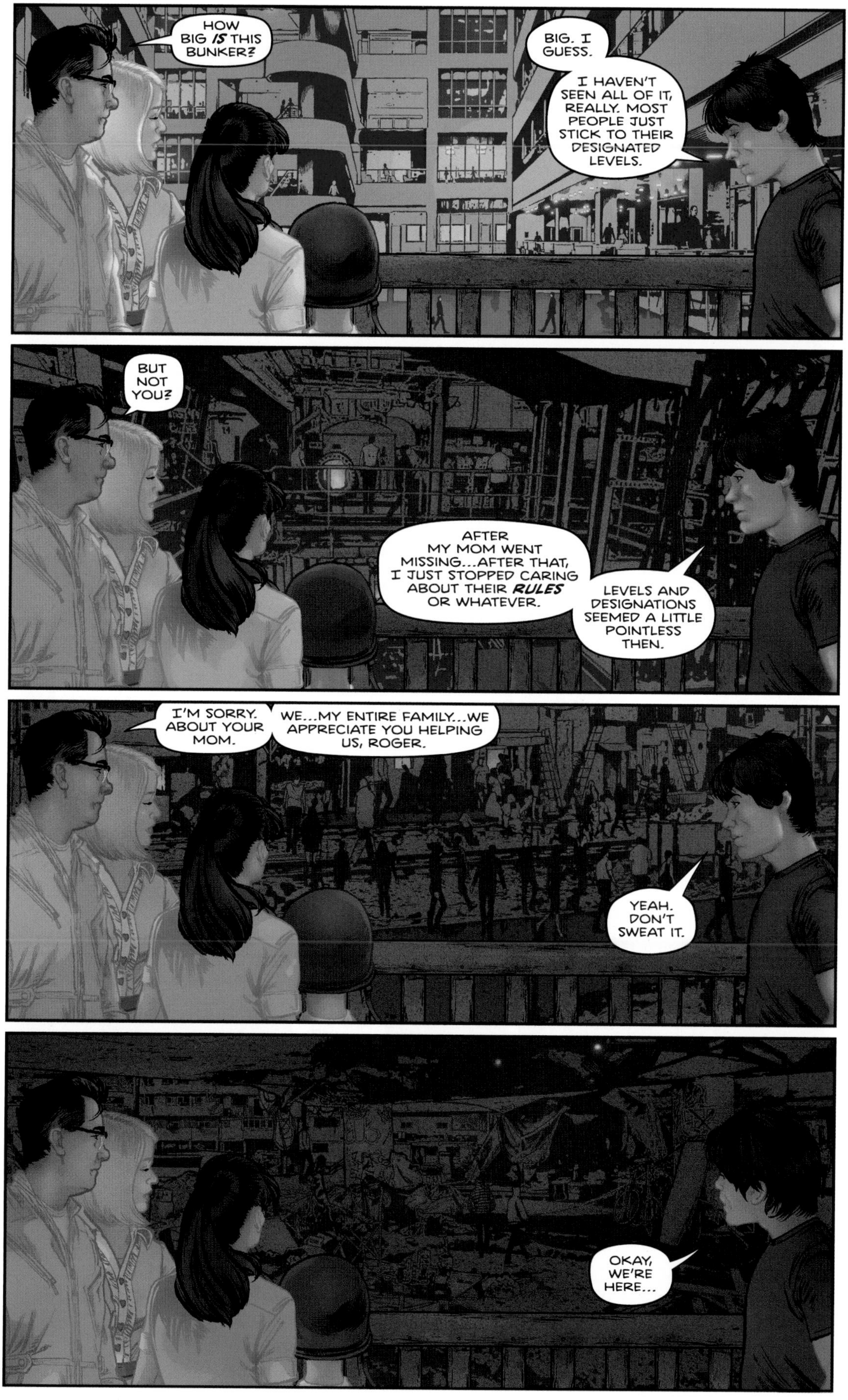
HOW BIG IS THIS BUNKER?
BIG. I GUESS.
I HAVEN'T SEEN ALL OF IT, REALLY. MOST PEOPLE JUST STICK TO THEIR DESIGNATED LEVELS.
BUT NOT YOU?
AFTER MY MOM WENT MISSING...AFTER THAT, I JUST STOPPED CARING ABOUT THEIR RULES OR WHATEVER.
LEVELS AND DESIGNATIONS SEEMED A LITTLE POINTLESS THEN.
I'M SORRY. ABOUT YOUR MOM.
WE...MY ENTIRE FAMILY...WE APPRECIATE YOU HELPING US, ROGER.
YEAH. DON'T SWEAT IT.
OKAY, WE'RE HERE...

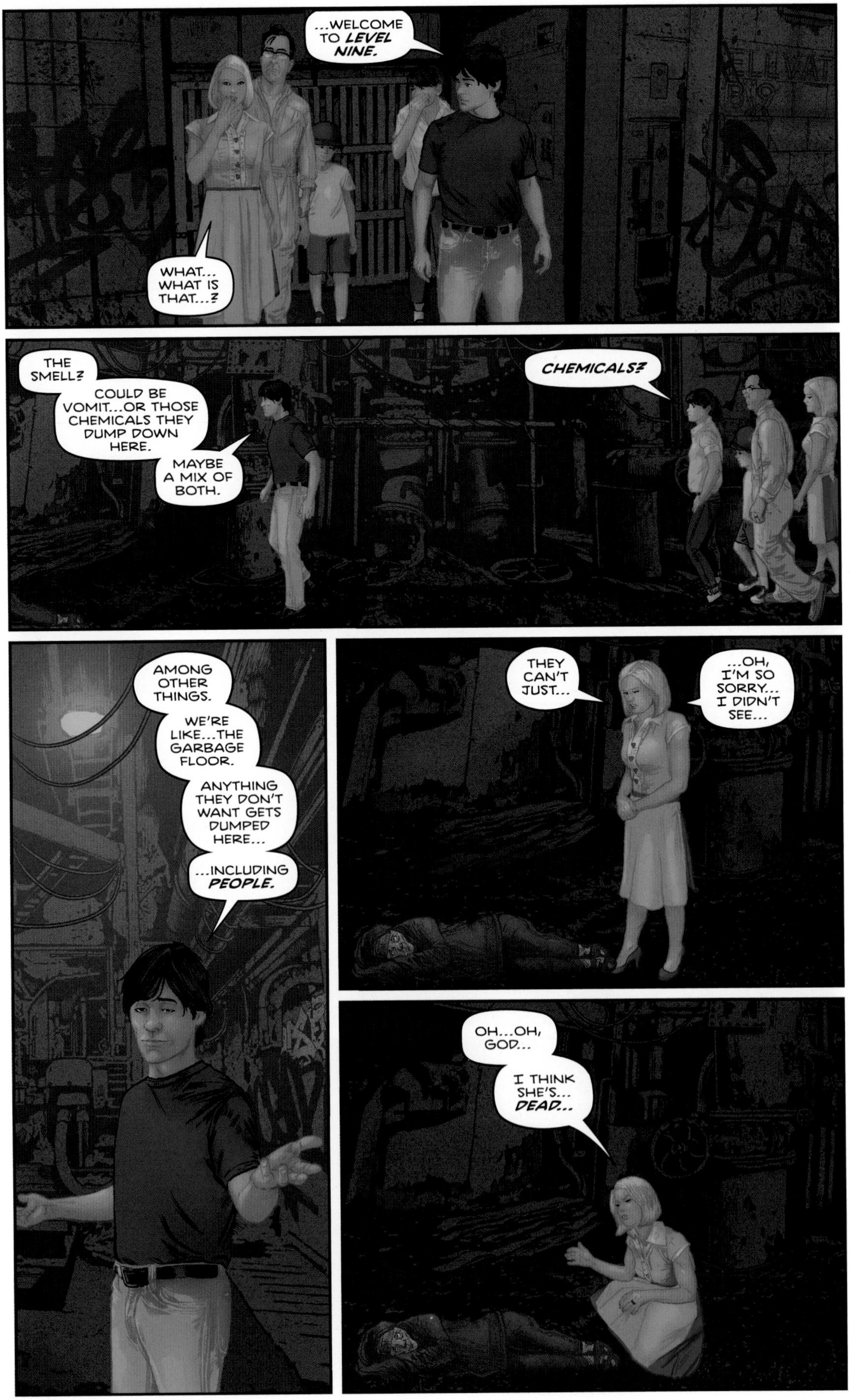
...WELCOME TO LEVEL NINE.
WHAT... WHAT IS THAT...?
THE SMELL?
COULD BE VOMIT...OR THOSE CHEMICALS THEY DUMP DOWN HERE.
MAYBE A MIX OF BOTH.
CHEMICALS?
AMONG OTHER THINGS.
WE'RE LIKE...THE GARBAGE FLOOR.
ANYTHING THEY DON'T WANT GETS DUMPED HERE...
...INCLUDING PEOPLE.
THEY CAN'T JUST...
...OH, I'M SO SORRY... I DIDN'T SEE...
OH...OH, GOD...
I THINK SHE'S... DEAD...

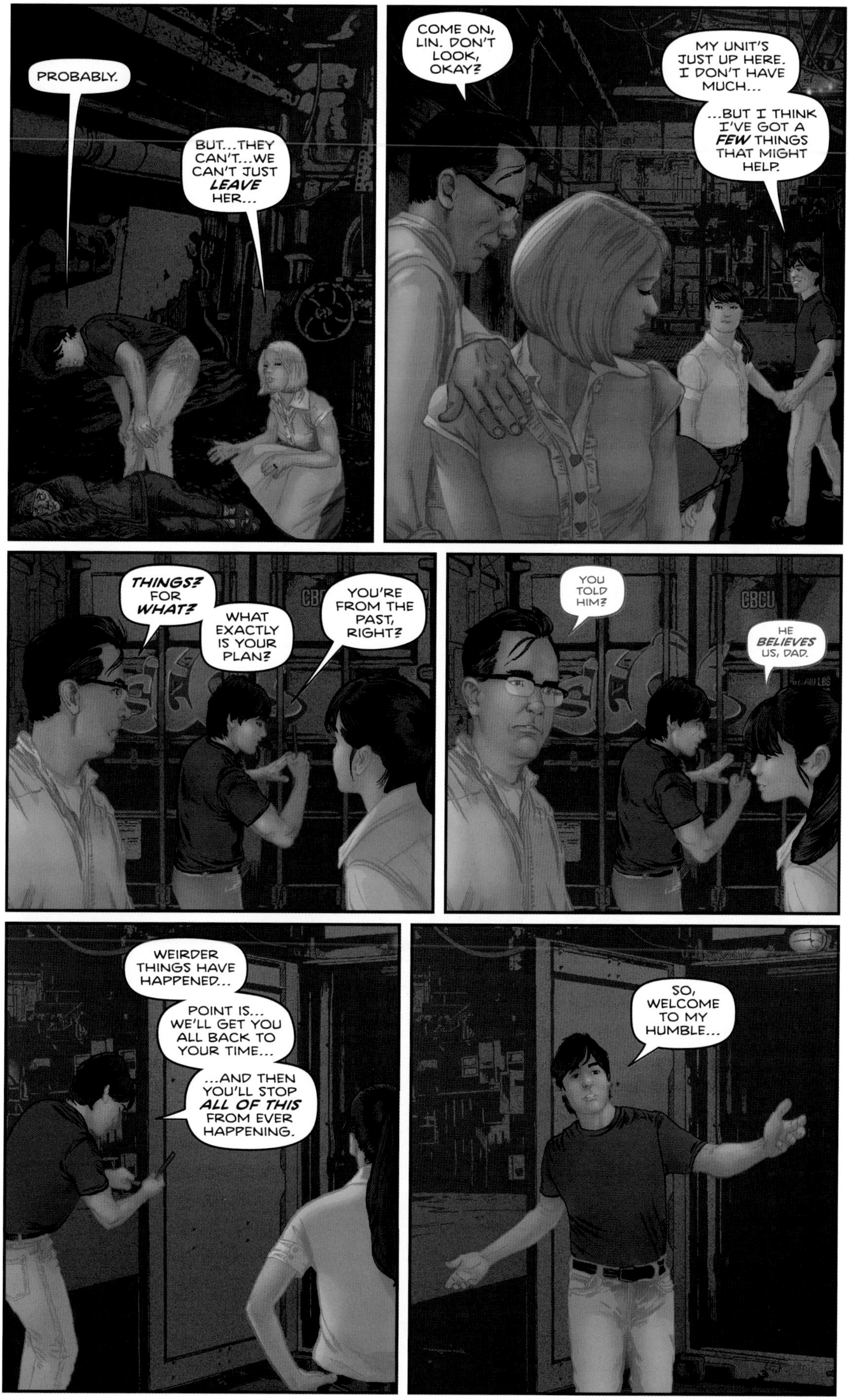
PROBABLY.
BUT...THEY CAN'T...WE CAN'T JUST LEAVE HER...
COME ON, LIN. DON'T LOOK, OKAY?
MY UNIT'S JUST UP HERE. I DON'T HAVE MUCH...
...BUT I THINK I'VE GOT A FEW THINGS THAT MIGHT HELP.
THINGS? FOR WHAT?
WHAT EXACTLY IS YOUR PLAN?
YOU'RE FROM THE PAST, RIGHT?
YOU TOLD HIM?
HE BELIEVES US, DAD.
WEIRDER THINGS HAVE HAPPENED...
POINT IS... WE'LL GET YOU ALL BACK TO YOUR TIME...
...AND THEN YOU'LL STOP ALL OF THIS FROM EVER HAPPENING.
SO, WELCOME TO MY HUMBLE...

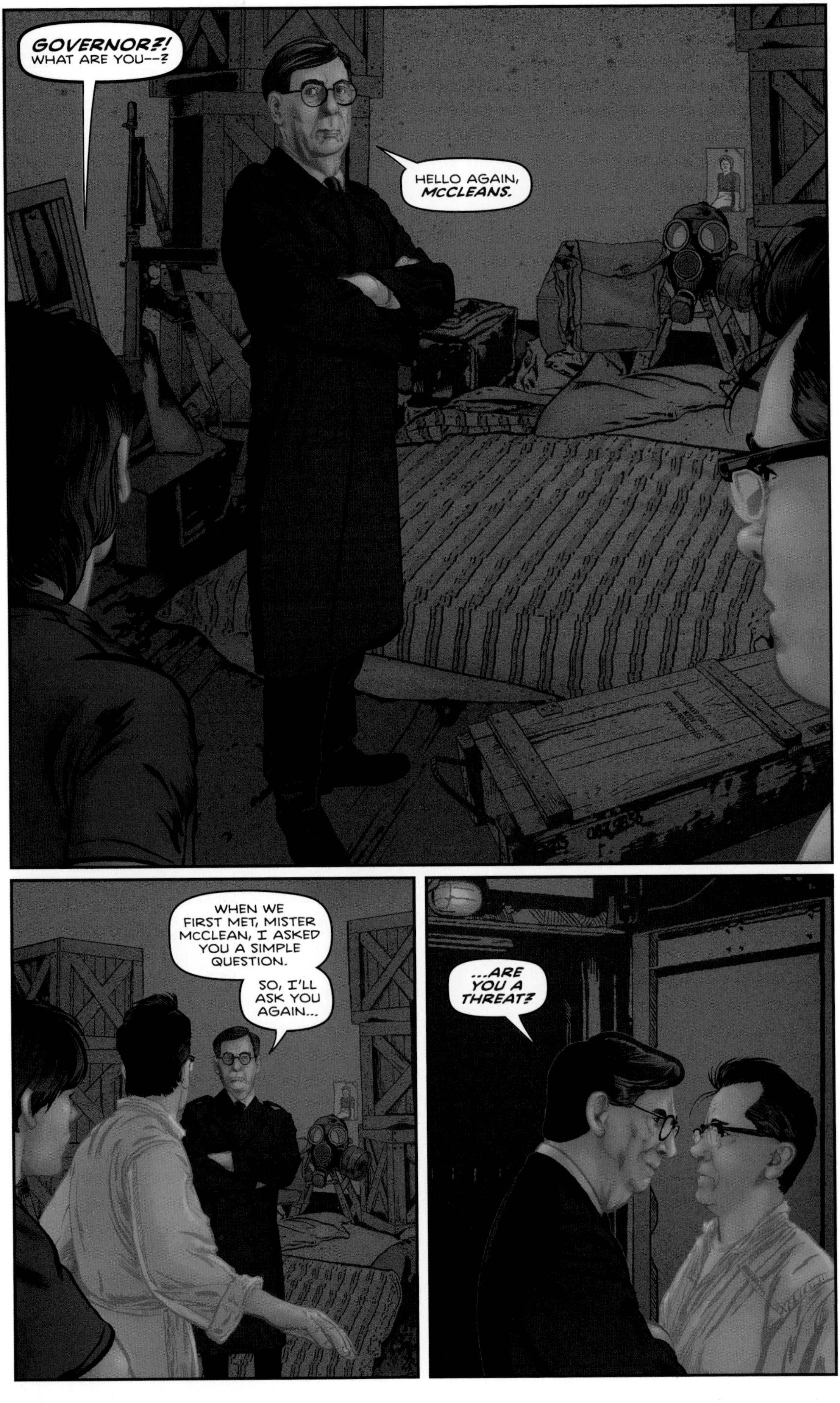
GOVERNOR?! WHAT ARE YOU--?
HELLO AGAIN, MCCLEANS.
WHEN WE FIRST MET, MISTER McCLEAN, I ASKED YOU A SIMPLE QUESTION.
SO, I'LL ASK YOU AGAIN...
...ARE YOU A THREAT?

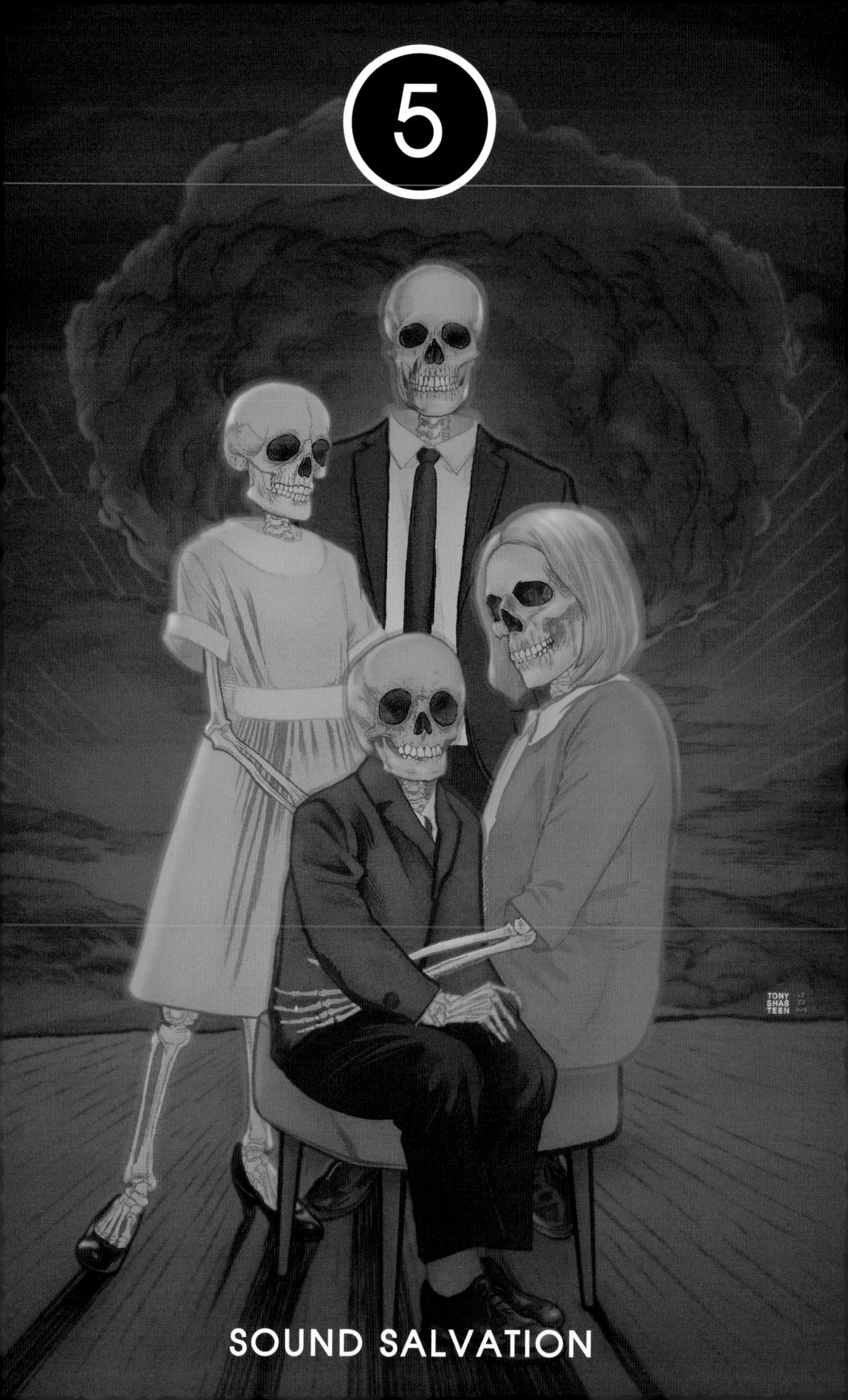
5
TONY
SHAS
TEEN
SOUND SALVATION

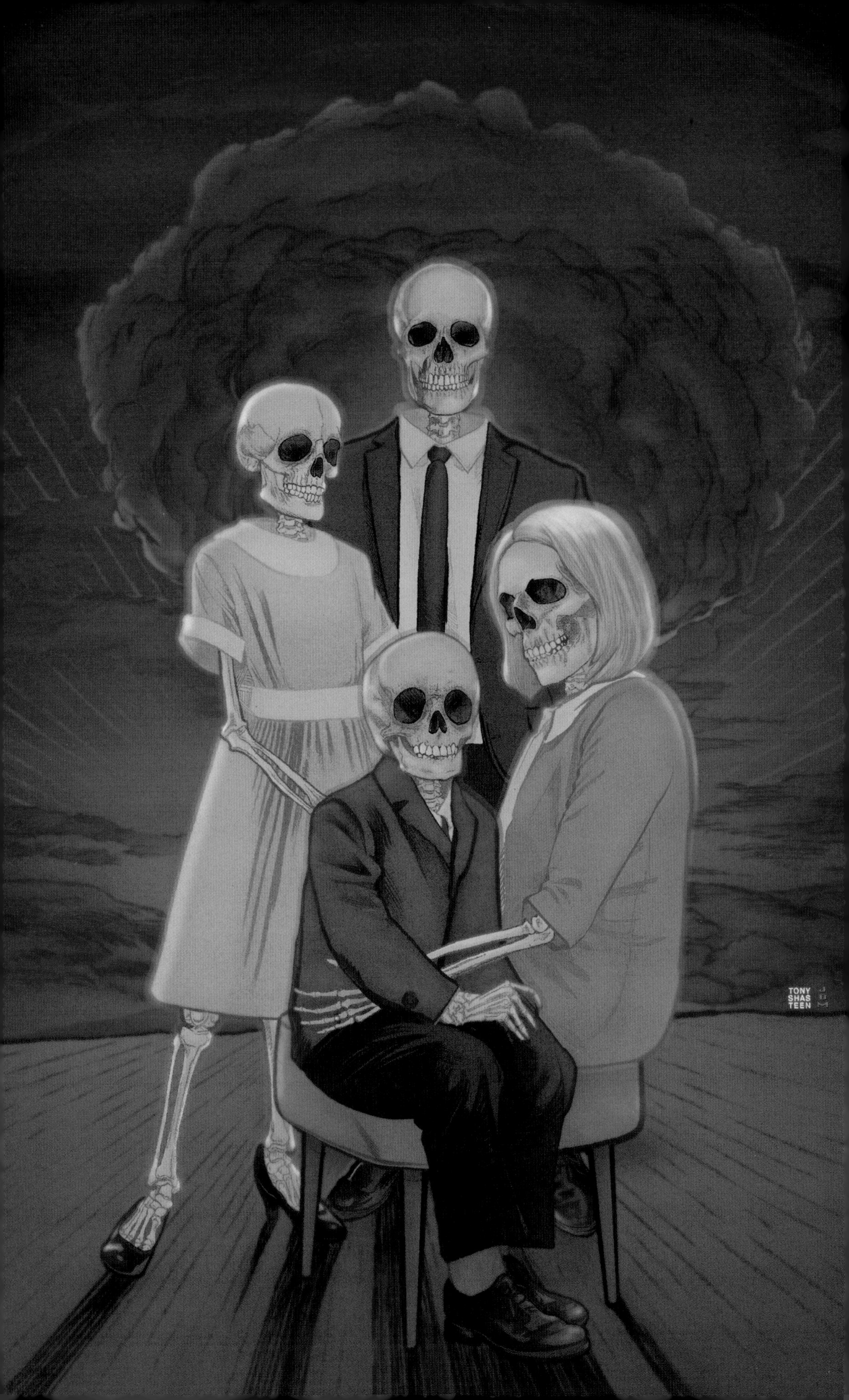
TONY
SHAS
TEEN
JBM

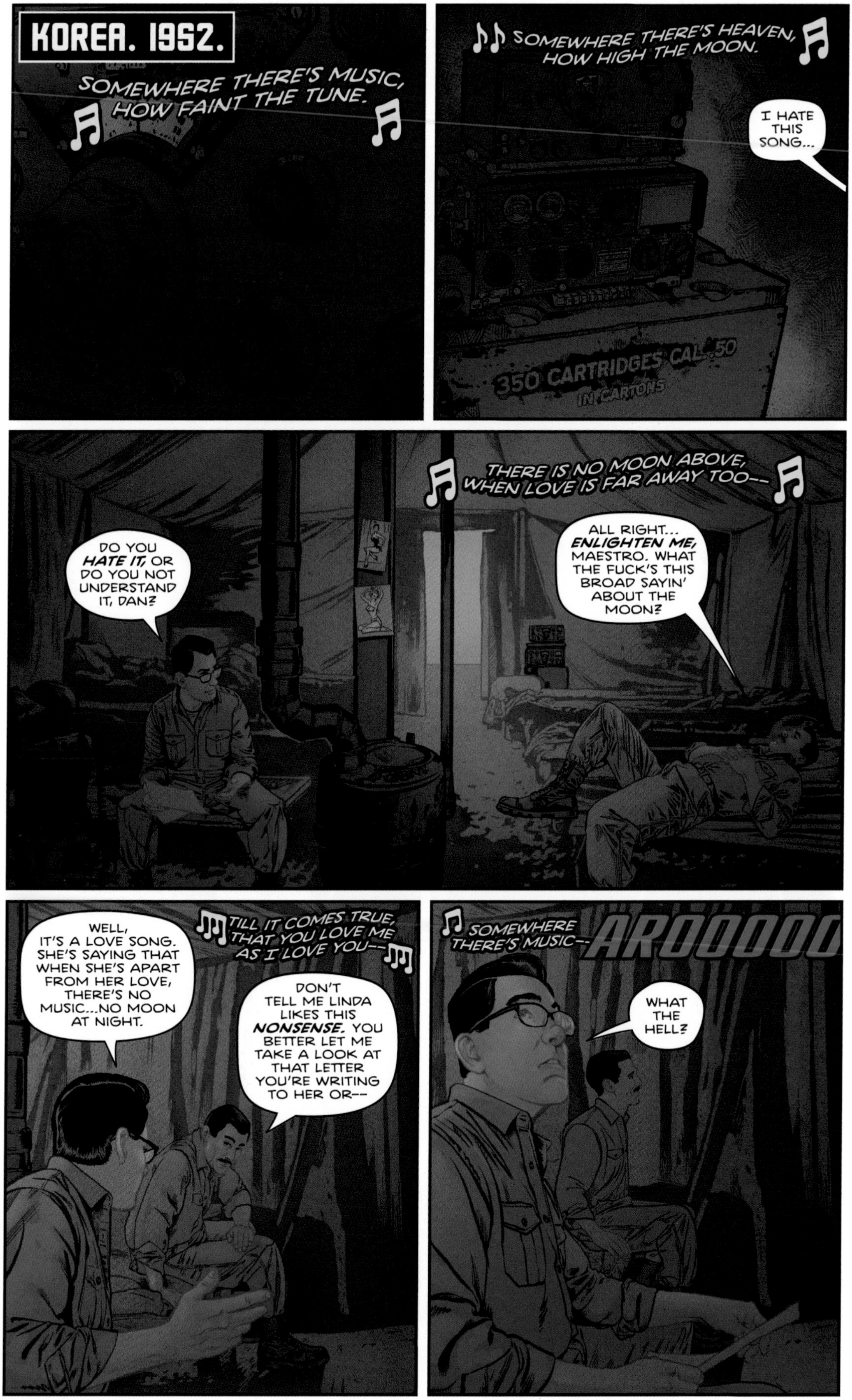
KOREA. 1952.
SOMEWHERE THERE'S MUSIC, HOW FAINT THE TUNE.
SOMEWHERE THERE'S HEAVEN, HOW HIGH THE MOON.
I HATE THIS SONG...
350 CARTRIDGES CAL. .50
IN CARTONS
THERE IS NO MOON ABOVE, WHEN LOVE IS FAR AWAY TOO--
DO YOU **HATE IT,** OR DO YOU NOT UNDERSTAND IT, DAN?
ALL RIGHT... **ENLIGHTEN ME,** MAESTRO. WHAT THE FUCK'S THIS BROAD SAYIN' ABOUT THE MOON?
TILL IT COMES TRUE, THAT YOU LOVE ME AS I LOVE YOU--
WELL, IT'S A LOVE SONG. SHE'S SAYING THAT WHEN SHE'S APART FROM HER LOVE, THERE'S NO MUSIC...NO MOON AT NIGHT.
DON'T TELL ME LINDA LIKES THIS **NONSENSE.** YOU BETTER LET ME TAKE A LOOK AT THAT LETTER YOU'RE WRITING TO HER OR--
SOMEWHERE THERE'S MUSIC--
AROOOOO
WHAT THE HELL?

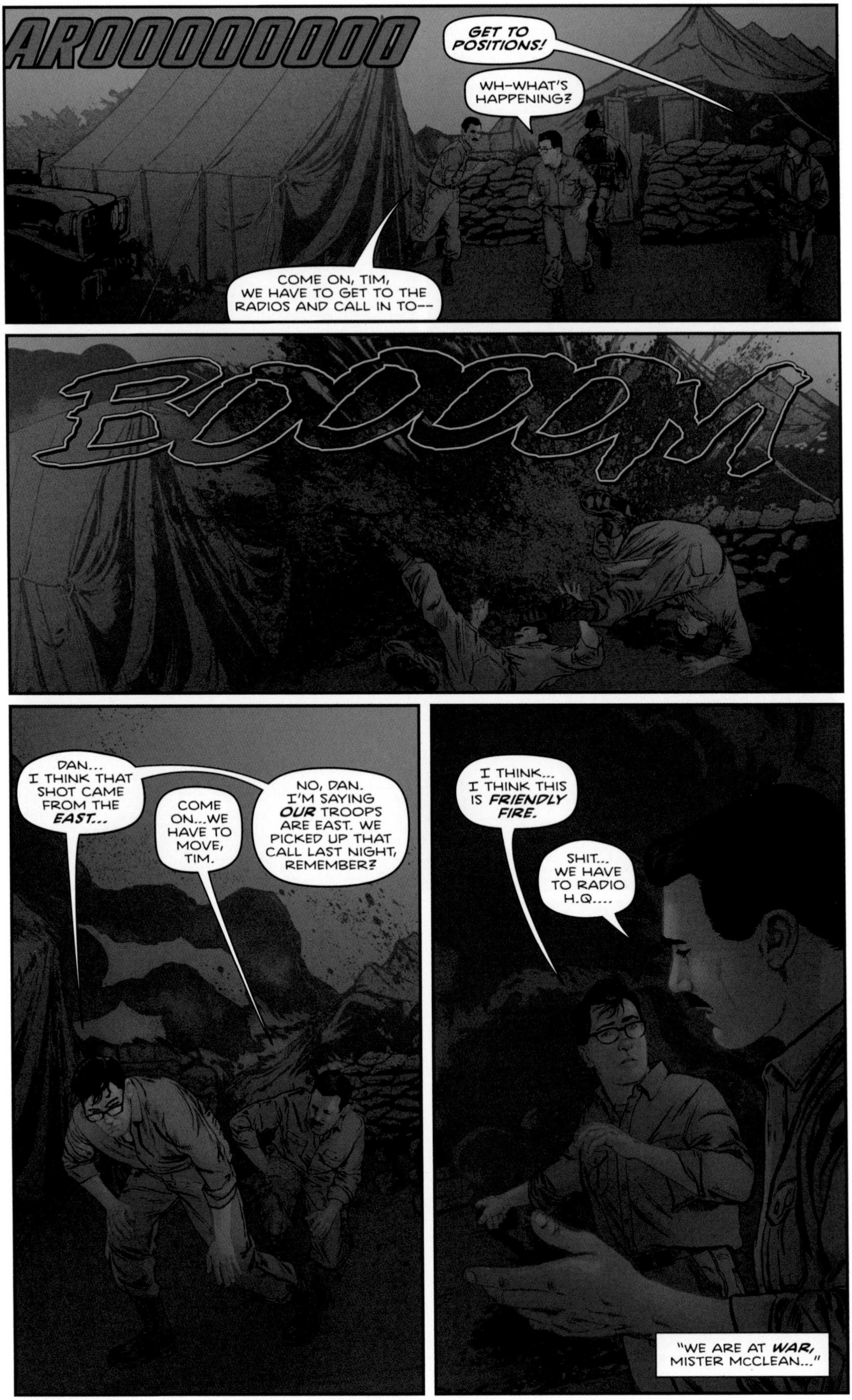
AROOOOOOOOO
GET TO POSITIONS!
WH-WHAT'S HAPPENING?
COME ON, TIM, WE HAVE TO GET TO THE RADIOS AND CALL IN TO--
BOOOOM
DAN... I THINK THAT SHOT CAME FROM THE EAST...
COME ON...WE HAVE TO MOVE, TIM.
NO, DAN. I'M SAYING OUR TROOPS ARE EAST. WE PICKED UP THAT CALL LAST NIGHT, REMEMBER?
I THINK... I THINK THIS IS FRIENDLY FIRE.
SHIT... WE HAVE TO RADIO H.Q....
"WE ARE AT WAR, MISTER MCCLEAN..."

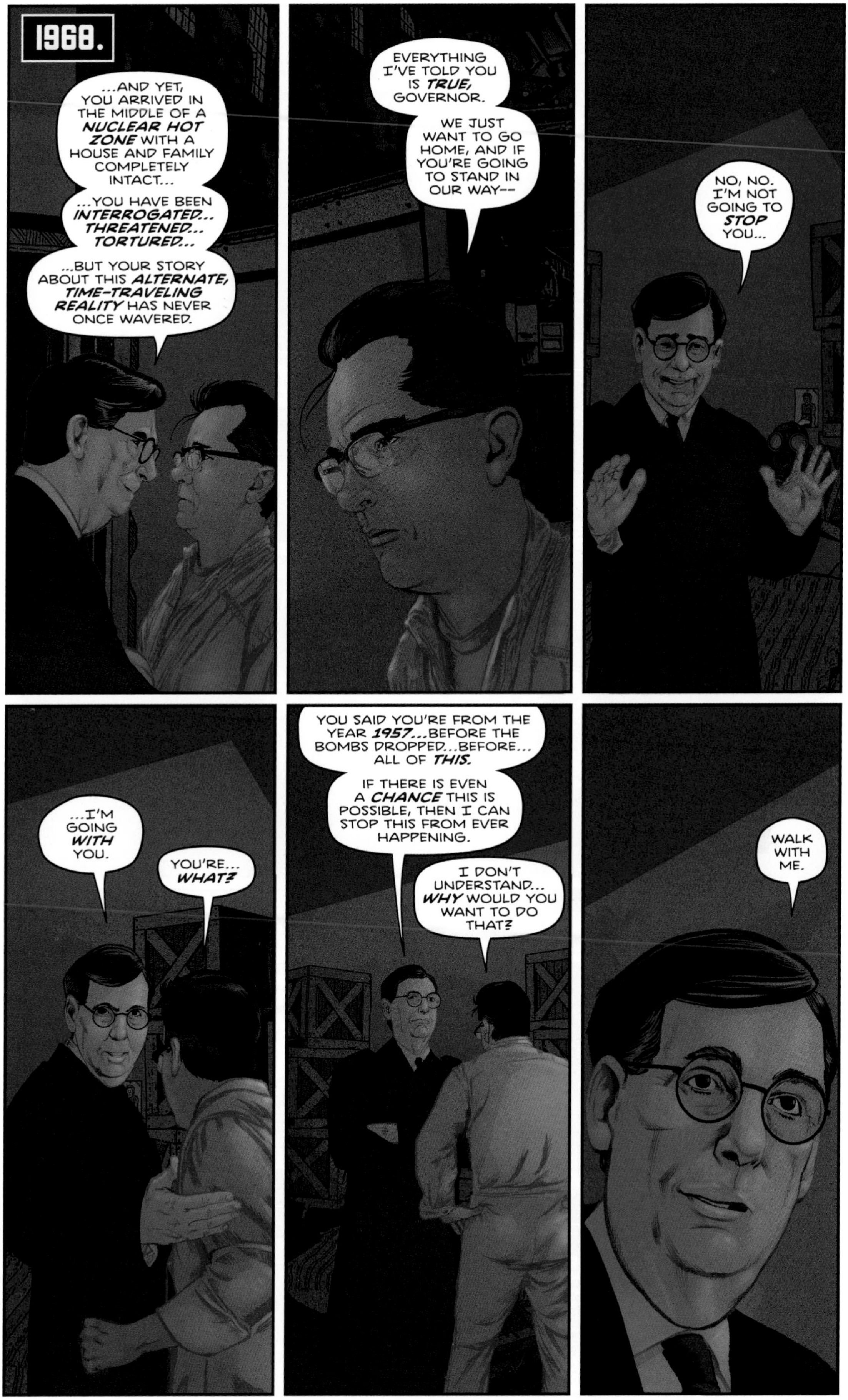
1968.
...AND YET, YOU ARRIVED IN THE MIDDLE OF A NUCLEAR HOT ZONE WITH A HOUSE AND FAMILY COMPLETELY INTACT...
...YOU HAVE BEEN INTERROGATED... THREATENED... TORTURED...
...BUT YOUR STORY ABOUT THIS ALTERNATE, TIME-TRAVELING REALITY HAS NEVER ONCE WAVERED.
EVERYTHING I'VE TOLD YOU IS TRUE, GOVERNOR.
WE JUST WANT TO GO HOME, AND IF YOU'RE GOING TO STAND IN OUR WAY--
NO, NO. I'M NOT GOING TO STOP YOU...
...I'M GOING WITH YOU.
YOU'RE... WHAT?
YOU SAID YOU'RE FROM THE YEAR 1957...BEFORE THE BOMBS DROPPED...BEFORE... ALL OF THIS.
IF THERE IS EVEN A CHANCE THIS IS POSSIBLE, THEN I CAN STOP THIS FROM EVER HAPPENING.
I DON'T UNDERSTAND... WHY WOULD YOU WANT TO DO THAT?
WALK WITH ME.

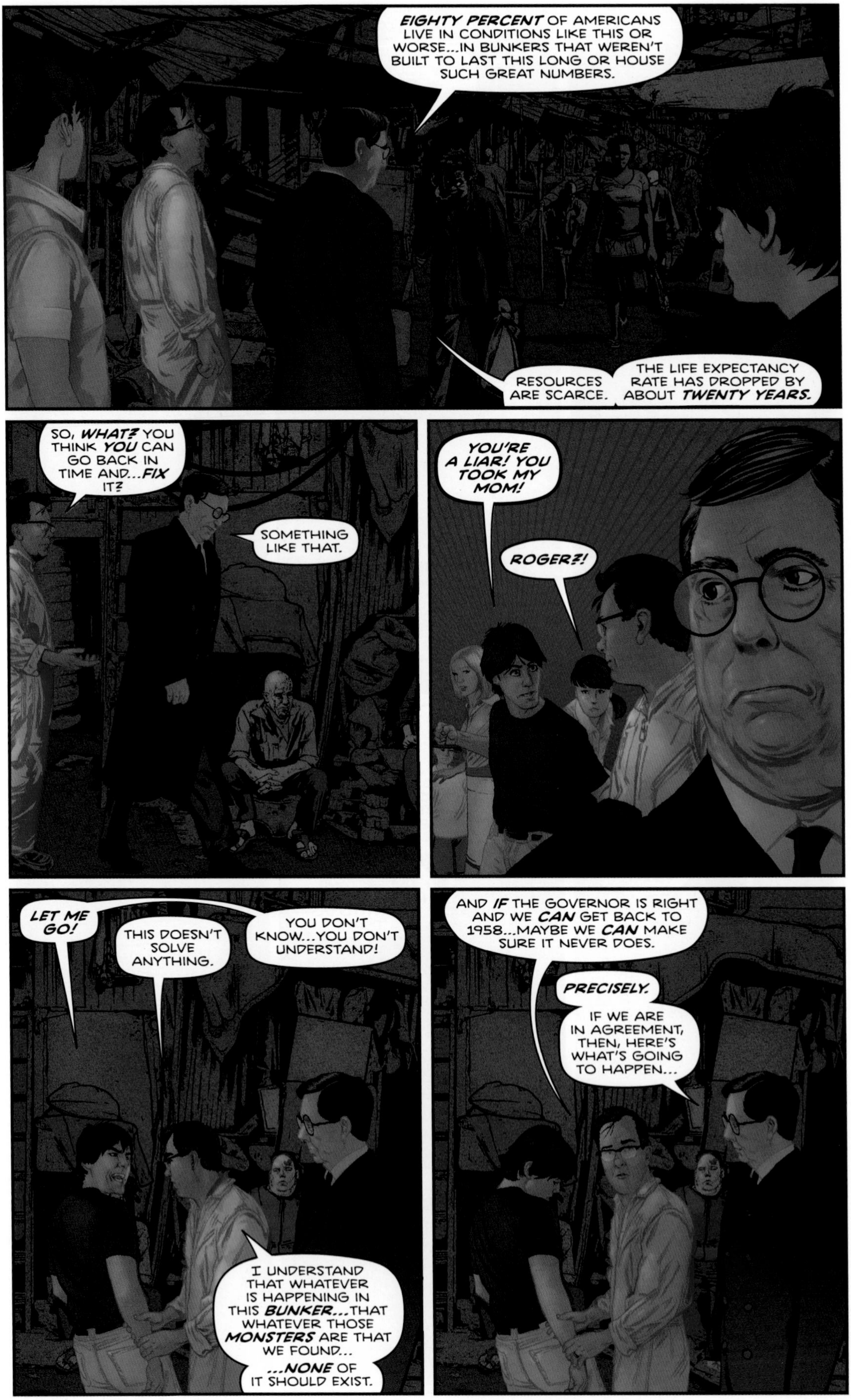
EIGHTY PERCENT OF AMERICANS LIVE IN CONDITIONS LIKE THIS OR WORSE...IN BUNKERS THAT WEREN'T BUILT TO LAST THIS LONG OR HOUSE SUCH GREAT NUMBERS.
RESOURCES ARE SCARCE.
THE LIFE EXPECTANCY RATE HAS DROPPED BY ABOUT TWENTY YEARS.
SO, WHAT? YOU THINK YOU CAN GO BACK IN TIME AND...FIX IT?
SOMETHING LIKE THAT.
YOU'RE A LIAR! YOU TOOK MY MOM!
ROGER?!
LET ME GO!
THIS DOESN'T SOLVE ANYTHING.
YOU DON'T KNOW...YOU DON'T UNDERSTAND!
I UNDERSTAND THAT WHATEVER IS HAPPENING IN THIS BUNKER...THAT WHATEVER THOSE MONSTERS ARE THAT WE FOUND...
...NONE OF IT SHOULD EXIST.
AND IF THE GOVERNOR IS RIGHT AND WE CAN GET BACK TO 1958...MAYBE WE CAN MAKE SURE IT NEVER DOES.
PRECISELY.
IF WE ARE IN AGREEMENT, THEN, HERE'S WHAT'S GOING TO HAPPEN...

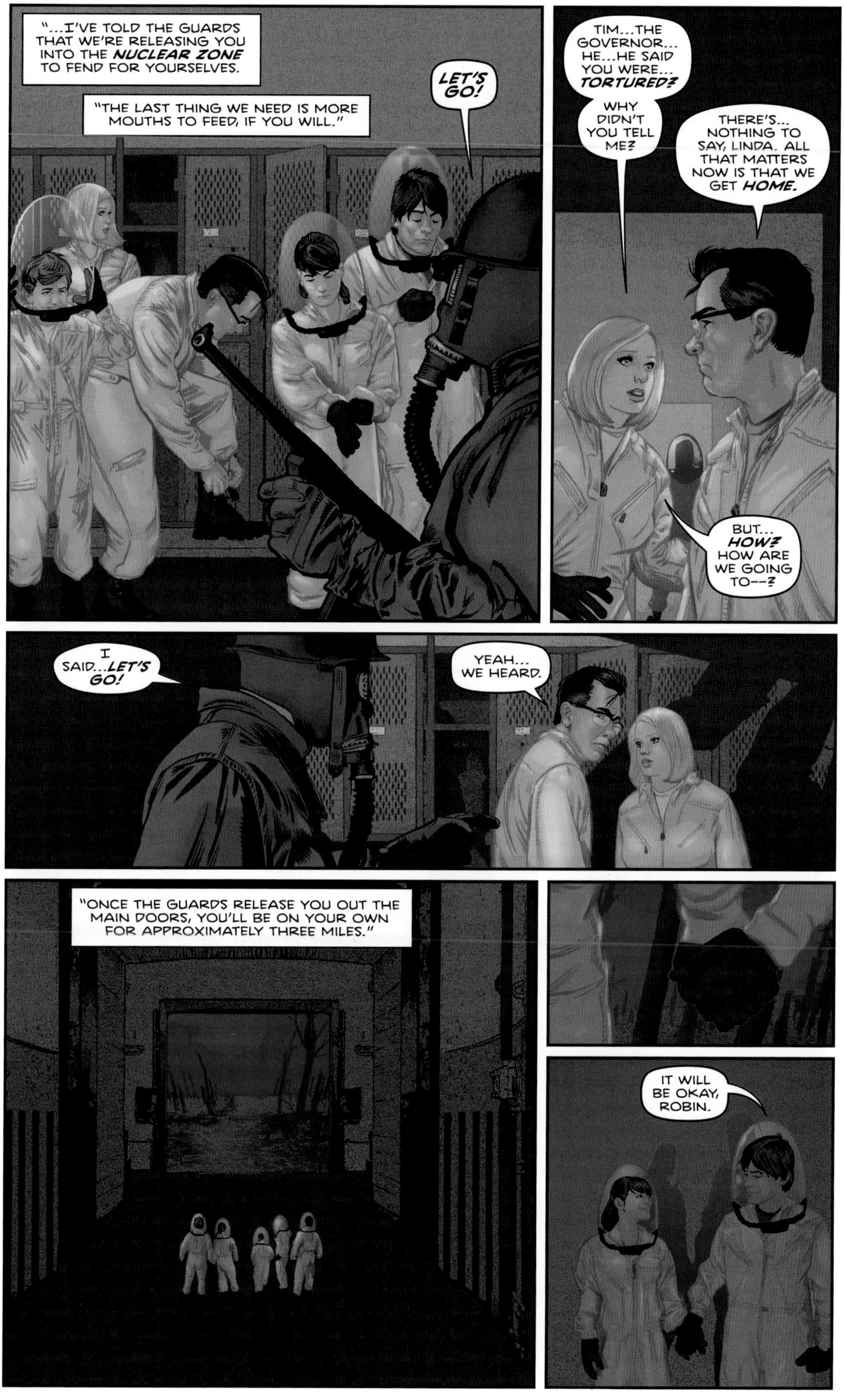
"...I'VE TOLD THE GUARDS THAT WE'RE RELEASING YOU INTO THE NUCLEAR ZONE TO FEND FOR YOURSELVES.
"THE LAST THING WE NEED IS MORE MOUTHS TO FEED, IF YOU WILL."
LET'S GO!
TIM...THE GOVERNOR... HE...HE SAID YOU WERE... TORTURED?
WHY DIDN'T YOU TELL ME?
THERE'S... NOTHING TO SAY, LINDA. ALL THAT MATTERS NOW IS THAT WE GET HOME.
BUT... HOW? HOW ARE WE GOING TO--?
I SAID...LET'S GO!
YEAH... WE HEARD.
"ONCE THE GUARDS RELEASE YOU OUT THE MAIN DOORS, YOU'LL BE ON YOUR OWN FOR APPROXIMATELY THREE MILES."
IT WILL BE OKAY, ROBIN.

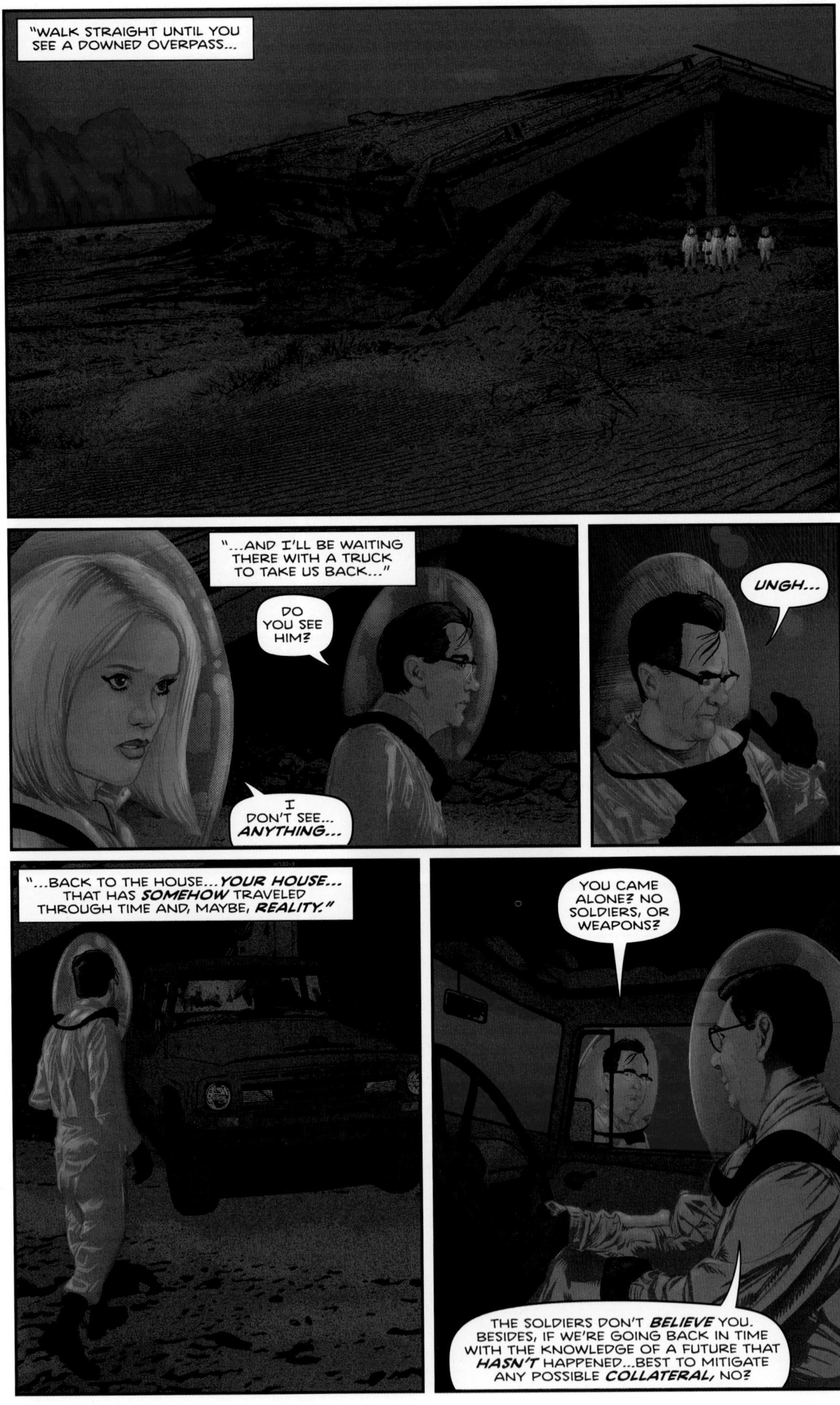
"WALK STRAIGHT UNTIL YOU SEE A DOWNED OVERPASS...
"...AND I'LL BE WAITING THERE WITH A TRUCK TO TAKE US BACK..."
DO YOU SEE HIM?
I DON'T SEE... ANYTHING...
UNGH...
"...BACK TO THE HOUSE...YOUR HOUSE... THAT HAS SOMEHOW TRAVELED THROUGH TIME AND, MAYBE, REALITY."
YOU CAME ALONE? NO SOLDIERS, OR WEAPONS?
THE SOLDIERS DON'T BELIEVE YOU. BESIDES, IF WE'RE GOING BACK IN TIME WITH THE KNOWLEDGE OF A FUTURE THAT HASN'T HAPPENED...BEST TO MITIGATE ANY POSSIBLE COLLATERAL, NO?

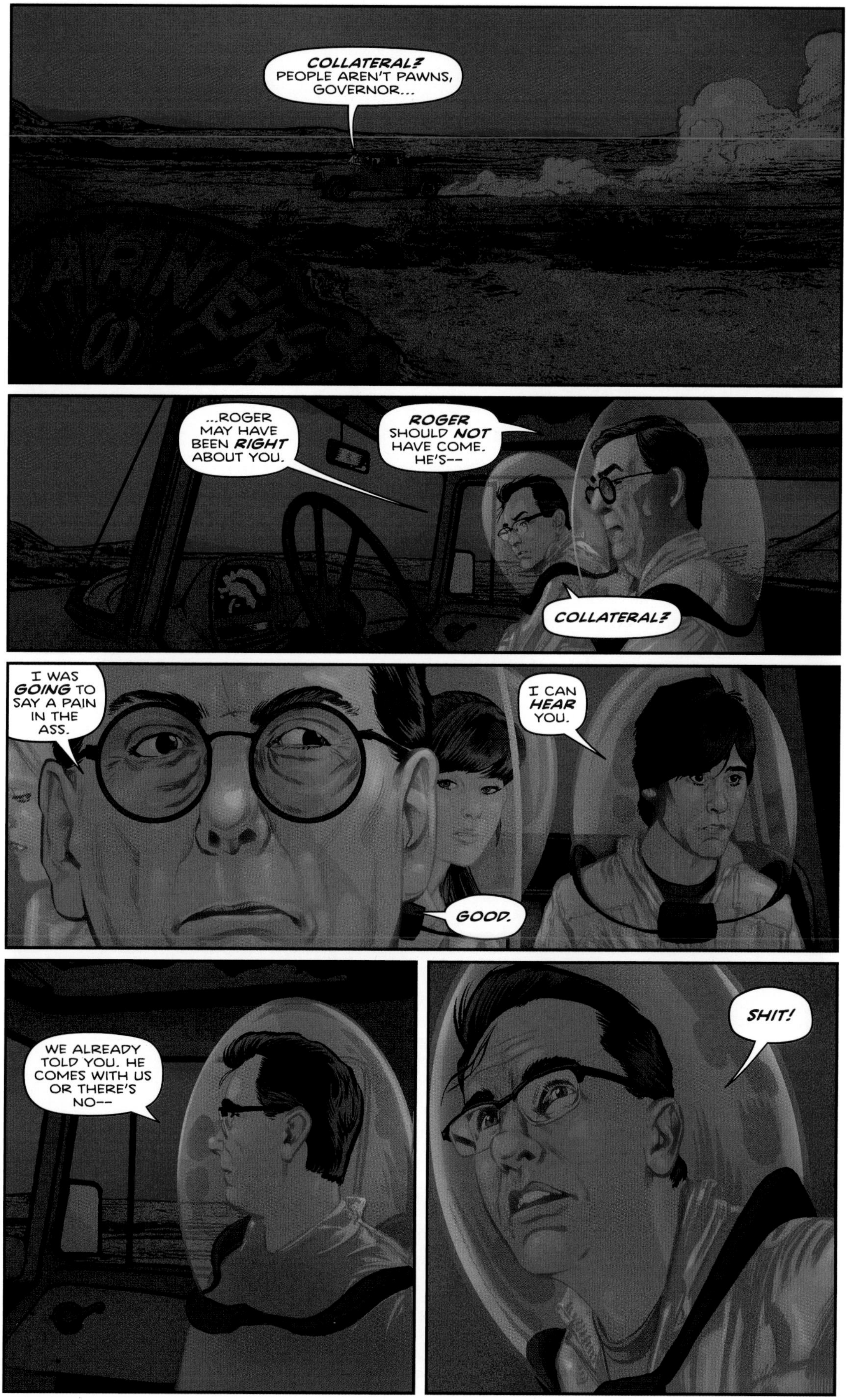
COLLATERAL? PEOPLE AREN'T PAWNS, GOVERNOR...
...ROGER MAY HAVE BEEN RIGHT ABOUT YOU.
ROGER SHOULD NOT HAVE COME. HE'S--
COLLATERAL?
I WAS GOING TO SAY A PAIN IN THE ASS.
I CAN HEAR YOU.
GOOD.
WE ALREADY TOLD YOU. HE COMES WITH US OR THERE'S NO--
SHIT!

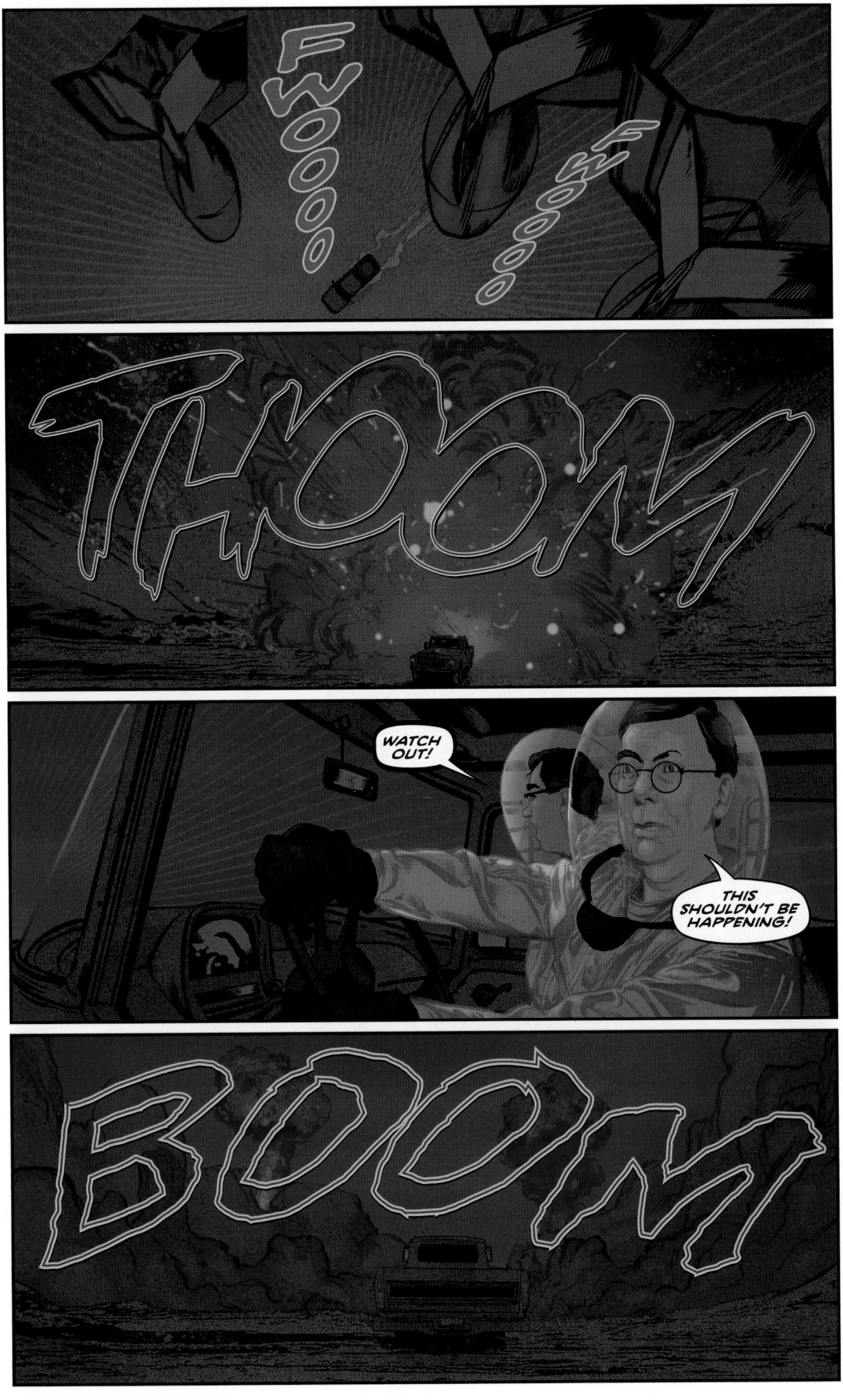
FWOOOO
FWOOOOO
THOOM
WATCH OUT!
THIS SHOULDN'T BE HAPPENING!
BOOM

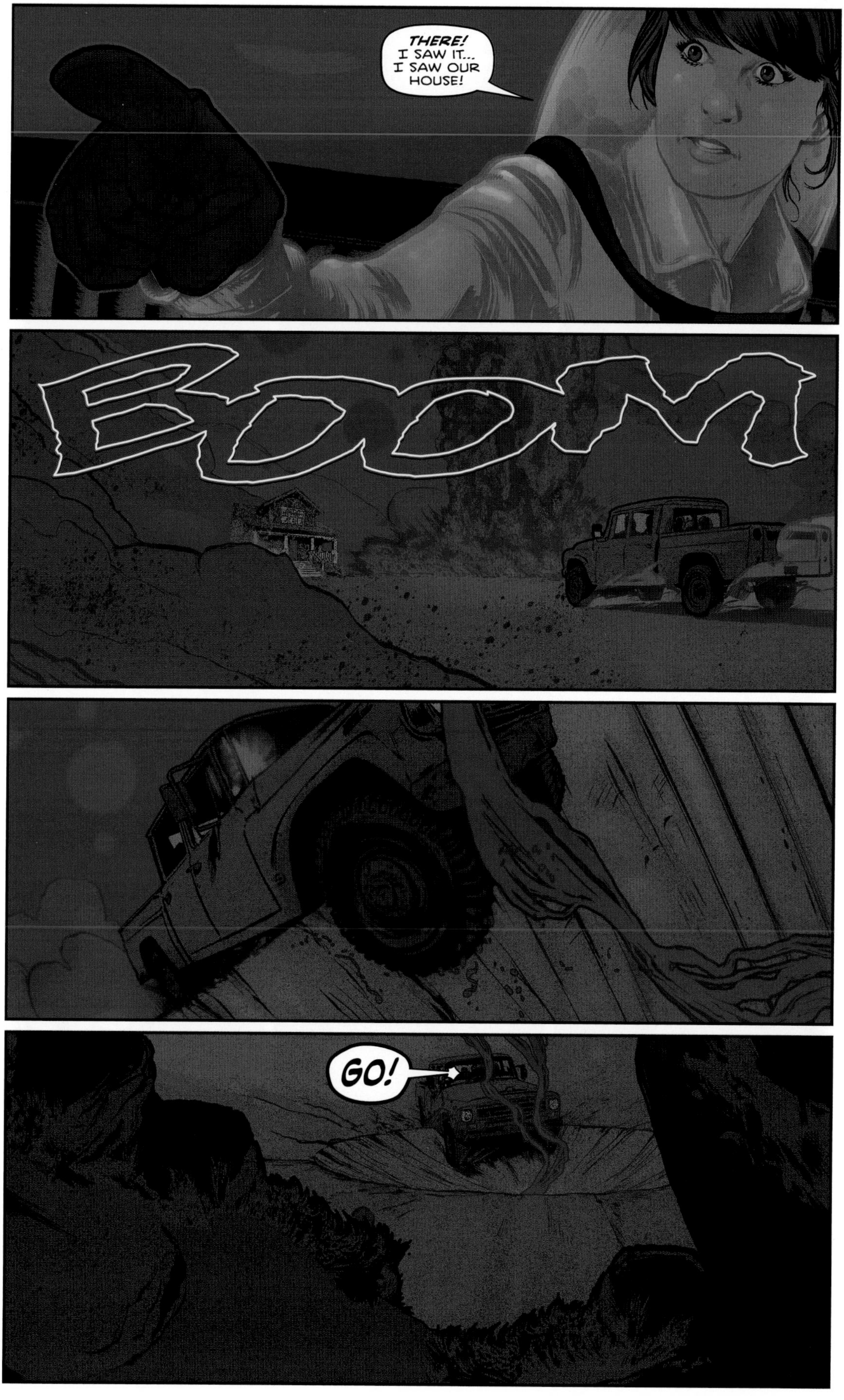
THERE! I SAW IT... I SAW OUR HOUSE!
BOOM
GO!

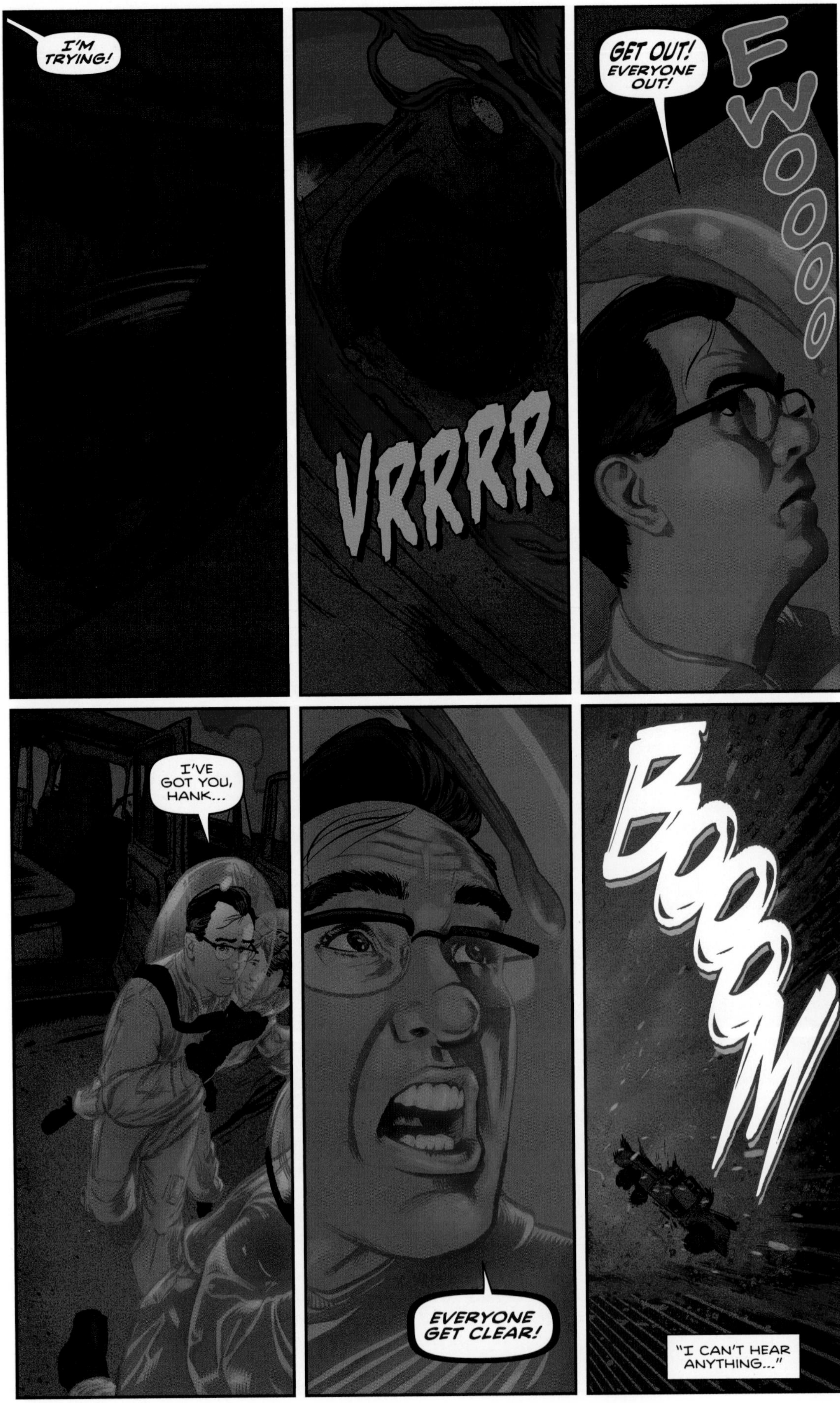
I'M TRYING!
VRRRR
GET OUT! EVERYONE OUT!
FWOOOO
I'VE GOT YOU, HANK...
EVERYONE GET CLEAR!
BOOOOM
"I CAN'T HEAR ANYTHING..."

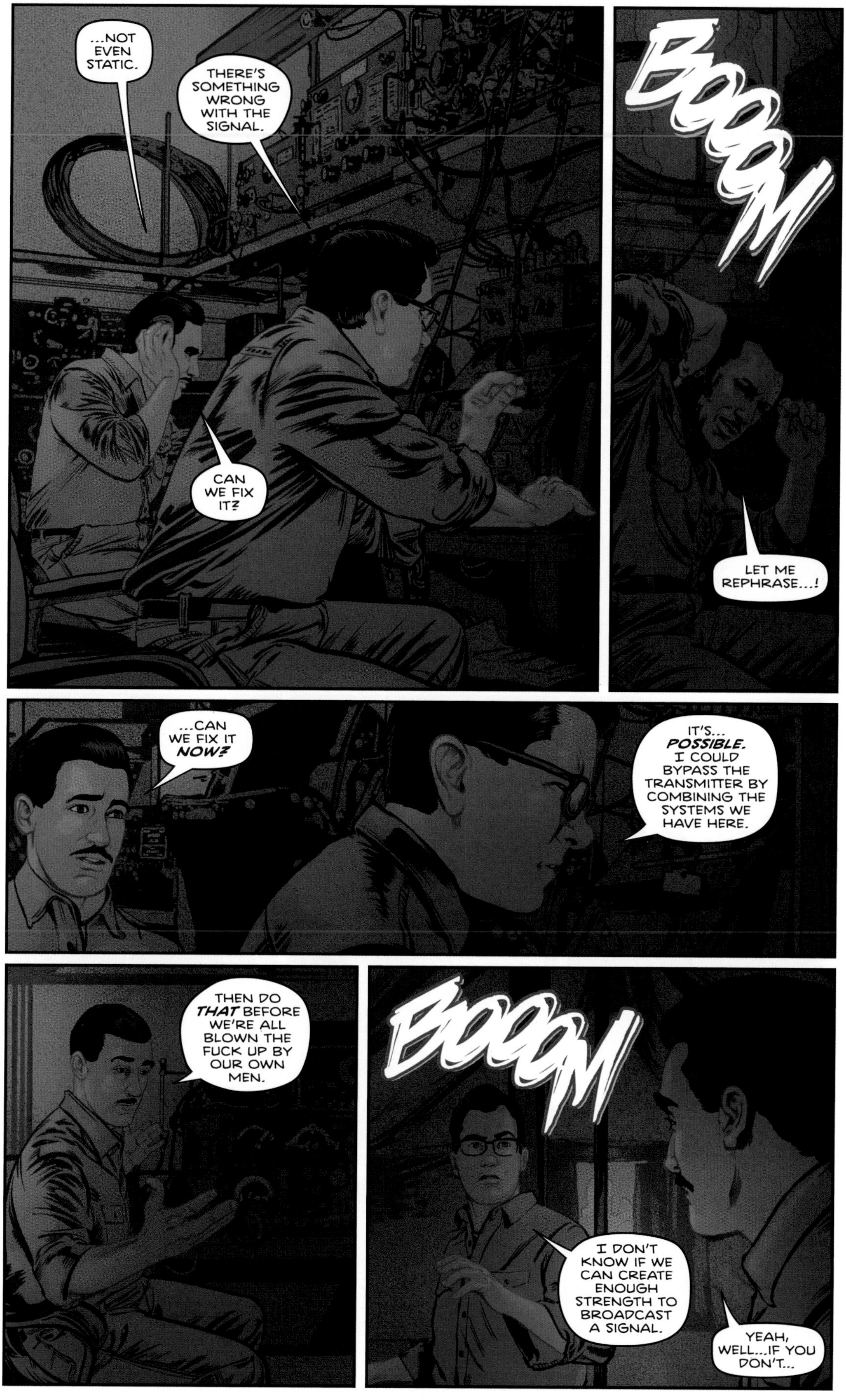
...NOT EVEN STATIC.
THERE'S SOMETHING WRONG WITH THE SIGNAL.
CAN WE FIX IT?
BOOOM
LET ME REPHRASE...!
...CAN WE FIX IT *NOW?*
IT'S... ***POSSIBLE.*** I COULD BYPASS THE TRANSMITTER BY COMBINING THE SYSTEMS WE HAVE HERE.
THEN DO ***THAT*** BEFORE WE'RE ALL BLOWN THE FUCK UP BY OUR OWN MEN.
BOOOM
I DON'T KNOW IF WE CAN CREATE ENOUGH STRENGTH TO BROADCAST A SIGNAL.
YEAH, WELL...IF YOU DON'T...

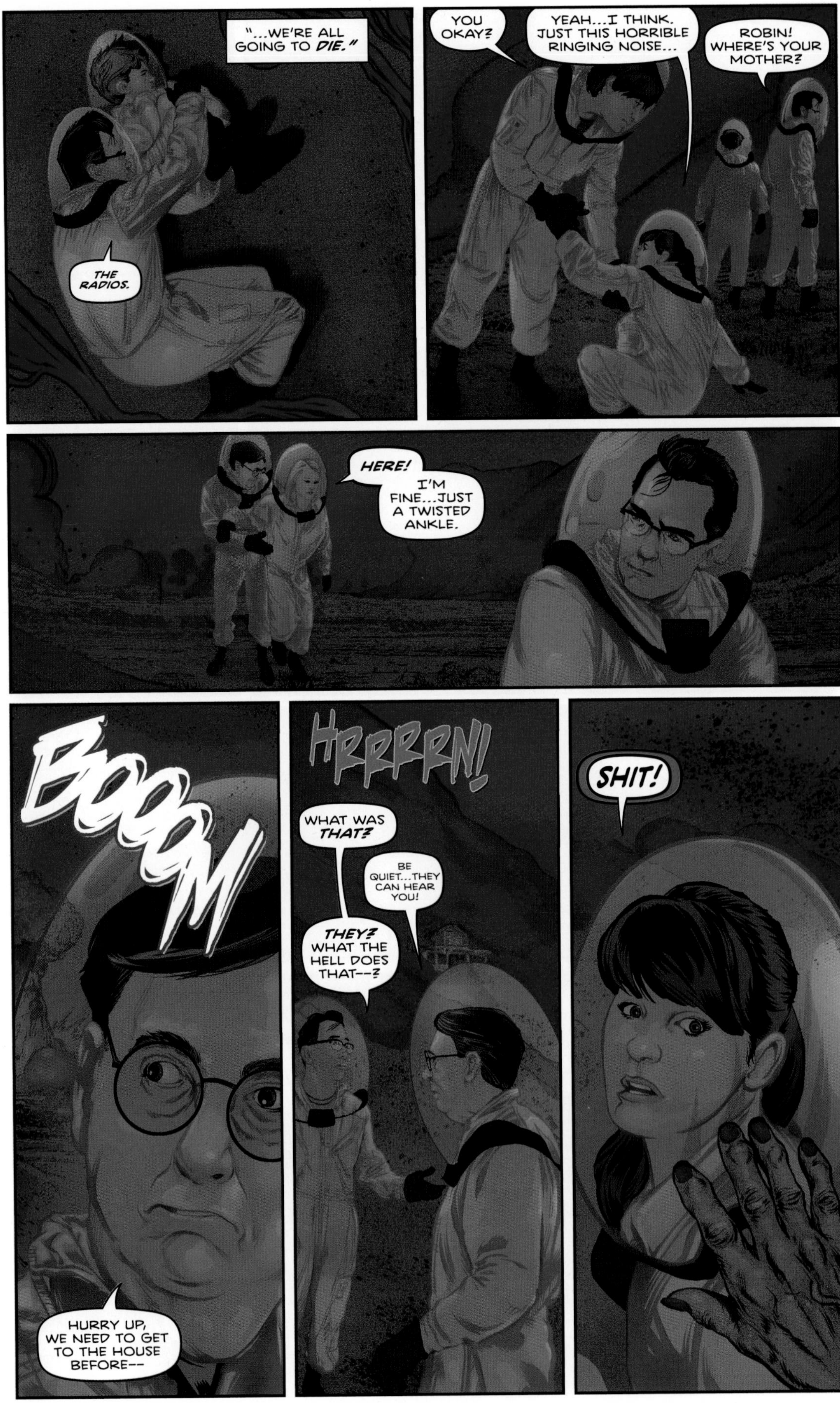
"...WE'RE ALL GOING TO DIE."
THE RADIOS.
YOU OKAY?
YEAH...I THINK. JUST THIS HORRIBLE RINGING NOISE...
ROBIN! WHERE'S YOUR MOTHER?
HERE!
I'M FINE...JUST A TWISTED ANKLE.
BOOOM
HURRY UP, WE NEED TO GET TO THE HOUSE BEFORE--
HRRRRN!
WHAT WAS THAT?
BE QUIET...THEY CAN HEAR YOU!
THEY? WHAT THE HELL DOES THAT--?
SHIT!

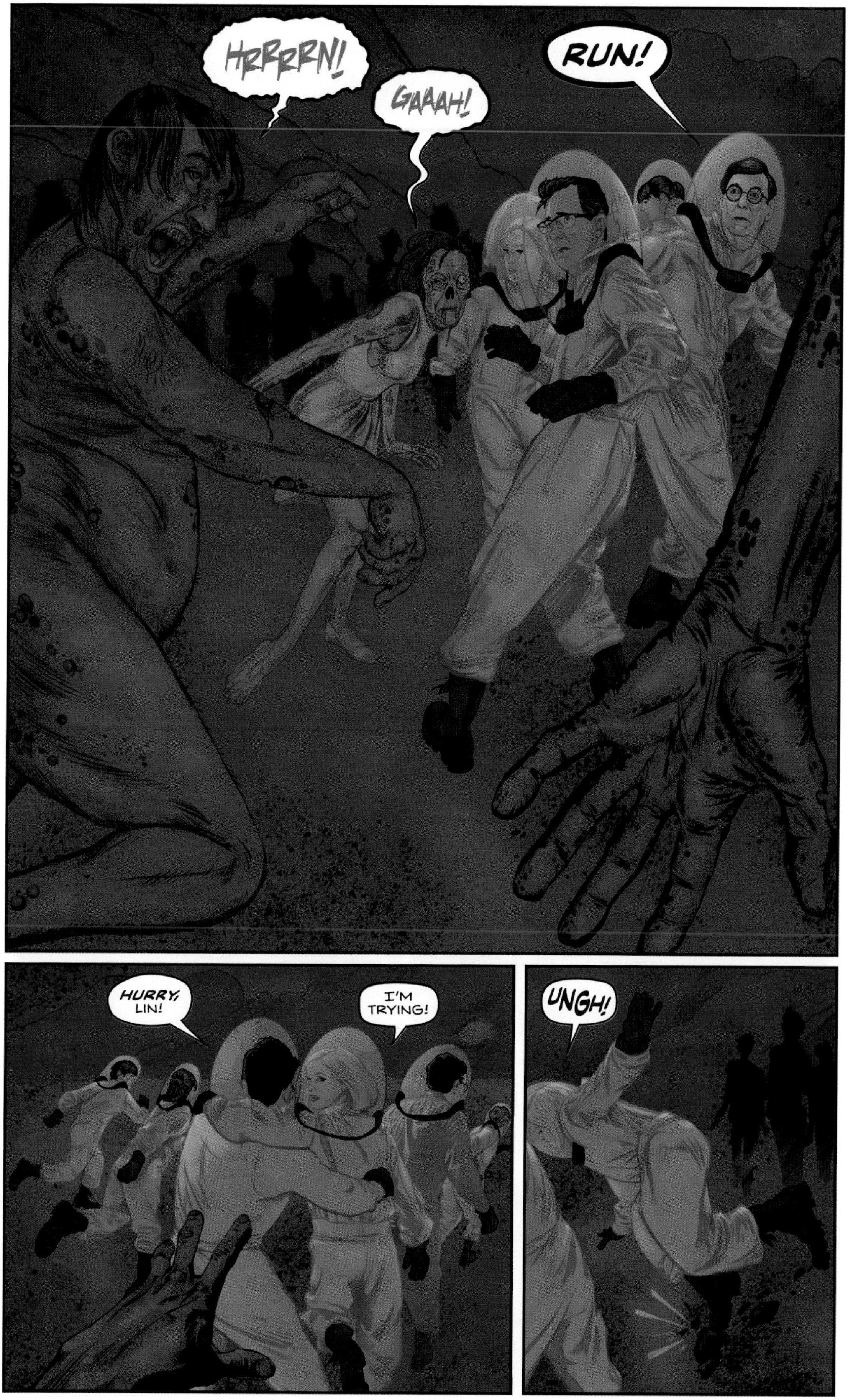
HRRRRN!
GAAAH!
RUN!
HURRY, LIN!
I'M TRYING!
UNGH!

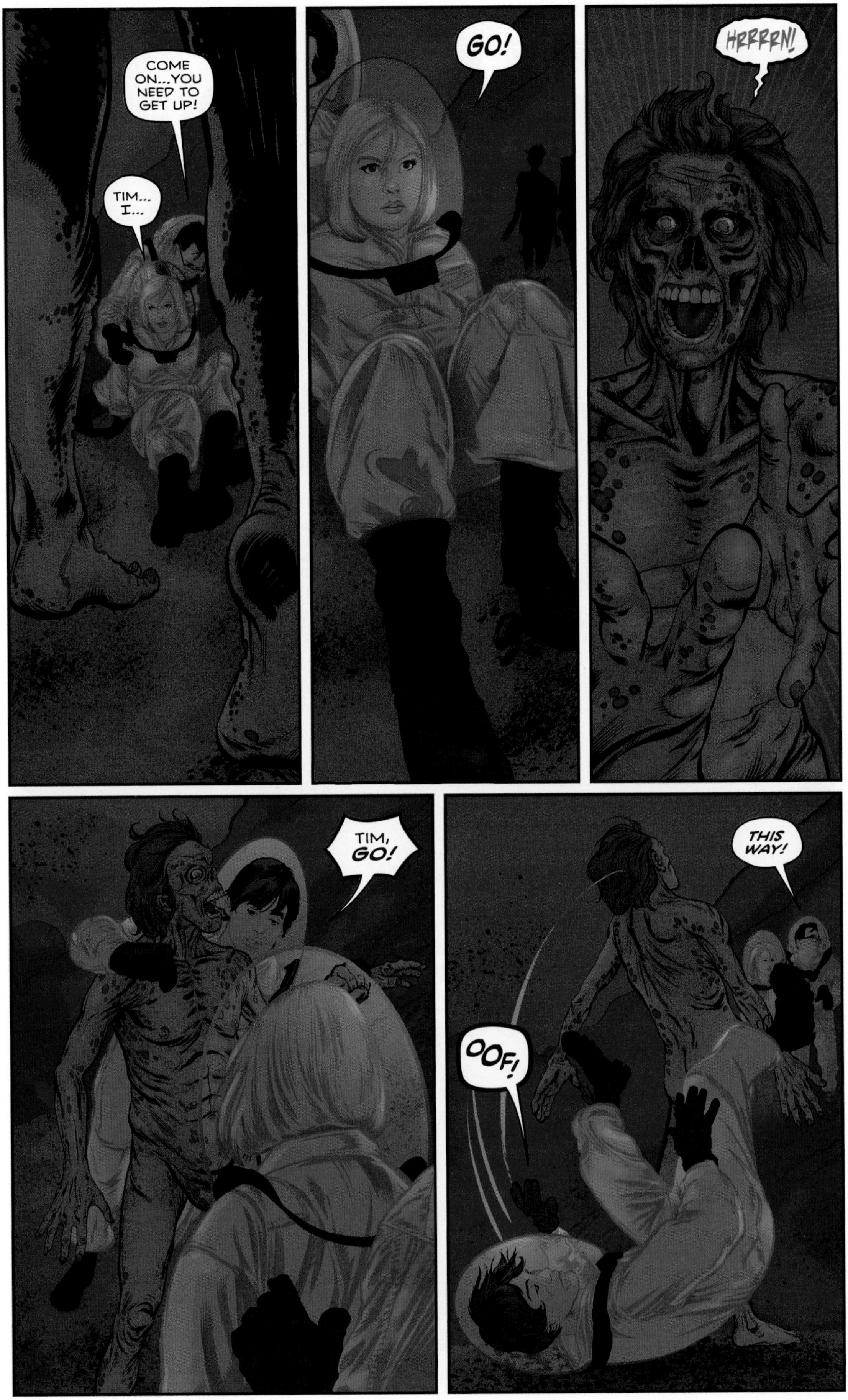
COME ON...YOU NEED TO GET UP!
TIM... I...
GO!
HRRRRN!
TIM, GO!
THIS WAY!
OOF!

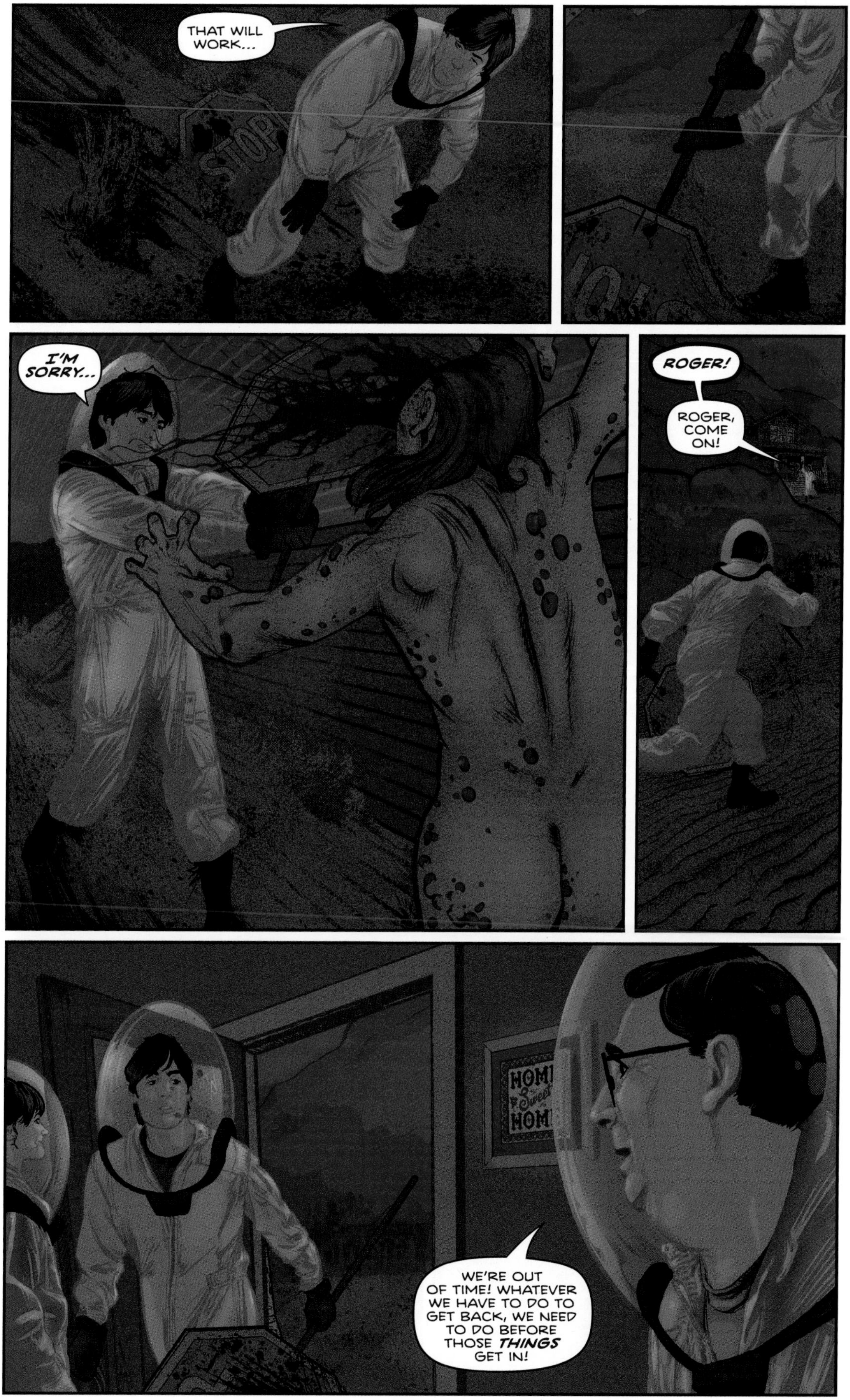
THAT WILL WORK...
STOP
I'M SORRY...
ROGER!
ROGER, COME ON!
HOME Sweet HOME
WE'RE OUT OF TIME! WHATEVER WE HAVE TO DO TO GET BACK, WE NEED TO DO BEFORE THOSE *THINGS* GET IN!

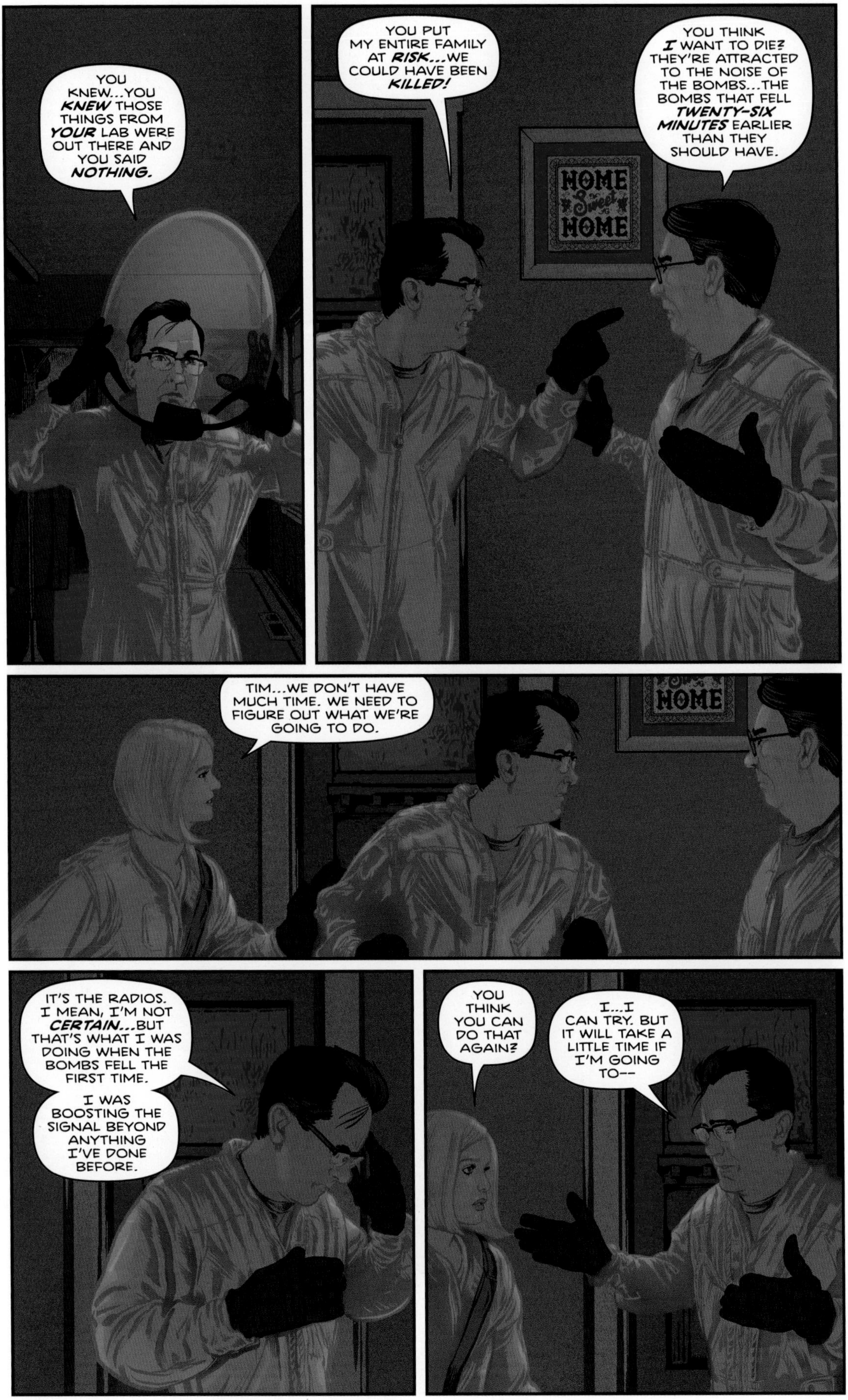
YOU KNEW...YOU KNEW THOSE THINGS FROM YOUR LAB WERE OUT THERE AND YOU SAID NOTHING.
YOU PUT MY ENTIRE FAMILY AT RISK...WE COULD HAVE BEEN KILLED!
YOU THINK I WANT TO DIE? THEY'RE ATTRACTED TO THE NOISE OF THE BOMBS...THE BOMBS THAT FELL TWENTY-SIX MINUTES EARLIER THAN THEY SHOULD HAVE.
HOME Sweet HOME
TIM...WE DON'T HAVE MUCH TIME. WE NEED TO FIGURE OUT WHAT WE'RE GOING TO DO.
HOME
IT'S THE RADIOS. I MEAN, I'M NOT CERTAIN...BUT THAT'S WHAT I WAS DOING WHEN THE BOMBS FELL THE FIRST TIME.
I WAS BOOSTING THE SIGNAL BEYOND ANYTHING I'VE DONE BEFORE.
YOU THINK YOU CAN DO THAT AGAIN?
I...I CAN TRY. BUT IT WILL TAKE A LITTLE TIME IF I'M GOING TO--

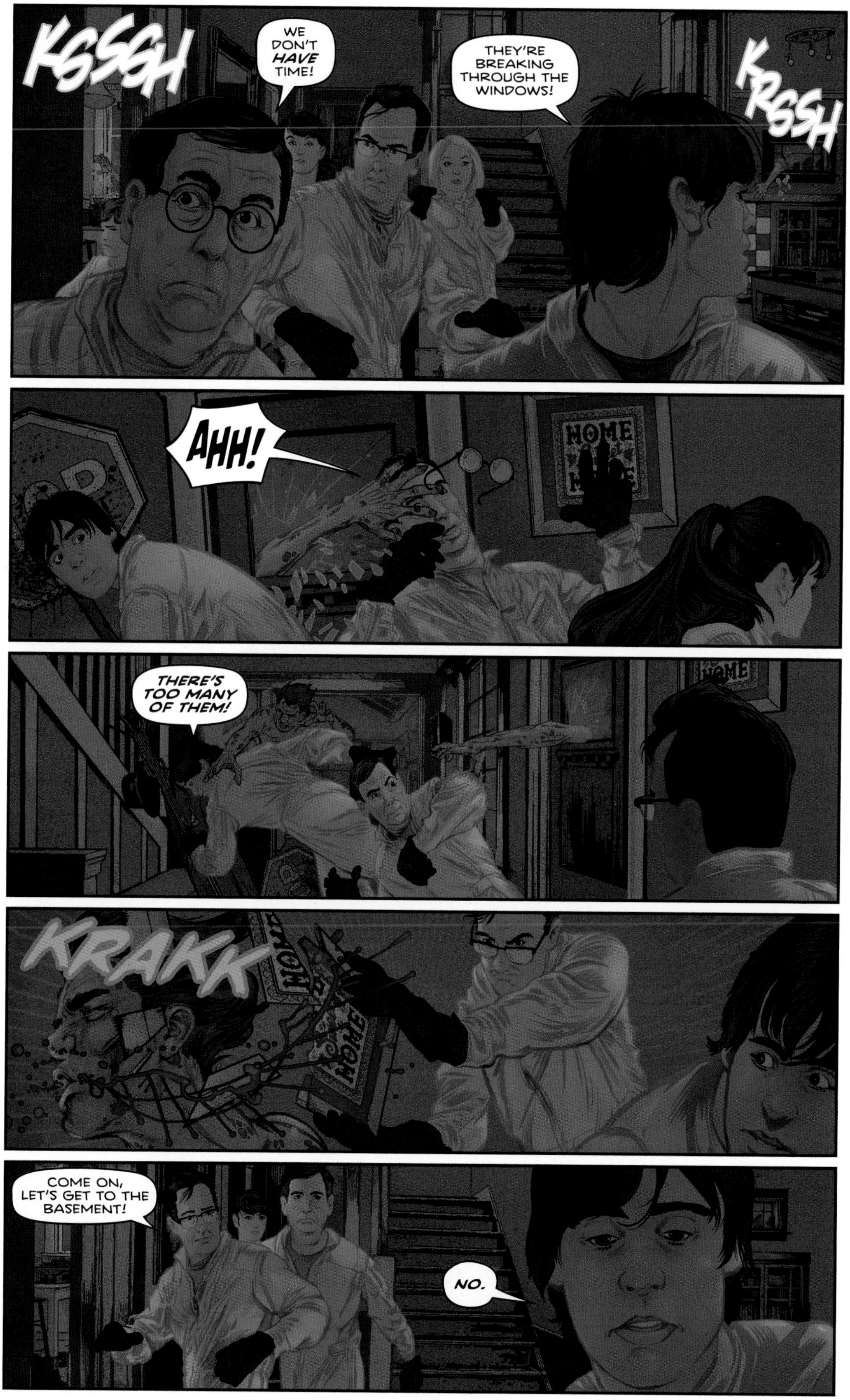
KSSSH
WE DON'T *HAVE* TIME!
THEY'RE BREAKING THROUGH THE WINDOWS!
KRSSH
AHH!
HOME
THERE'S TOO MANY OF THEM!
KRAKK
COME ON, LET'S GET TO THE BASEMENT!
NO.

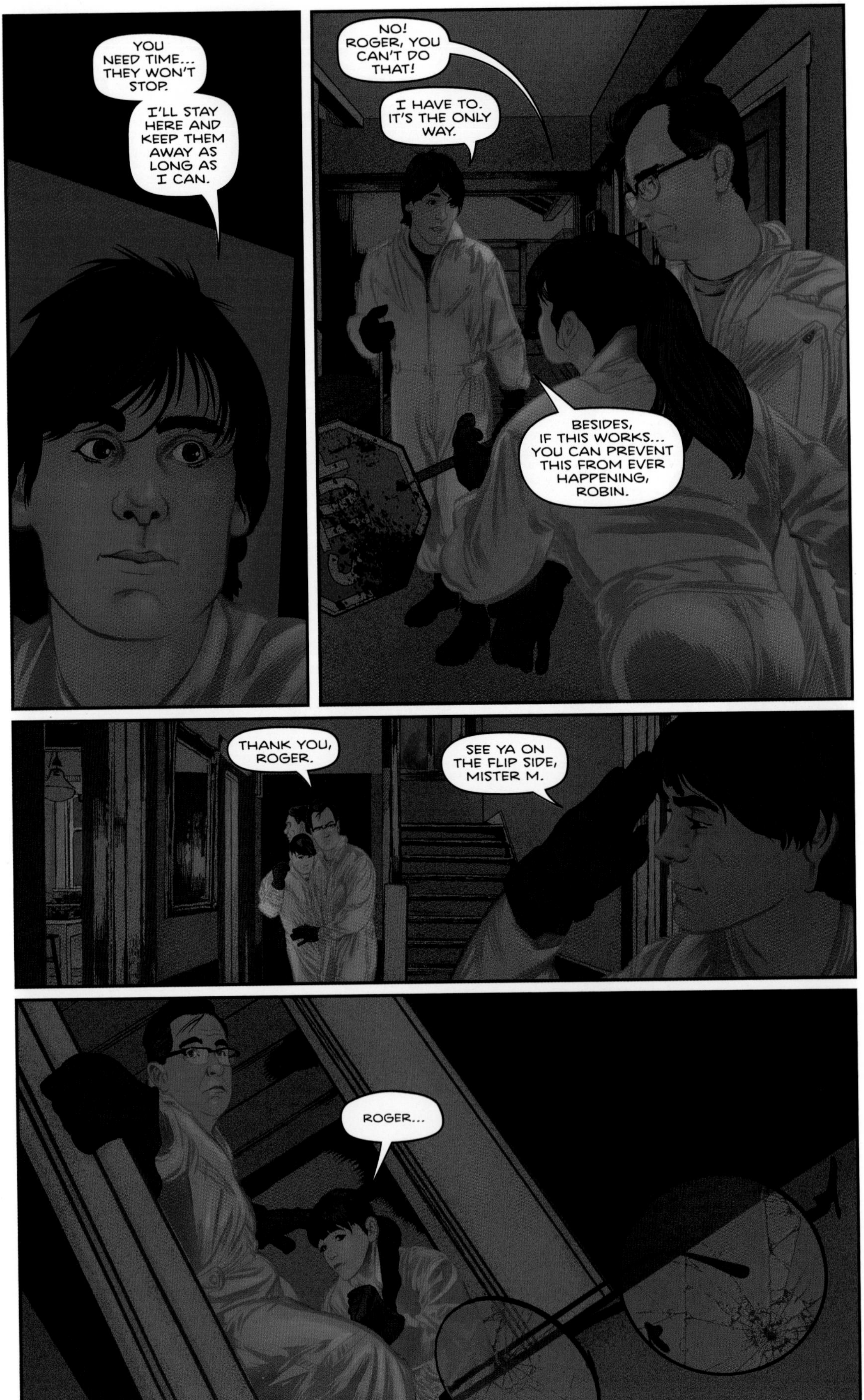
YOU NEED TIME... THEY WON'T STOP.
I'LL STAY HERE AND KEEP THEM AWAY AS LONG AS I CAN.
NO! ROGER, YOU CAN'T DO THAT!
I HAVE TO. IT'S THE ONLY WAY.
BESIDES, IF THIS WORKS... YOU CAN PREVENT THIS FROM EVER HAPPENING, ROBIN.
THANK YOU, ROGER.
SEE YA ON THE FLIP SIDE, MISTER M.
ROGER...

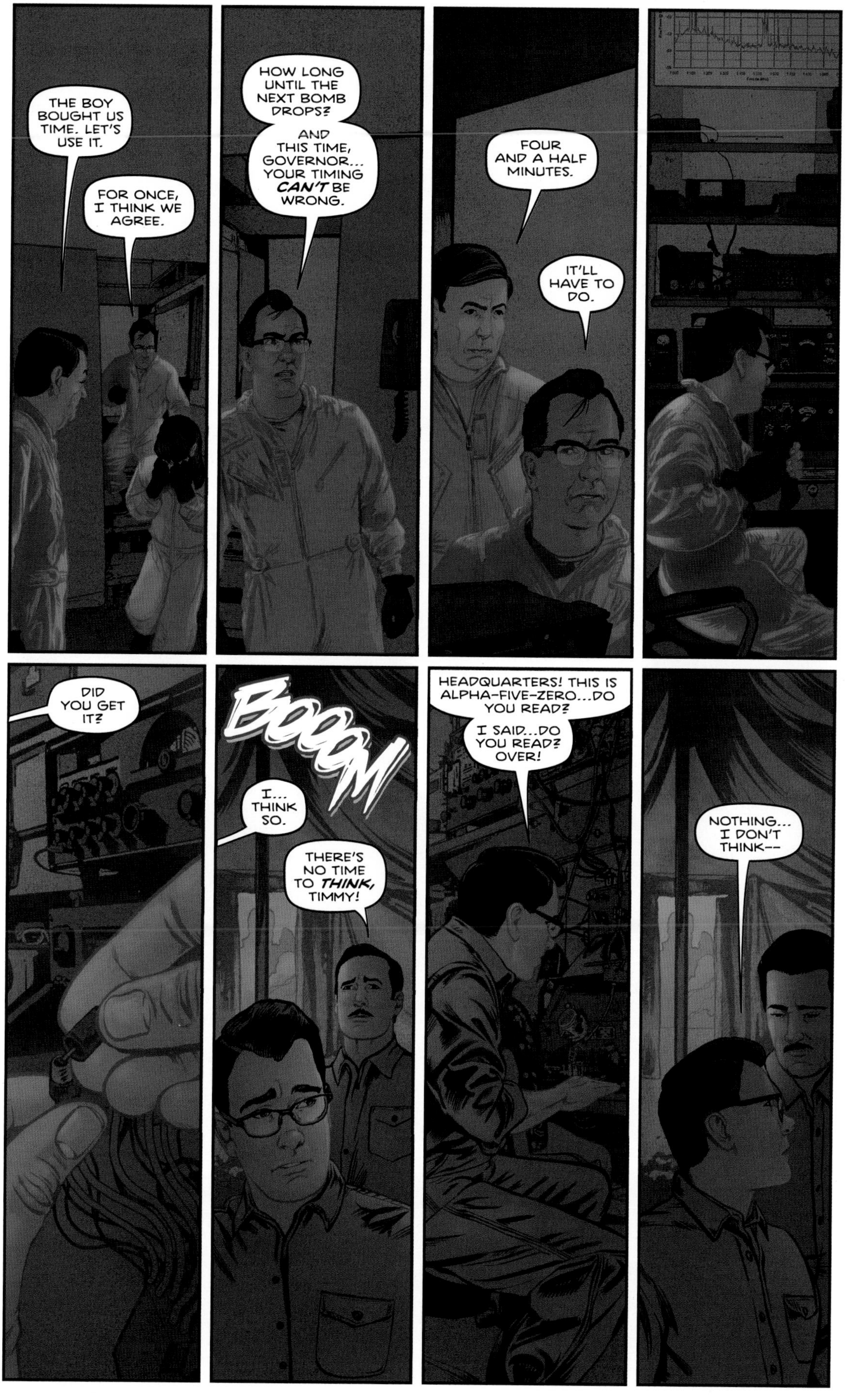
THE BOY BOUGHT US TIME. LET'S USE IT.
FOR ONCE, I THINK WE AGREE.
HOW LONG UNTIL THE NEXT BOMB DROPS?
AND THIS TIME, GOVERNOR... YOUR TIMING *CAN'T* BE WRONG.
FOUR AND A HALF MINUTES.
IT'LL HAVE TO DO.
DID YOU GET IT?
BOOOM
I... THINK SO.
THERE'S NO TIME TO *THINK,* TIMMY!
HEADQUARTERS! THIS IS ALPHA-FIVE-ZERO...DO YOU READ?
I SAID...DO YOU READ? OVER!
NOTHING... I DON'T THINK--

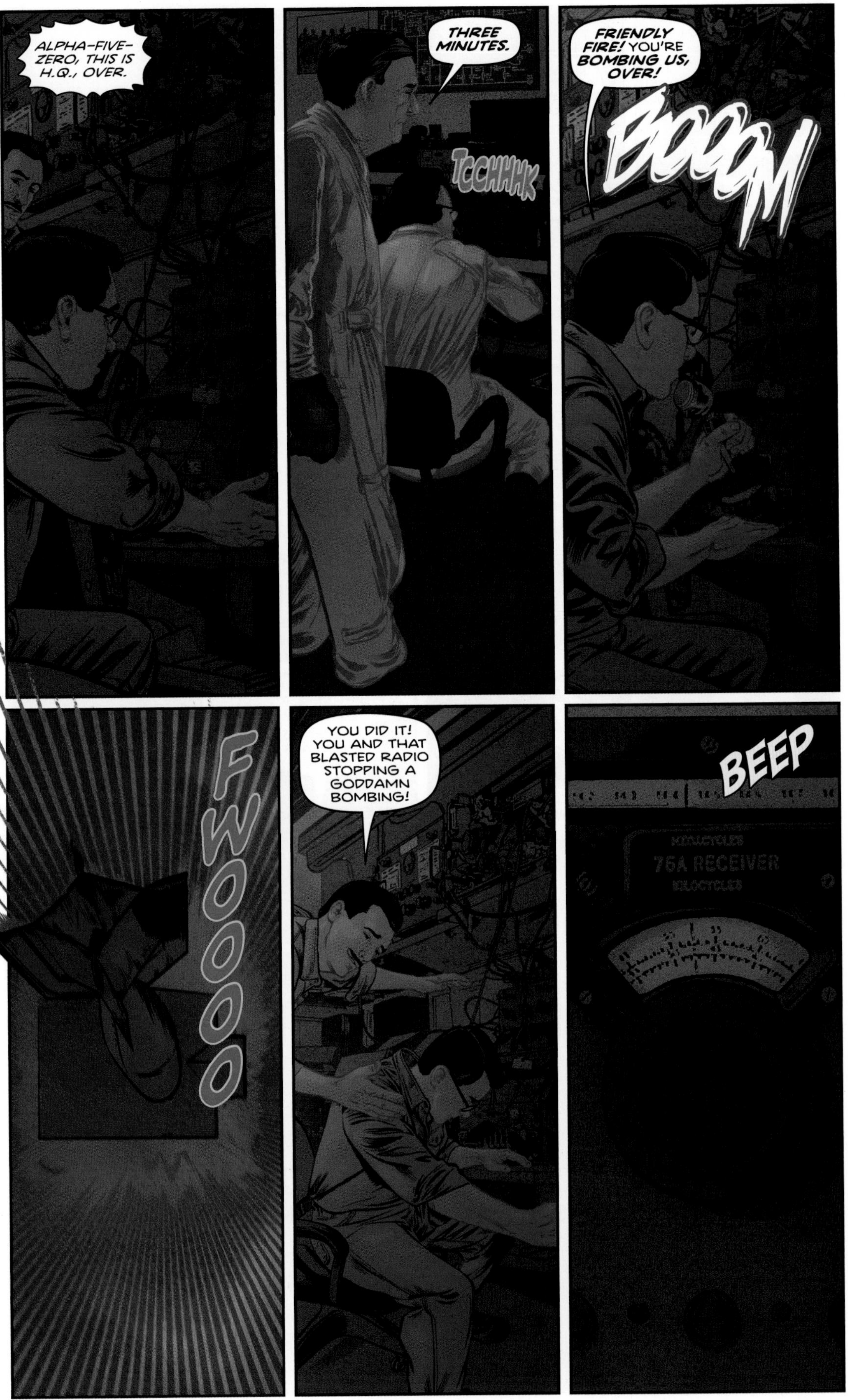
ALPHA-FIVE-ZERO, THIS IS H.Q., OVER.
THREE MINUTES.
TCCHHHK
FRIENDLY FIRE! YOU'RE BOMBING US, OVER!
BOOOM
FWOOOO
YOU DID IT! YOU AND THAT BLASTED RADIO STOPPING A GODDAMN BOMBING!
BEEP
76A RECEIVER

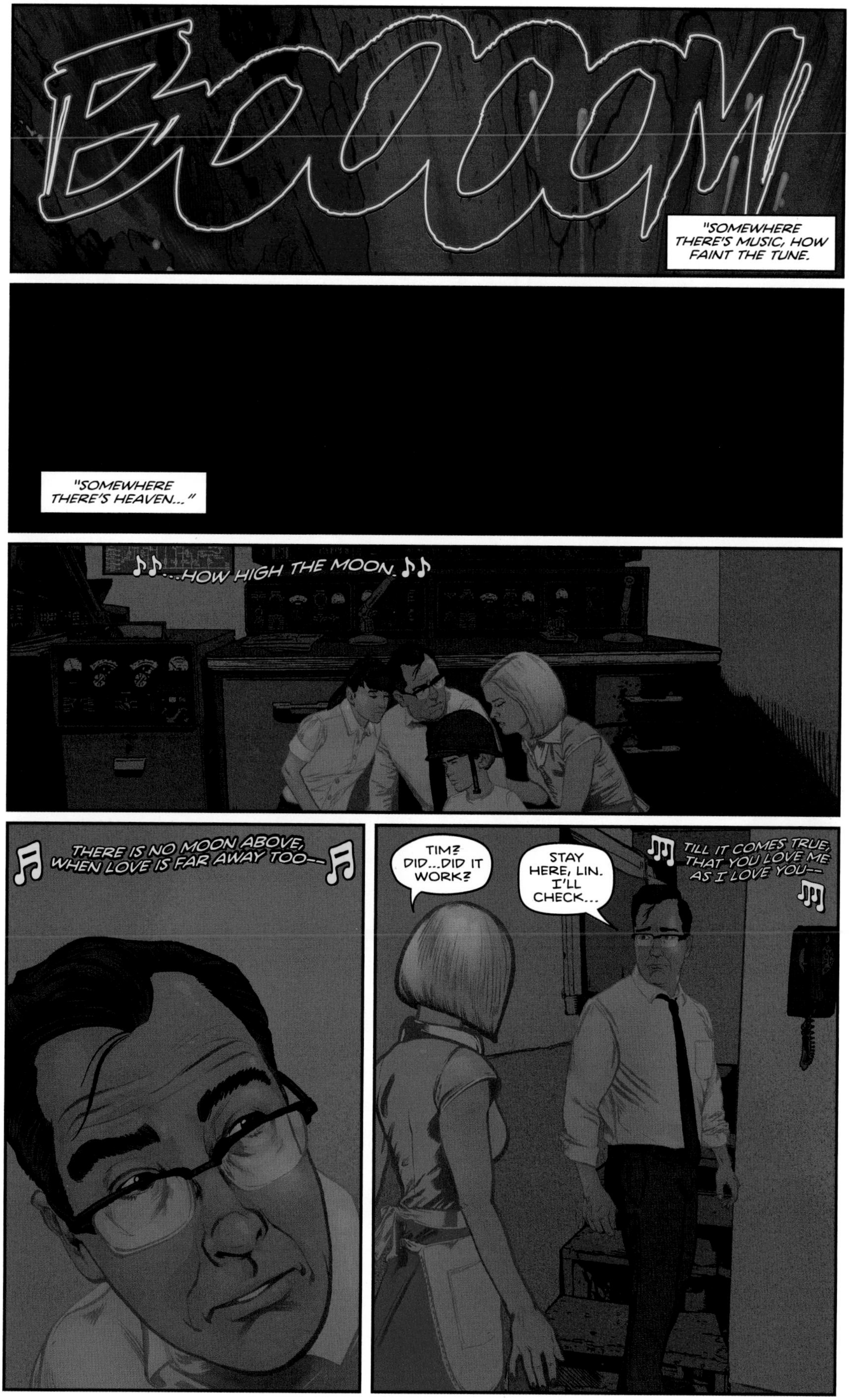
BOOOOM
"SOMEWHERE THERE'S MUSIC, HOW FAINT THE TUNE.
"SOMEWHERE THERE'S HEAVEN..."
♪♪...HOW HIGH THE MOON.♪♪
THERE IS NO MOON ABOVE, WHEN LOVE IS FAR AWAY TOO--
TIM? DID...DID IT WORK?
STAY HERE, LIN. I'LL CHECK...
TILL IT COMES TRUE, THAT YOU LOVE ME AS I LOVE YOU--

♪ ...THAT YOU LOVE ME AS I LOVE YOU... ♪

♪♪ SOMEWHERE THERE'S MUSIC--

YOU USED TO SEND THOSE LYRICS TO ME WHEN YOU WERE IN KOREA.

I WOULD IMAGINE YOU SINGING THEM TO ME AS I FELL ASLEEP.

WAS...WAS THAT *REAL?* WHAT HAPPENED TO THE GOVERNOR?

HONESTLY? I...I DON'T KNOW, LIN. I DON'T KNOW WHAT TO THINK.

BUT I DO KNOW OUR FAMILY IS SAFE. AND RIGHT NOW, THAT'S ALL I CARE ABOUT.

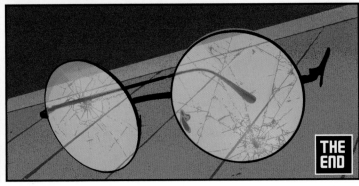

THE END

Issue 1
TONY HARRIS
Incentive Cover

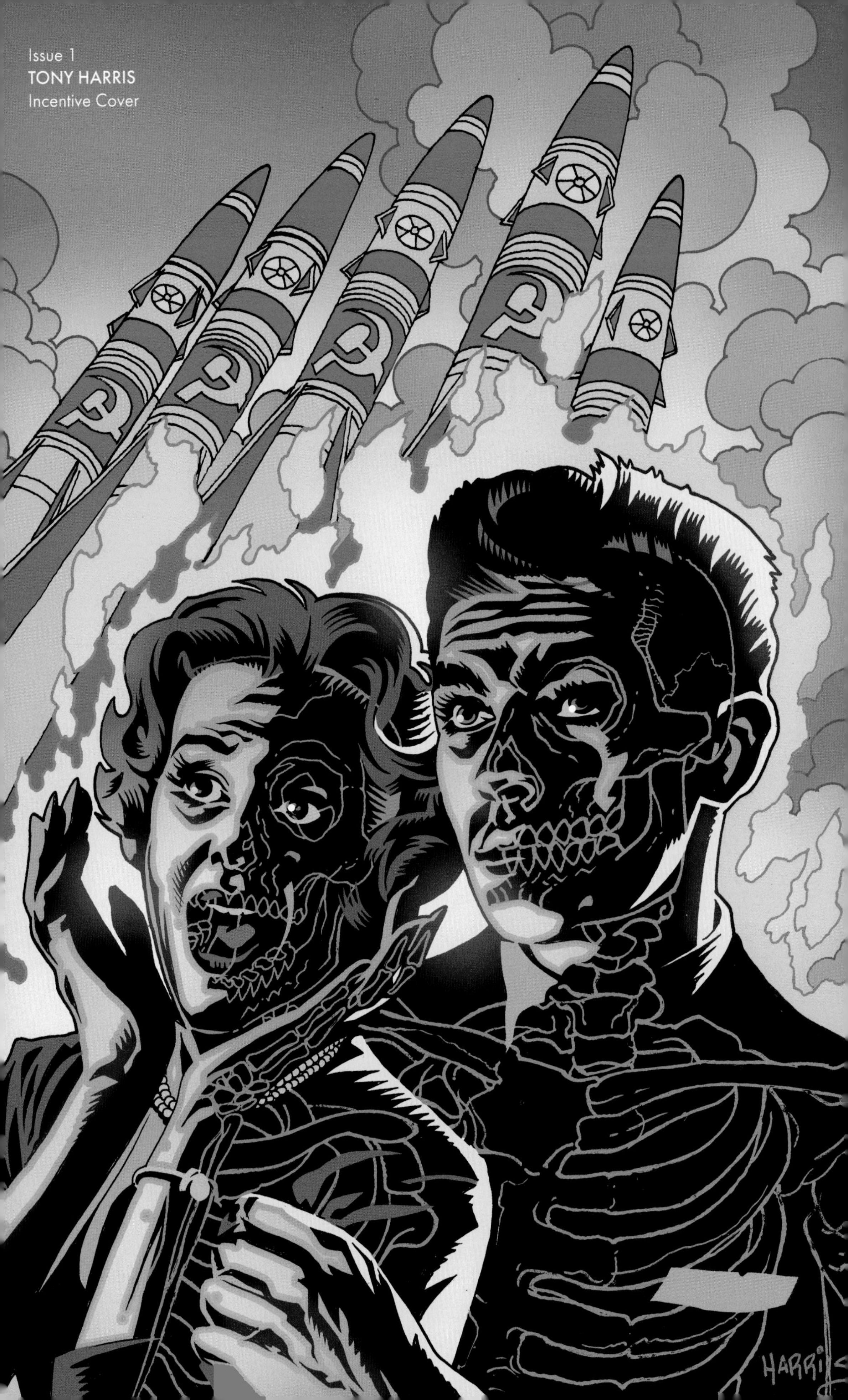

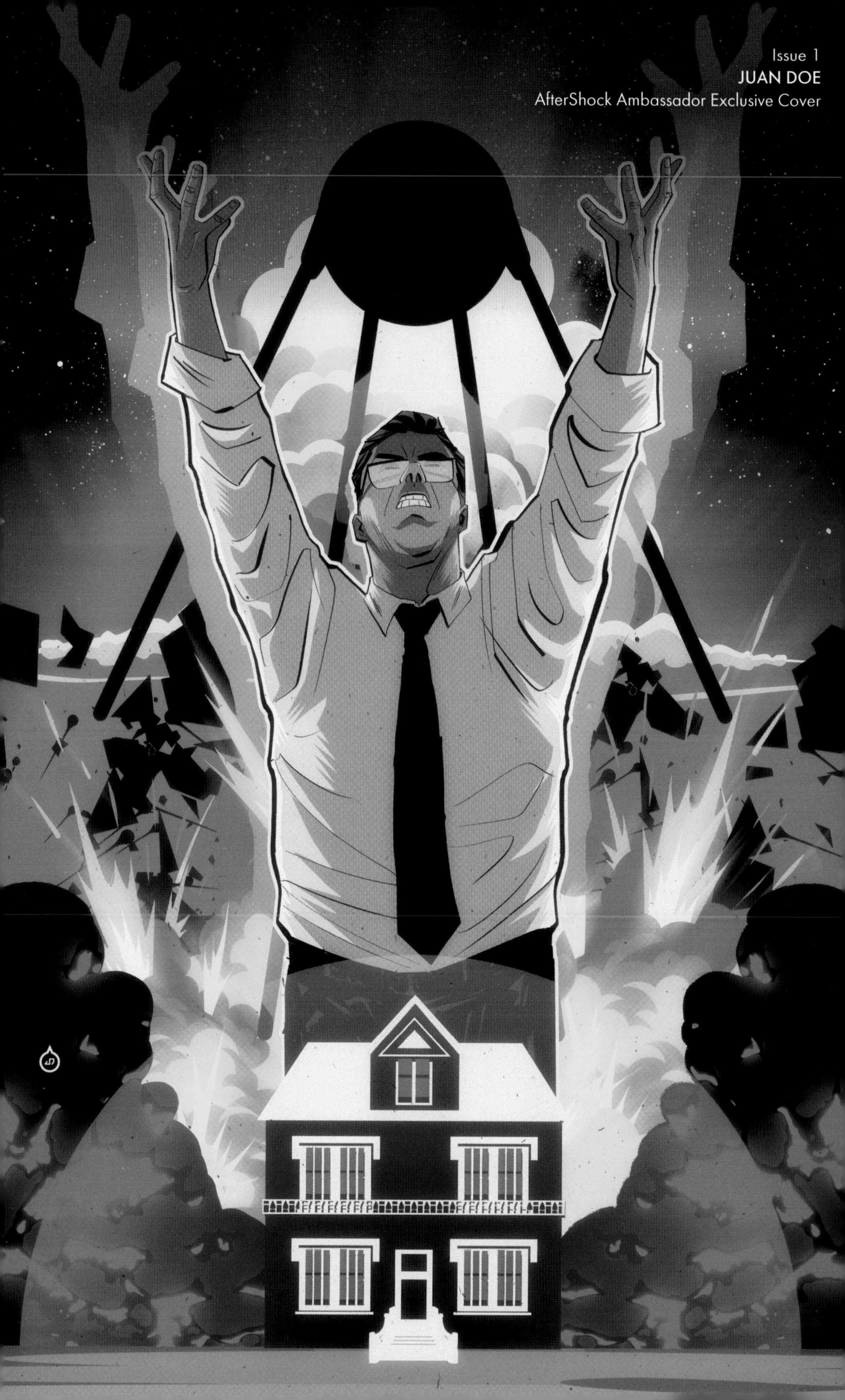

Issue 1
JUAN DOE
AfterShock Ambassador Exclusive Cover

Issue 1
RYAN GARY BROWNE
Comic Blend Exclusive Variant Cover

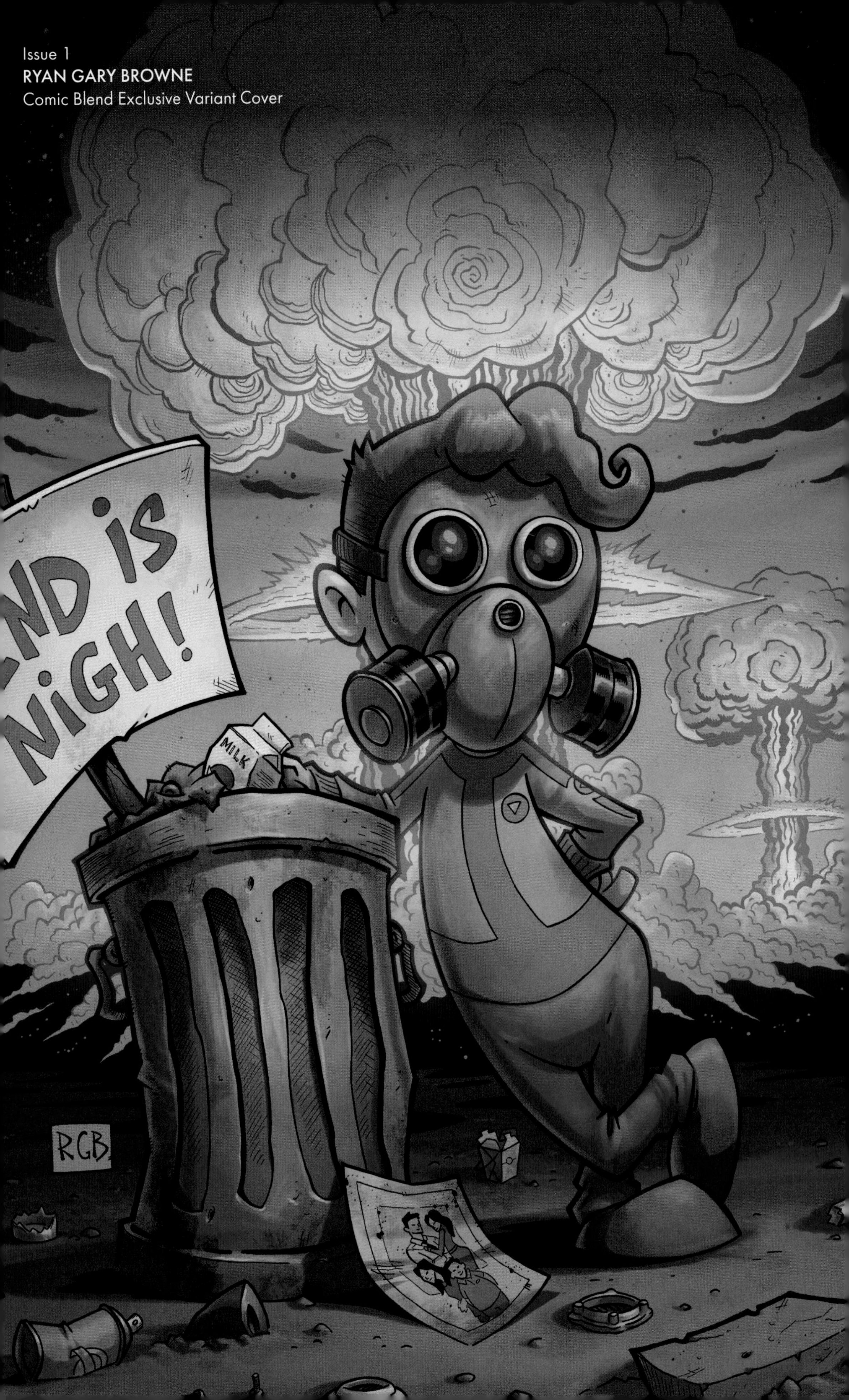

ND IS
NiGH!
MILK
RGB

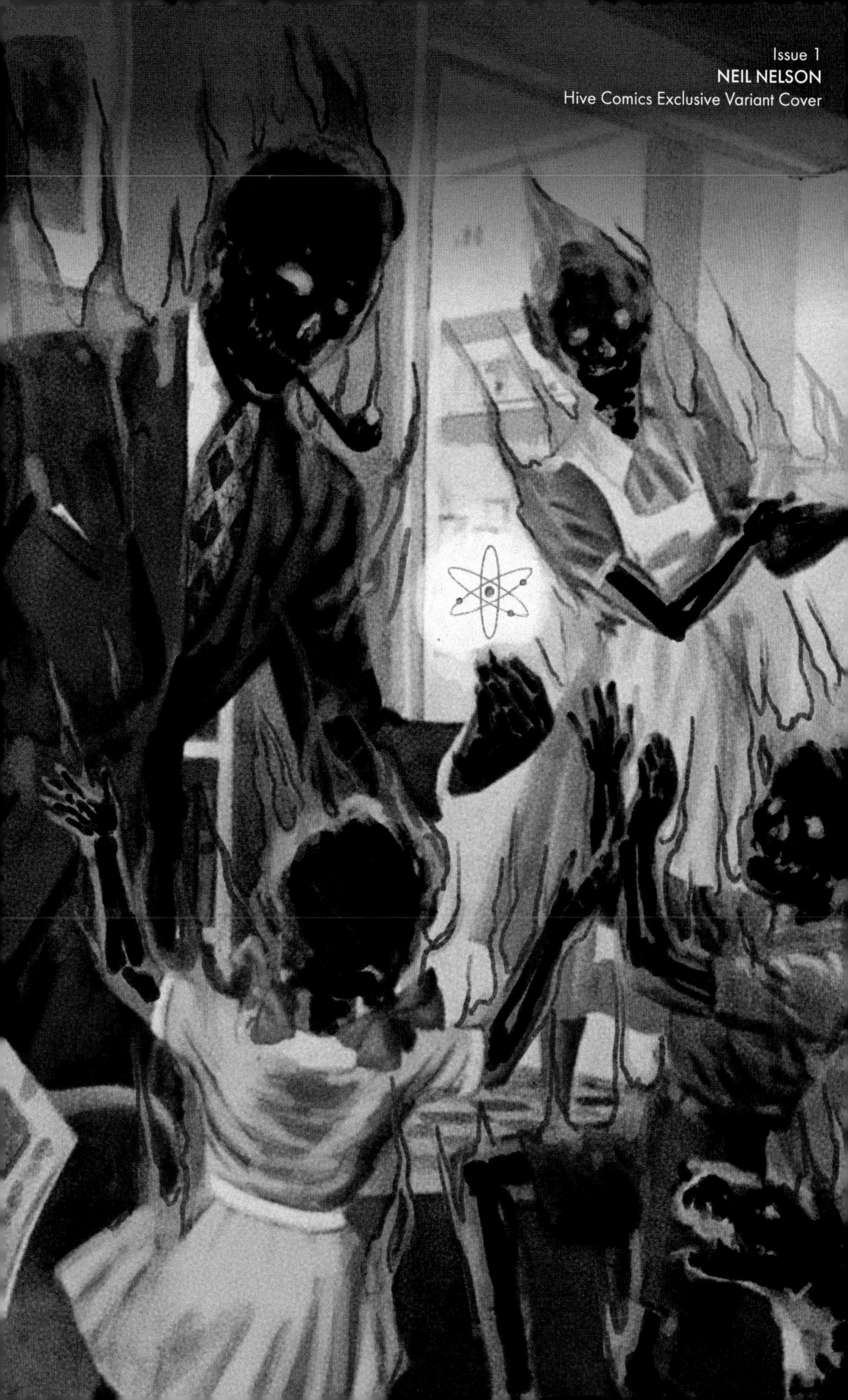

Issue 1
NEIL NELSON
Hive Comics Exclusive Variant Cover

A TRUE AMERICAN'S GUIDE TO
COMMUNISM!

Do *You* know what a Communist *looks* like?

How about what a Communist *sounds* like?

Or *smells* like?

That's right, folks, **Communism** is on the rise right here on American soil. Spotting Commies is more important now than ever before. While the **Communist Party** has made a concerted effort to go underground and infiltrate our great country from the **inside**, a **true** American can spot the signs of Communism, however subtle they might be.

WHAT SHOULD YOU BE
ON THE LOOKOUT FOR?

Communists have a preference for long sentences with a distinct vocabulary and penchant for hyperbolic diction that will often include words and phrases like **integrative thinking, comrade, hootenanny, chauvinism, syncretistic faith, bourgeois-nationalism, colonialism, hooliganism, ruling class, progressive, demagogy, dialectical, reactionary, exploitation, oppressive** and **materialist.**

Make sure *you* can identify the language of a **Communist.**

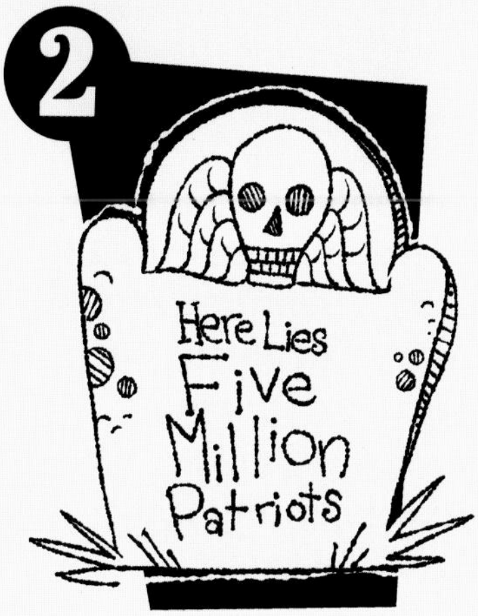
2
Here Lies
Five
Million
Patriots

Communists are quick to condemn our great Nation and criticize our global commitment to prevent the red scare from spreading. A **Communist** will criticize even the most insignificant occurrences in our great country's history, like the five million lives lost in Korea, or how 50% of those deaths belonged to Korean civilians.

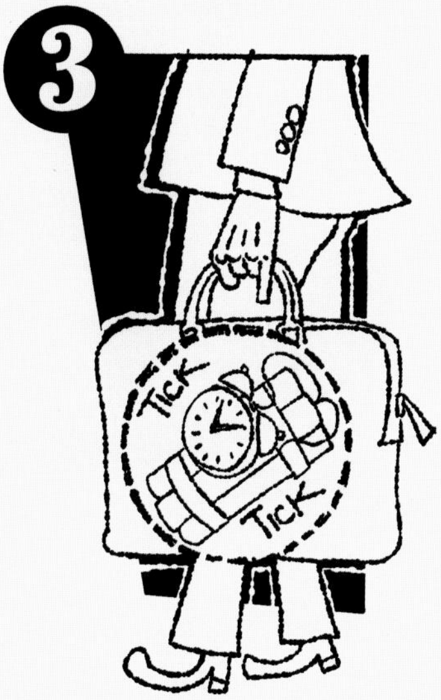
3
TICK
TICK

Communists are often secretive about their contacts, whereabouts, and even personal belongings. If you see a man, typically with a beard, walking with a briefcase and he will not tell you the contents of his personal item, nor will he share his destination, he most likely has bombs in his briefcase and is headed to meet his fellow Communist counterparts.

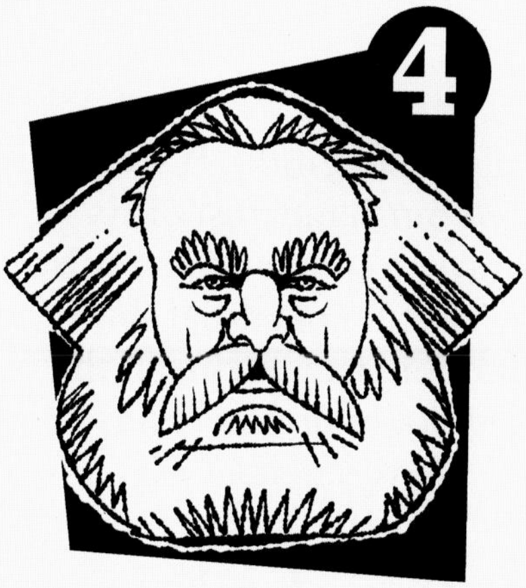
4

Communists cling stubbornly to their Marxist agenda and will not relent the issue of resources for all, regardless of class. Any **true** American understands the value of a country divided by economic status.

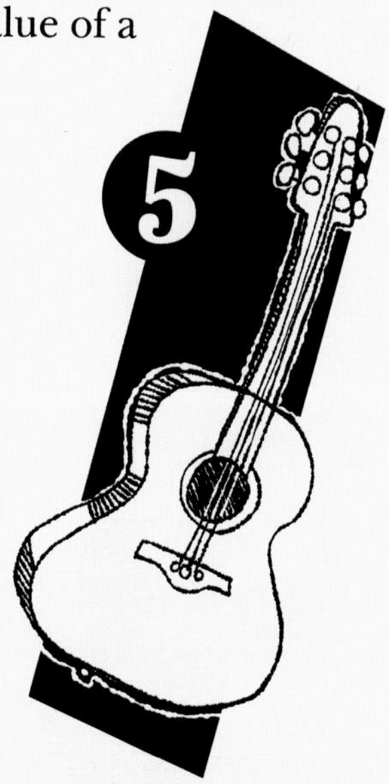
5

While showing standard opposition to certain standard issues, the U.S. **Communist** has traditionally identified himself with certain activities in the hope of furthering his ultimate purposes. Such hobbies as **"folk dancing"** and **"folk music"** have been traditionally allied with the Communist movement in the United States.

6 A **Communist** will use common tactics and arguments to appeal to the public regarding their "faith" and principles. The **Communist** arsenal might include such issues as: "McCarthyism", violation of civil rights, racial or religious discrimination, immigration laws, anti-subversive legislation, any legislation concerning labor unions, the military budget, "peace."

IS MY NEIGHBOR A COMMUNIST?!

He just might be, Linda! If you've consulted our handy list of six sure-fire ways to spot a Communist and you're still not sure if that man next door is an enemy of the United States of America, ask yourself:

DOES HE *look* LIKE A COMMUNIST?

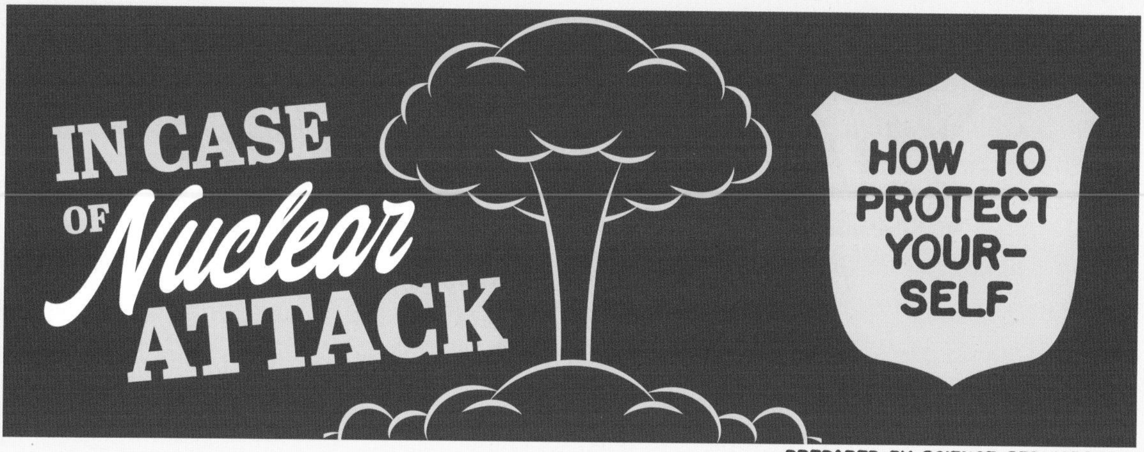
IN CASE
OF Nuclear
ATTACK
HOW TO
PROTECT
YOUR-
SELF

PREPARED BY SCIENCE SERVICES INC.

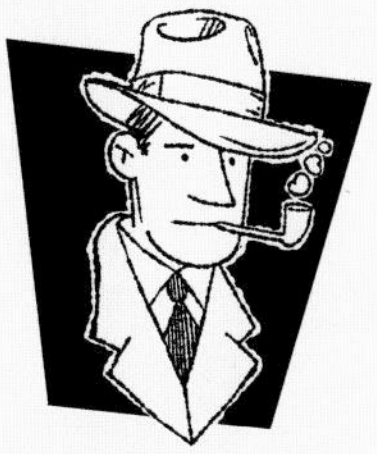

1. Remain calm.

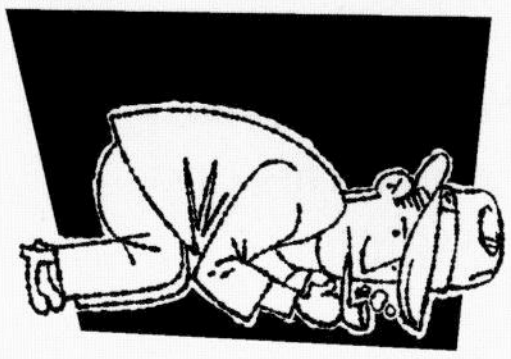

2. Make yourself small as to appear less threatening.

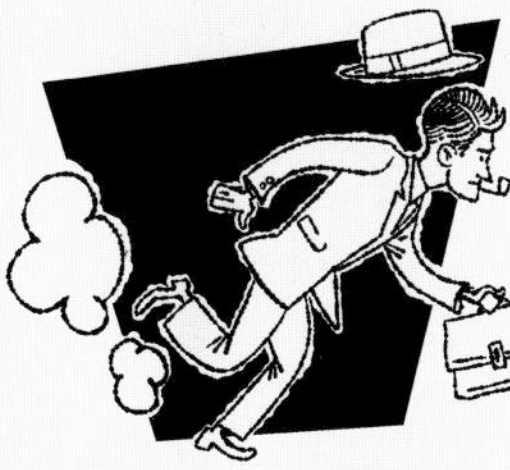

3. If problem persists, run in a zig-zag pattern to your nearest fallout shelter.

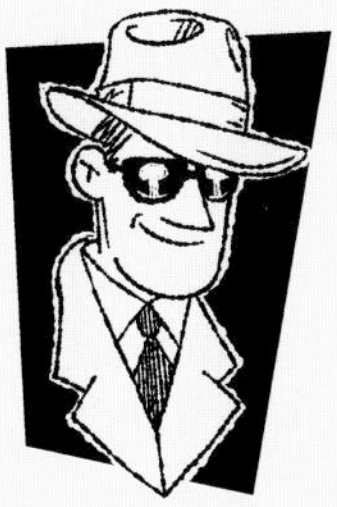

4. Don't look directly at the flash. For $9.99 you can purchase your very own pair of *Nuclear Visions* Watch the fall of humanity while protecting your retinas.

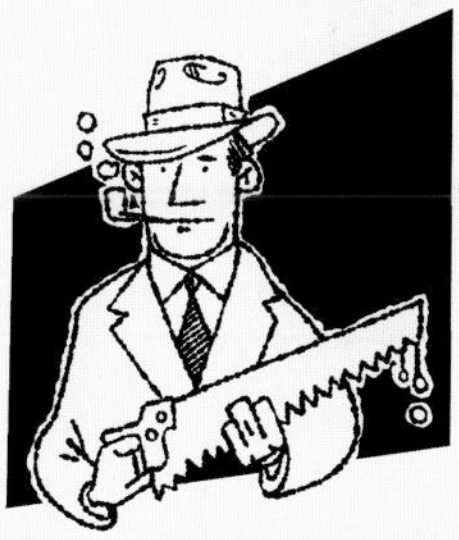

5. Find and care for the injured. Perform amputations as you see fit.

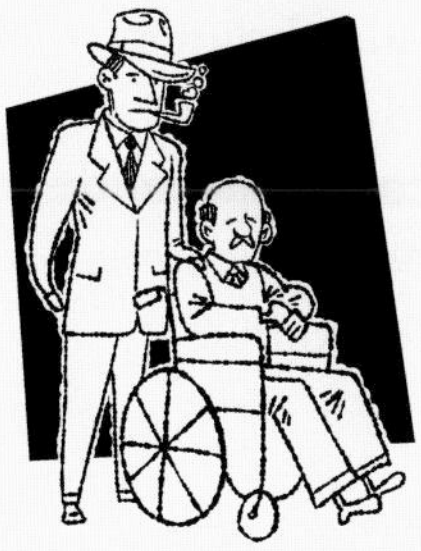

6. Comfort the dying.

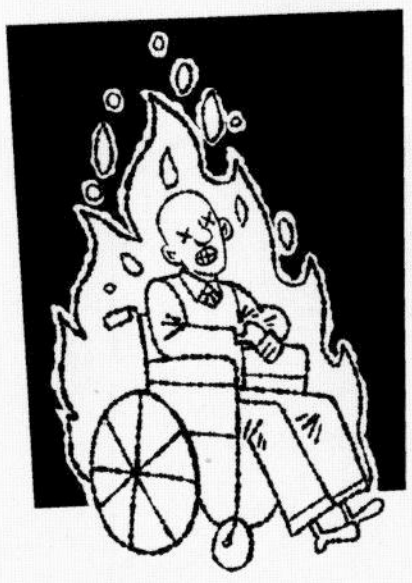

7. Contain the dead bodies so as not to spread diseases.

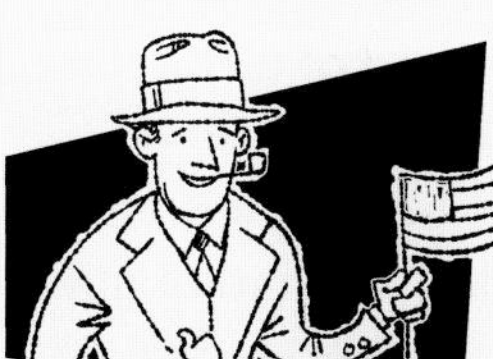

8. Stay positive and thank God you're an American!

PHILLIPS & SHASTEEN: BACKMATTER WORDS AND ART

Nuclear Family™

Sketchbook & Artist Interview:
TONY SHASTEEN

AFTERSHOCK COMICS: **What were your influences behind the military uniforms and overall look of NUCLEAR FAMILY?**

TONY SHASTEEN: My influences were a mix of traditional military uniforms of the era, pop sci-fi references and simply thinking about what would be functional in an underground post-apocalyptic city. Jumpsuits and coveralls could be mass-produced, fit everyone even if it was a poor fit, and could be sealed like a hazmat suit to protect them from radiation. From there, I just layered different gear based on the character's individual role in the bunker.

Storytelling-wise, I needed to differentiate the ranks visually because we see the characters in gas masks so often. We need to know if we were seeing a grunt or an officer, so the field officers got a jacket and a sidearm, whereas the regular soldiers had no jacket and a Thompson submachine gun.

ASC: **Do you have a favorite character? A favorite panel?**

HOME
Sweet
HOME

TS: It's hard to pick a favorite character. By the end of the book, I grew really fond of all of them. If I was forced to choose, I'd have to go with Roger. He's just a fun laid-back guy even in the face of certain death. He's the kind of guy I'd want on my team.

A favorite panel would be the big reveal of the bunker city. That thing was a monster to draw—

it took me days to complete, so it certainly sticks out in my mind. I don't usually love drawing architecture, but that was a fun one.

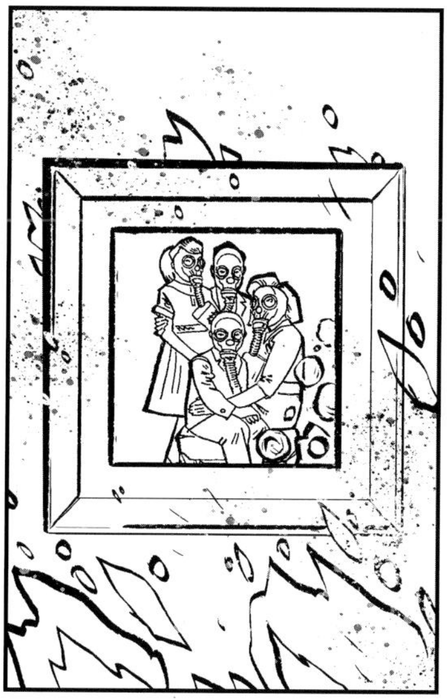

ASC: **What is your process when coming up with cover compositions?**

TS: I read the script a couple times, or a synopsis if that's all I have, and I take notes of any visuals that might jump out to me. I start by sketching a couple dozen rough thumbnails. These little roughs are very loose and are usually just putting together basic design elements.

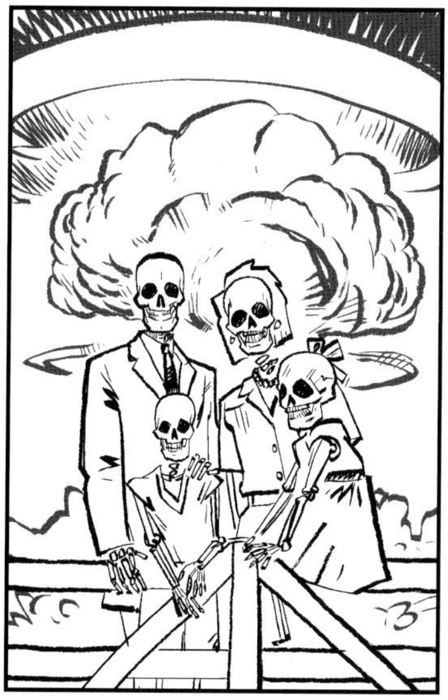

Then I choose a handful of the strongest designs and refine them. I'm trying to come up with a concept that stands out on the shelves. We see enough superhero books with characters fighting or jumping towards the camera, so I stay away from those tropes. Once I have what I think is a decent concept, I try to take it one step further. If you have a zombie soldier, take it one more step and make it a recruiting poster. If you have a family portrait with everyone in gas masks, maybe have them decimated by an atomic blast.

ASC: **What influenced you when creating the NUCLEAR FAMILY logo?**

TS: I wanted it to feel like it came from that era. I love the design from the 50s. The typefaces and design elements had a certain look, and you know it as soon as you see it. Once I came up with a black and white design, I wanted to take it one step further, like I do when I'm designing a cover. Instead of having a flat, clean logo, I wanted it to look like a motel sign from the 50s that's been rusting in the nuclear wasteland.

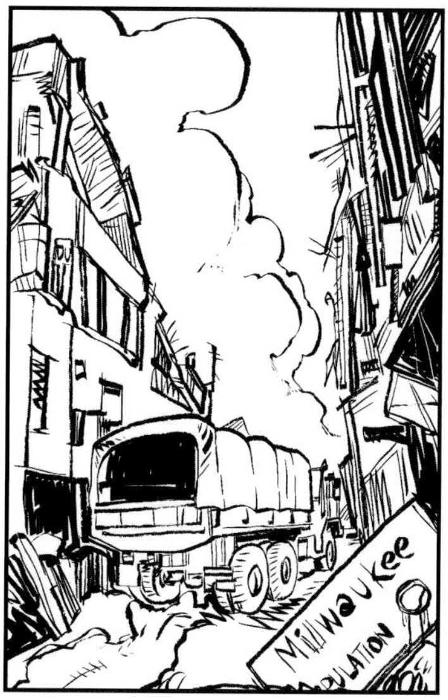
Milwaukee

ASC: **Any advice for artists trying to break into the industry?**

TS: Everyone wants to know how to break-in, but it's just as important to understand how to *stay in* once you've broken in.

You always have to remember there are thousands of people right behind you that want your job. Treat freelancing like a business, because it is. It's a very difficult business. If you're in it for the long haul, you need to treat yourself well. Remember that your body can only take so many years of working seven days a week and pulling all-nighters. Set a reasonable work schedule and stick to it.

ASC: What was the most challenging aspect for you when illustrating NUCLEAR FAMILY?

TS: I never feel like I fully get the story that's in my head onto the page. It's my biggest challenge with all the books I work on. The scale of the story that Steph wrote and what was in my head when I read the script was much bigger. I always want another stab at drawing a book.

ASC: Do you have a favorite Cold War-themed film, television show or book?

TS: Tough question! There are so many to choose from that I've watched a million times. *The Hunt for Red October* is up there on my list. They have horrible accents, but I can listen to a Scottish man play a Russian Captain all day long. *The Iron Giant* has always been a huge influence. Brad Bird is a master storyteller. I'd even throw *The Abyss* in as well. There are too many to choose just one!

DETENTION BLOCK
D-45

BASE FATIGUES

DRIVER

GUARD

JOIN TODAY
SERVE FOREVER

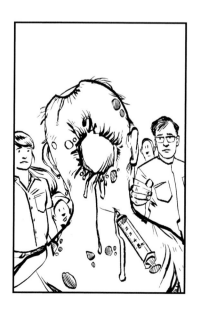

FIELD SOLDIER

FIELD OFFICER

SCIENTIST/HAZMAT

PROTECT OUR
LIBERTY
BUY
WAR
BONDS

line art

Nuclear Family

base colors

Nuclear Family

finished textures

Nuclear Family

Colorist Interview:
JD METTLER

AFTERSHOCK COMICS: For anyone who might not be familiar with what coloring a comic book entails, can you describe what your job is?

JD METTLER: For color, my job is to read the script, look at the line art and interpret what I believe they're going for in mood/tone/feel... and then turn in the finished pages on time. I get to manipulate your emotions, just by changing up the lighting—that's fun for me! Deadlines aren't as fun, but are part of the deal and can actually kick my creative-drive into gear.

ASC: **What is your typical approach to coloring a book?**

JDM: The line art is sent to me as bitmapped files. Then I do any research/reference gathering that's needed after reading the script. All coloring is done digitally in Photoshop, using as many layers/channels/groups as I need in the working PSD file. After JPEG previews are approved by editorial, the hi-res TIFFs are uploaded for the letterer, and finally a lettered/colored PDF is sent to everyone for final proofing before print.

ASC: **What were your influences for NUCLEAR FAMILY?**

JDM: Paintings mostly—but film directors & directors of photography have been and continue to be a huge influence on my work, as well. Also—lots of old ad designs.

ASC: **Any advice for artists who are trying to break into coloring?**

JDM: RUN AWAY!!!! Kidding...*sorta*. It ain't for everyone.

Have a few fallback skills that you can make money with. Even if/when you break in and do it full time, having a second or even third skillset that pays may prove invaluable over the years. Even if it's only to pay rent occasionally until that next/extra/steady color gig comes in. It could actually help you to stay in comics, in the long term. The trick is prioritizing, trying to keep all your clients happy, staying healthy and not burning out. Like I said—it ain't for everyone. If it's in your blood to do it, you're going to do it no matter what I tell you anyways, so you'll see what I mean soon enough!

ASC: **If you found yourself in the world of NUCLEAR FAMILY, what character would you seek out to befriend?**

JDM: I'd probably be down in the lower levels with Roger, squirreling away supplies and learning all the ways to get around the city without getting caught. But only because Robin went home—if she stayed, *she'd* be The Governor eventually and we'd all end up working for *her*, I bet!

ASC: **Do you listen to specific music while working on a book or do you like your studio to be quiet?**

JDM: It depends on what I'm doing. Coloring and design work—I like background noise. Usually it's movies or tv shows with a good score or soundtrack that I've played a thousand times before. When I'm writing I can't have that stuff going, though—*shhhhhhh.*

ASC: **Do you have a favorite Cold War-themed film, television show or book?**

JDM: Too many great titles to list a best. If there's solid Cold War intrigue in a movie, show or book—I'm in. An odd-ball personal favorite would have to be Joe Dante's *Matinee.* I was living on Key West when it was filmed, and getting to see some of the process was both impressive & fun.

THANK YOU

I can't thank everyone enough for coming on this journey with us through time... through reality...through history...and through the radio waves.

NUCLEAR FAMILY has been an absolute joy to work on and a highlight of my career. From the incredible team I've gotten to work with—Tony Shasteen, JD Mettler and Troy Peteri—to the entire crew at AfterShock, including editors Mike Marts and Christina Harrington, who helped make this book possible, every moment working on this story has been energizing. And, of course, seeing the reactions of you readers each month as you descend further into this radioactive wasteland with us... that was truly something special.

Thank you for reading and supporting this project. "See you on the flipside."

Stephanie Phillips

NUCLEAR FAMILY has been a fantastic experience over one of the strangest years of my life, and I couldn't have asked for a better quarantine team.

The AfterShock crew gave me the luxury of time that I don't usually have. Stephanie created an amazing world, and was generous enough to include me in the creative process. Working with Stephanie has been on my bucket list since we became fast friends and convention neighbors. I look forward to working together again soon. Troy did an amazing job with the deceptively difficult job of lettering. I've tried my hand at lettering in the past, and I have a lifelong appreciation for Troy's skills. JD Mettler will always be my hero. He's a loyal friend and collaborator. I don't know how I got lucky enough to work with JD for so many years, and it will always be appreciated far beyond anything I can write here.

Lastly, thank you all for coming along for the ride and choosing to spend your hard-earned money on our book. It's greatly appreciated, and we wouldn't be here without you.

Tony Shasteen

ABOUT THE CREATORS OF

STEPHANIE PHILLIPS writer
🐦 @Steph_Smash

Stephanie Phillips is an American writer known for comics and graphic novels such as *Harley Quinn, Sensational Wonder Woman, Taarna* and *The Butcher of Paris*. Her stories and comics have appeared with DC, AfterShock, Dark Horse, Oni Press, Top Cow/Image Comics, Heavy Metal, and more. Along with comics, Stephanie holds a PhD in rhetoric and composition. Her other AfterShock work includes DESCENDENT, ARTEMIS & THE ASSASSIN and RED ATLANTIS.

TONY SHASTEEN artist
🐦 @TonyShasteen

Tony has been an illustrator and graphic designer since graduating from the Art Institute of Atlanta many years ago. His work has been featured in publications such as *Communication Arts, and Spectrum: The Best in Contemporary Fantastic Art*. He lives in Portland, OR with his wife, two sons and as many cats as the law will allow.

JD METTLER colorist

JD Mettler was born in London, England, and raised in Florida/Georgia. Mettler is a digital colorist (*Star Trek, The Royals: Masters of War, Ex Machina, JSA, Supernatural, Spider-Man, Batman, Nightmare on Elm Street, Conan,* etc.) who was given his first assignment in the comics industry in 2001, by a (then) young editor named Mike Marts. He now resides in Oregon with his wife (Amy), a Husky (Loki), a mixed Xoloitzquintli/Lab (Batgirl), a cat (Greywind), a couple of chickens (Hei & Hei), many giant wild turkeys (unnamed) & a smallish Sasquatch (JJ).

TROY PETERI letterer
🐦 @A_Larger_World

Troy Peteri, Dave Lanphear and Joshua Cozine are collectively known as A Larger World Studios. They've lettered everything from *The Avengers, Iron Man, Wolverine, Amazing Spider-Man* and *X-Men* to more recent titles like *The Spirit, Batman & Robin Eternal* and *Pacific Rim*. They can be reached at studio@largerworld.com for your lettering and design needs.